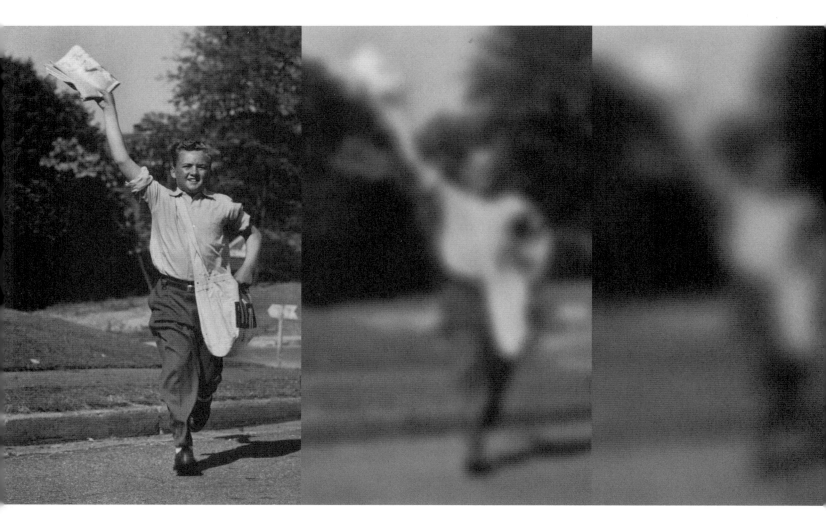

Going Going Gone

G
Going

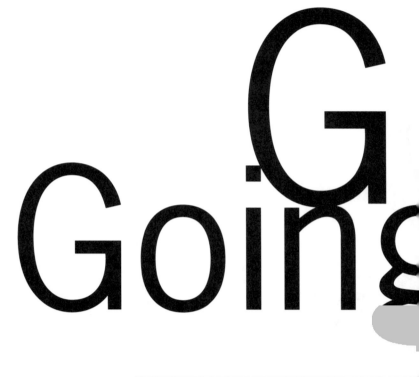

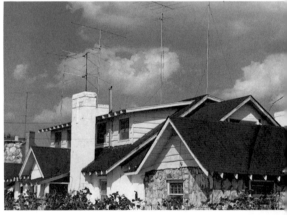

ing
Gone

Vanishing Americana
Susan Jonas & Marilyn Nissenson
Chronicle Books · San Francisco

Page 172 constitutes a continuation
of the copyright page.

Printed in the United States of
America.

Library of Congress Cataloging-in-
Publication Data

Jonas, Susan.
    Going, going, gone :
Vanishing Americana / Susan Jonas
& Marilyn Nissenson.
        p.   cm.
    Includes bibliographical
references (p.).
    ISBN 0-8118-0292-2
    1. Americana. 2. United
States—Social life and customs—
20th century. 3. Material culture—
United States. I. Nissenson,
Marilyn, 1939-   . II. Title.
E169.02.J64   1994
973.9—dc20   93-11548
                        CIP

Editing: Judith Dunham

Intern: Anastacia Leach

Book and cover design:

Eric Baker Design Assoc.

Cover photograph:

Sam Falk/National Archives

Distributed in Canada by

Raincoast Books,

112 East Third Avenue, Vancouver,

B.C. V5T 1C8

10 9 8 7 6 5 4 3 2 1

Chronicle Books

275 Fifth Street

San Francisco, CA 94103

For Sarah, Phoebe, Katherine, and Kore,
to whom the future belongs

Table of Contents

Introduction 8

American Elms 10

The Automat 12

Balsa-Wood Model Airplanes 14

Bank Checks 16

Baseball Players Who Stay With One Team 18

Black-and-White Movies 20

Black Smoke 24

Blue Laws 26

Bridge Parties 28

Carbon Paper 30

Card Catalogs 32

Cavities 34

Chop Suey 36

Civil Defense 38

DDT 42

The Dining Room 44

The Draft 46

Drive-in Movies 50

Enclosed Telephone Booths 52

Family Farms 54

Fan Mags 56

Fire Escapes 60

Fur Coats 62

Gas Station Attendants 64

Girdles 66

Handkerchiefs 68

Hitchhiking 70

Hotel Keys 72

House Calls 74

Landfills 76

Leisure Suits 78

Marbles 80

Mending 82

The Menopause Taboo 84

Men's Clubs 86

Men's Garters 88

The Milkman 90

The Motion Picture Production Code 92

The Navy Blue Suit 96

The Nuclear Family 98

Nuns 100

Organized Labor 102

Paperboys 104

Paper Dolls 106

Parietal Rules 108

Penmanship 110

Polio Scares 112

Political Bosses 116

Psychoanalysis 120

The Red Menace 122

Rotary Phones 126

Sanitary Napkin Belts 128

Security-Free Airports 130

Shoe-Fitting Fluoroscopes 132

Slide Rules 134

The Smell Of Burning Leaves 136

Smoking 138

Soda Fountains 140

Stockings 142

Suntans 144

Teenage Dating 146

Telegrams 148

Tonsillectomies 150

TV Antennas 152

Two-Newspaper Towns 154

Typewriters 156

The Unanswered Phone 160

Unfixed Domestic Male Animals 162

Vinyl Records 164

Wedding-Night Virgins 166

White Gloves 168

Acknowledgments 170

Credits 172

Bibliography 174

Introduction

Remember LPs? They were made of old-fashioned black vinyl, with music recorded on both sides. They were protected by paper sleeves and cardboard jackets, but no matter how carefully they were handled, they got scratched.

Whatever happened to vinyl records? For that matter, where did the milkman go? Has anyone bought a girdle recently, or made multiple copies with carbon paper, or ordered a malted at a soda fountain?

Modern life is predicated on change. In the first half of the twentieth century, the horse and buggy gave way to the car, the gas jet to the light bulb; the authority of religion was challenged by Marxism and psychoanalysis. Those astonishing technological and sociological changes have been well documented. Since 1945, another revolution has taken place. Many objects and concepts that we once took for granted as part of everyday life either have vanished or seem destined to disappear. Shoe-fitting fluoroscopes, blue laws, and men's garters are distant memories. Landfills and hotel keys are just beginning to pass into history. The departure of some items has been televised, analyzed, and eulogized. Others have slipped away without being noticed. Some are gone for good; a few may reappear in different forms. Though we feel nostalgic about many of them, others we'll never even miss.

Technology is responsible for most of the changes in everyday life. Typewriters are an obvious victim of computerization, but the silicon chip has killed off slide rules and imperils bank checks as well. Scientific research has routed polio scares and cavities but also has doomed the smell of burning leaves.

The swiftness of telecommunications has fostered the illusion that time has speeded up. Why send a telegram when a fax arrives faster? Why take ten seconds to dial when you can punch in a number in half the time? The incessant demands of work and play compete for our attention; we feel there are more things to do and fewer hours to do them in. This altered perception of time has transformed significant aspects of family life from the demise of dining rooms to the passing of doctors' house calls.

The evolving role of women has far-reaching social consequences. On the broadest scale, the women's movement is both a cause and an effect of changes in the nuclear family; it has also done away with mending, taboos about menopause, and the exclusivity of men's clubs. Women's assertiveness has overturned some venerated rules in the world of fashion. The navy blue suit was the spring uniform until freedom of expression encouraged women to desert the standard of fashion propriety; the disappearance of white cotton gloves marked the devaluation of "ladylike" as an ideal; nylon stockings were replaced when women redefined convenience and their own comfort.

As the list of subjects for this book expanded, we developed ground rules. We rejected Pet Rocks, propeller beanies, and Hula-Hoops—fads that were created to be ephemeral. We eliminated objects that vanished too early in the century; razor strops and running boards on cars are barely part of the collective memory of most Americans. We dropped things that seemed too similar in function to their replacement: wooden tennis rackets, wooden skis with leather bindings, leather subway straps, Checker cabs.

Contrary to published reports, some subjects turned out to be alive and well: diners, fossil fuel reserves, hair nets and bobby pins, watches that wind, bedroom slippers, double beds, the Fuller Brush man. Ocean liners may cross the Atlantic infrequently, but Mediterranean and Caribbean cruises have never been more popular.

The projected life expectancy of some items was controversial. For every expert who predicted the imminent end of department stores and urban zoos, we found equally informed sources who said they would play an important role in the future. Opinions about the manned exploration of space are similarly divided.

Every man we met suggested we talk about various parts of cars. Manual windows, chokes, and carburetors all provoked nostalgia. Someone mentioned hand signals. Our research revealed they were all replaced by better technology, but unlike slide rules or typewriters, for example, the transition did not reflect wider changes in society. Convertibles, with and without roll bars, are making a comeback.

Some categories we included are Going, Going, but probably never will be Gone. About one in four adults still smokes; people still get sunburns; half the children in America have cavities. But the burden of scientific information and the pressure of public opinion surely guarantee that the numbers will never go back up.

In every instance we were drawn to subjects that elucidated some aspect of our country's recent social history. We were interested in how an item was used or perceived, what it represented in its heyday, what quickened its decline, and why anyone cared.

It may be that Americans have always been comfortable with change. After all, everyone who settled here was uprooted from someplace else, and the effect of the frontier on our national restlessness has been often discussed. As the pace of change has quickened in this century, we expect and even anticipate that many things will become obsolete even before we've gotten used to them. Nonetheless we lead our daily lives as if our routines and resources have permanence. We buy a desktop computer though we know it will soon be obsolete. We marry though we know the divorce rate remains high.

Our purpose as authors is neither to lament days gone by nor to argue in favor of preserving a status quo. We know that not all change is progress. We have tried to stop time for a moment to acknowledge transitions, both major and minor, to provide a nostalgic journey through the American landscape of the twentieth century, and to say goodbye to those things that will be the anachronisms of the twenty-first. ☐

American Elms

The American elm was our most popular shade tree. Rows of hundred-foot elms once lined city streets, college campuses, and country lanes.

George Washington is said to have taken command of the Continental Army under a famous elm tree in Cambridge, Massachusetts. William Penn signed his treaty with the Delaware Indians in the shade of an elm. Under a massive elm in central Ohio, Chief Logan of the Mungoes, a longtime ally of the American colonists, delivered a protest to the governor of Virginia about the murder of his family by a frontier trader. As settlers pushed west from New England, they took elms with them. Eventually American elms flourished in every state except Hawaii.

Elms are vulnerable to pests; they suffer from root rot, leaf wilt, stem cankers, and bacterial wetwood. But as a species, the American elm held its own until thousands of trees were suddenly stricken with Dutch elm disease in the early 1930s. The disease, first identified in Holland early in the century, had already decimated European elms. It is a deadly fungus that spreads rapidly from tree to tree, either by hitching a ride on the bodies of invading beetles or by passing directly through root systems joined beneath the earth. It was probably brought to America in a shipment of European burled elm logs headed for a furniture factory. Beetles in the logs migrated to American trees, and disaster followed.

The fungus cuts off the circulation of water and nutrients within the tree. The outermost leaves turn yellow, the twig ends gnarl, and the limbs shrivel. Quickly pruning the visibly damaged area can prolong the tree's life, but there is no cure. Soon only a leafless graying skeleton remains. The orioles and other birds that nest in elms disappear. In Syracuse, New York, the loss of four hundred miles of elms dating

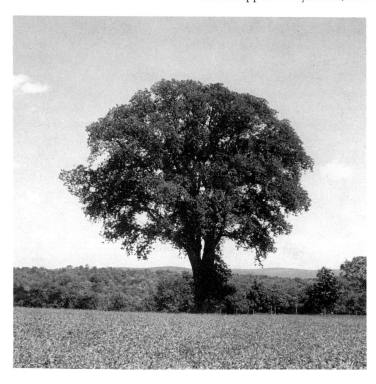

from the Civil War raised the temperature of formerly shady streets so much that twenty-two thousand maples died of the heat.

Some cities tried to kill the beetles with DDT, which did in the birds without deterring the bugs. Other cities cut down infected trees at once, hoping to protect remaining elms in the same stand. Nothing worked. In the last fifty years, perhaps one hundred million trees have died.

In the wild, other hardwoods and opportunistic evergreens soon reseeded the areas that elms once dominated. Towns and cities that took pride in their dignified old elms have become sunnier but otherwise bleaker places.

A few pockets of original American elms still stand. Thousands remain in New York City's Central Park. But the fungus could strike at any moment. Since the mid-1970s, in New York and elsewhere, foresters have injected various antifungal chemicals into elms that are mildly infected or thought to be at risk. The injections are, according to one plant pathologist, "a holding action."

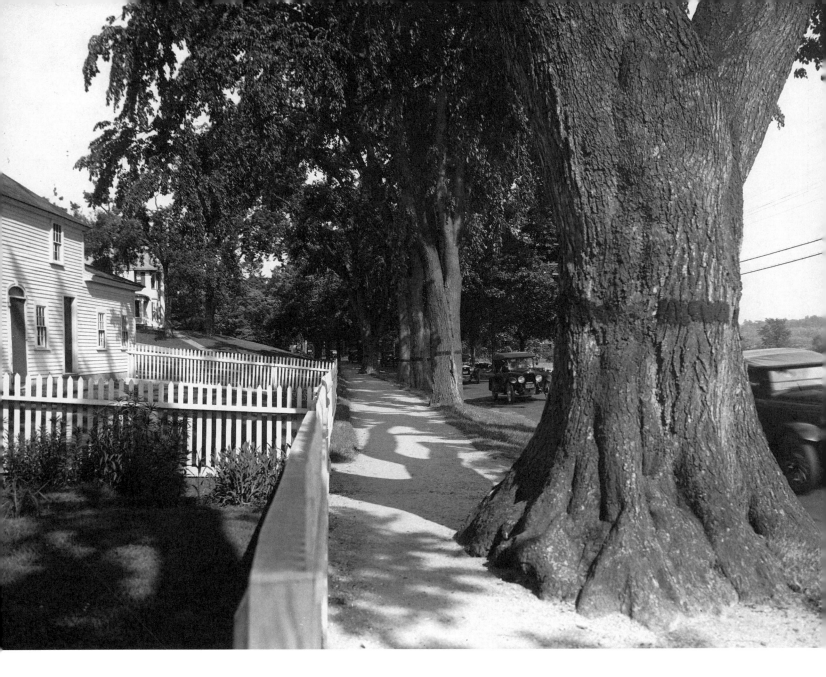

Dutch botanists have discovered that although there is no getting rid of the fungus, some varieties of elm are resistant to it. The Buisman elm, a smooth-leaved variety native to the Mediterranean, has been planted throughout the Netherlands. Some American towns seeking to replace their lost trees also planted Buismans. They are nice trees, but they lack the arched crown that makes American elms so special.

The Elm Research Institute of Harrisville, New Hampshire, funded by a businessman who mourns the trees that once grew in his hometown, has been trying for over twenty years to find a disease-resistant strain. The institute has distributed nearly one hundred thousand saplings called American Liberty elms. These trees, cloned from cross-pollinated hardy parents, grow into the characteristic shape of the classic American elm. The vessels of their capillary system are too narrow for the fungus to pass through. So far, the American Liberty elms, some of which are a decade old, have stayed healthy. □

The elms made archways over the street and the sun would shine through and on a day that was very bright, especially in the fall when the leaves were beginning to turn yellow, it was almost golden going through the street. Just to look down it, just like gold. — Native of Syracuse, New York, reminiscing about Oxford Street in the 1950s

11

The Automat

The first New York Automat opened in 1912 near Times Square, then considered the most glamorous address in America. Located on the west side of Broadway between Forty-sixth and Forty-seventh streets, the Automat had a stained-glass window thirty feet wide and two stories high, designed by Nicola D'Ascenzo, who also created windows for New York's Episcopal Cathedral of St. John the Divine. The moldings of the dining room were carved with leafy branches laden with apples and pears. From the tops of the interior pillars, plaster gargoyles clutching cups and bowls grinned down on the clientele. White marble tabletops gleamed above the white tile floor. Coffee spouted from dolphin-head spigots mounted on chrome urns.

On the first day the Automat took in 8,693 nickels. It became a magnet for tenants of nearby boardinghouses and office workers who couldn't get home for lunch. Soon actors and other celebrities were eager to be photographed at the chic new eatery. Within two years, a second Automat opened at 250 West Forty-second Street, and by 1939, there were forty of them in New York. At the height of their success, they served as many as eight hundred thousand meals a day.

The Automat was a New York institution and a national icon—a cheap, clean cafeteria with a great gimmick. Tasty, nourishing food of all kinds was displayed in individual glass compartments stacked up like mailboxes at the post office. There were no waiters. You dropped coins into the slots in a compartment and turned a knob. The glass door opened, and you helped yourself to a steaming bowl of oatmeal, or Boston baked beans, or a shimmering slice of lemon meringue pie.

The Automat chain was founded by Joseph Horn and Frank Hardart, who started their career in 1888 with a fifteen-stool luncheonette in Philadelphia. They made their reputation serving the French-style coffee that Hardart knew from his boyhood in New Orleans. As their first lunchroom prospered, the partners opened several more, plus a central commissary which ensured quality control and kept costs down.

In 1900, Hardart made a tour of Europe's fanciest hotels and restaurants. On his

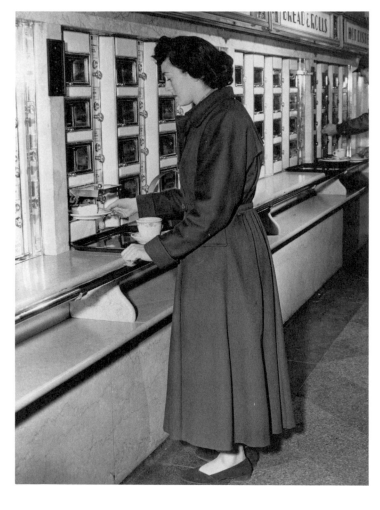

return, he announced proudly that he had paid the Quisisana Automat Company of Berlin $30,000 for equipment similar to the apparatus installed in that city's famous "waiterless" restaurant. Unfortunately, the ship bearing Hardart's purchase sank during a storm in the English Channel, and the partners had to reorder.

Horn & Hardart opened their first Automat in 1902 at 818 Chestnut Street in Philadelphia. The restaurant was an immediate success, at least in part because of the nation's fascination with gadgets and mechanization. Aside from novelty, the equipment's great virtue was its capacity to keep boiling water hot and ice cubes cold, an advantage over other low-cost restaurants, which had problems with hygiene and spoilage.

Messrs. Horn & Hardart stored their recipes in a safe. They provided each manager with a thick, leather-bound rule book containing detailed instructions for preparing and serving every item on the menu. It included diagrams showing how to put the food on the plate. "There is no trick to selling a poor item cheaply," Horn said. "The real trick is to sell a good item cheaply." Every day the top executives sampled food to check on quality control. Horn was the final arbiter. "Joe had the common palate," according to Alice Clements, who worked on the restaurant chain's advertising account for over forty years. "What he thought was good the public thought was good. He was hell on coffee and on mashed potatoes."

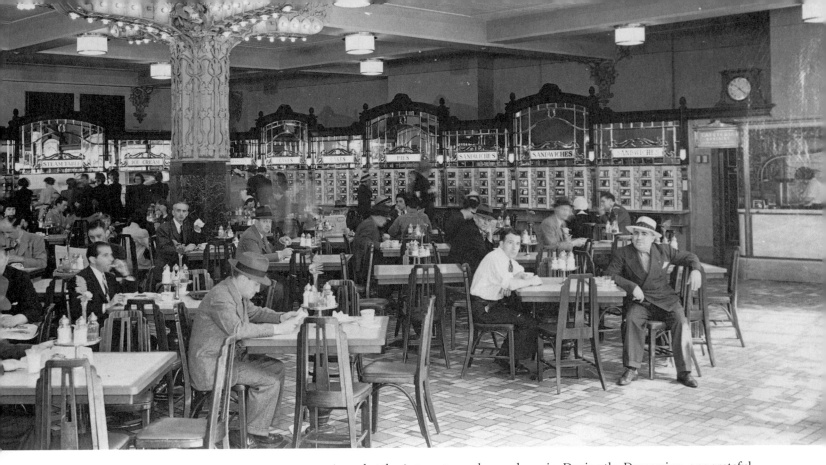

A meal at the Automat was always a bargain. During the Depression, one grateful customer remembers, seventy-five cents bought you a three-course dinner of fish cakes with a jar of tomato sauce, baked beans in a brown cup, coleslaw, a seeded roll with butter, a glass of cold milk (poured from the mouth of a bronzed fish), and two chocolate cupcakes with chocolate sprinkles. People without six bits to spare could sit at a table for several hours nursing a Depression cocktail—free ketchup in a glass of water.

Satisfied diners from the 1940s and 1950s recall the aroma of the beef potpie or the savor of macaroni and cheese. For value, it was hard to beat a vegetable plate. A combination of puréed squash, mashed potatoes, and creamed corn, with a dinner roll on the side, was especially filling.

Although Horn & Hardart operated in just two cities, the firm was one of the world's largest restaurateurs well into midcentury. But management was slow to respond to changes in America's eating habits. Horn & Hardart clung too long to their old downtown locations while their former customers moved out to suburban malls. The Automats maintained a large and varied menu that required talented cooks and elaborate preparation. Fast-food chains specializing in burgers, pizza, or tacos relied on unskilled labor to heat up, package, and push out a very limited choice of items to people on the run. By 1978, the restaurant on the corner of Forty-second Street and Third Avenue, which had opened twenty years earlier, was the only Automat left in New York.

The company tried to convert some locations to Burger King and Arby's, but the transition was unsuccessful. The Forty-second Street Automat closed in 1991. By 1992, after several changes of ownership, Horn & Hardart's primary operating division was a mail-order clothing company. It had sold or closed its food franchises, severing all links to a corporate tradition that once made the Automat the pride of New York. ☐

To this day, I dream of those Sunday nights in the Depression, when my mother—divorced, jobless, and taking in two boarders to help pay the rent—would treat me to dinner at the Automat. The Automat! The Maxim's of the disenfranchised. . . .

To have your own sack of nickels placed in your own tiny hands; to be able to choose your own food, richly on display like museum pieces; to make quick and final decisions at the age of eight, was a lesson in financial dealings that not even two years at the Wharton school could buy today.

Into the forties, I maintained my affection for the Automat. . . . The years went by and I turned from a day customer to a night patron, working on those first attempts at monologues and sketches at two in the morning over steaming black coffee and fresh cheese Danish. And a voice from the stranger opposite me. 'Where you from? California?' 'No I grew up in New York.' 'Is that so? Where in New York?' 'At this table.'
— Neil Simon, *New York Magazine*, December 21-28, 1987

Balsa-Wood Model Airplanes

In World War II, when American GIs cleared the Japanese off the beaches in the Solomons and secured the islands, they discovered stands of balsa trees in the interior. They chopped down a few trees, built a kiln to dry the wood, and began to build model airplanes.

Balsa trees grow not only in the South Pacific, but also in Central and South America. A balsa tree, which in ten years can reach ninety feet in height and fifteen inches in diameter, produces wood that is stronger than cork but half the weight. Thor Heyerdahl took advantage of this unique property when he made his raft, *Kon-Tiki*. Heyerdahl lashed together twelve giant balsa logs, which he sailed across the Pacific from Peru to prove his theory that the Polynesian islanders originally came from South America. Movie studios used balsa wood to make the building facades on Hollywood back lots and also the furniture that stuntmen broke over each others' heads.

But to most Americans, and certainly to those GIs on an island far from home, balsa trees meant model airplanes. Fitting together delicate wings and tails cut from thin sheets of balsa bonded generations of American boys. The first balsa-wood kits appeared in the 1920s, capitalizing on the glamour that fighter planes acquired in World War I. Boys put together replicas of Spads and Nieuports; they built the Red Baron's famous Fokker triplane. Models of the *Spirit of St. Louis*, commemorating Charles Lindbergh's 1927 solo flight across the Atlantic, gave the industry a big boost. Youngsters growing up in the 1940s built Spitfires or B-29s and pretended to be fighting in the Battle of Britain or engaged in a bombing mission over Tokyo.

Boys saved their allowance to buy the latest model kits. They spent hours and hours tracing the pattern onto the sheets of balsa wood and cutting out each piece— the ribs, the body, the wings. The wood often splintered. A day's work could end abruptly when a model maker sliced his thumb open with his X-acto knife. After the pieces were cut out, they were glued together with Duco wood cement—applied with a toothpick—then put aside on waxed paper to dry. Inhaling the glue produced a light-headed euphoria. (In the 1970s sniffing glue, which was toxic to the liver, became a serious problem. To stop the habit, manufacturers added a pungent oil of mustard to their product.)

When the cement dried, the planes were painted and the fuselage decorated with decals that came in the kit: a red bull's-eye inside a white ring inside a yellow circle for the RAF, a white star on a field of blue for the Eighth Air Force, and a black swastika for the Luftwaffe. Finishing a plane took up to two weeks.

The planes flew with a rubber-band engine. The propeller was attached to a shaft which had a hook at one end. There was a second hook in the tail assembly. A big red rubber band was stretched between the hooks. Turning the propeller counter-clockwise twisted and tightened the band. The trick was to keep it from unwinding until the plane was launched. Once released, the plane might stay in the air for thirty seconds—about as long as the Wright brothers' first flight at Kitty Hawk. When the power cut out, the plane glided to earth—or crashed. Sometimes planes were attached to a wire tether which controlled their flight path and landed them safely.

The first all-plastic model plane kits were marketed in 1952, although plastic landing gear, flight canopies, and rockets had been included in balsa kits for some time. Plastic parts didn't have to be cut out; they just snapped off the frame holding them. Because they were made in molds, plastic parts preserved design details and textures impossible to capture in balsa, such as the fittings on the fuselage. Plastic could also be shaped to eliminate the angles created at the juncture of wood parts. By 1960 the biggest manufacturer of balsa kits had converted completely to plastic.

Plastic came along just in time to capitalize on the Korean War. F-86 and MIG-17 fighters sold well through the 1970s. Since then, most successful models have continued to be up-to-the-minute military planes. The 1986 movie *Top Gun* stimulated demand for the F-14 Tomcat. Desert Storm made Stealth bomber models popular. But most young boys today aren't interested in military aircraft, and pilots are not their heroes. They're more likely to admire Arnold Schwarzenegger or the Ninja Turtles. Their fathers introduce them to model aircraft because they want to share a boyhood hobby with their sons.

A large percentage of the buyers of model airplane kits are grown men, shopping for themselves. Some haunt hobby shops for balsa-wood kits, which can't be found in toy stores at the mall. The kits are not cheap, but balsa is lighter than plastic, and weight counts in flight. The most elaborate balsa planes are commonly powered by two-cycle gas engines like the ones that drive chain saws. Learning to fly these planes by radio control takes hours. It is not a kid's game. □

I once spent ten days making a beautiful model of a Messerschmitt 109. I flew it in the field behind our house. Then in a kind of ritual sacrifice, I set it on fire, fantasizing that a German pilot was slumped over the controls.
— Sixty-year-old lawyer from New York

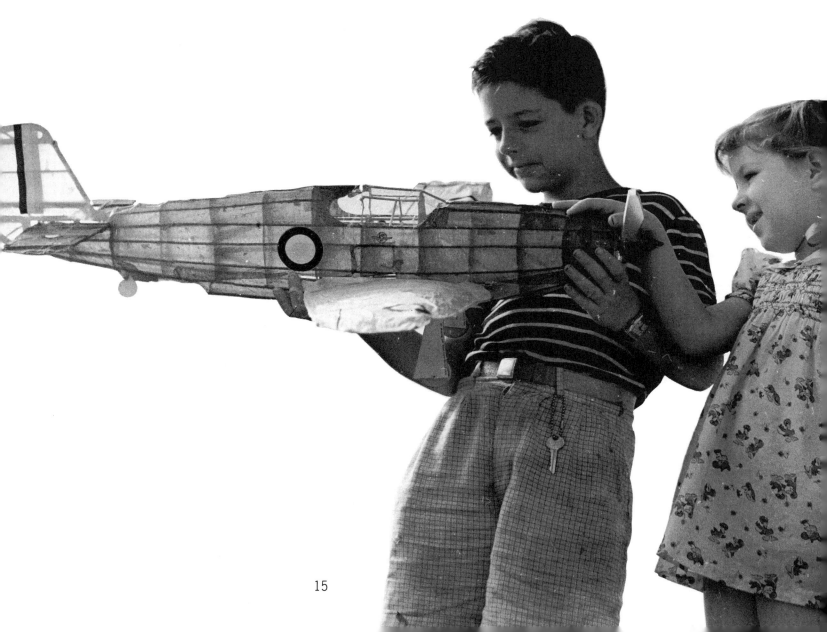

Bank Checks

When European colonists first settled in North America, they needed to trade with each other and the Native Americans. Barter worked for a while, but expanding commerce required a more flexible money system. Tobacco, corn, beaver skins, and wampum served briefly as legal tender in Massachusetts and Virginia, until the colonies began minting their own coins and experimenting with paper money, bank drafts, and personal IOUs.

Bank checks, a formal kind of IOU designed primarily for business use, appeared in New England in the late eighteenth century and spread west in the nineteenth. In the 1880s, the New York Chamber of Commerce reported with condescension that "the use of the modern instrument of checks is found on the remotest frontier." Private citizens discovered that checks were safer and easier to carry than cash, and the register or check stubs provided a convenient way of recording where their money went. Bankers marketed checking accounts to their middle-class and upper-class clients as a service, although as early as 1884 one prescient banker from Kansas warned his colleagues they were making a bad mistake by offering them free of charge.

During the first half of the twentieth century, the possessor of a checking account was likely to be a substantial member of the community. Wage earners expected their weekly pay envelope to be filled with legal tender, and working-class families felt more comfortable with cash. Only in the 1950s did paychecks become common, and not till the 1960s did over fifty percent of American households have personal checking accounts.

One young woman, who worked for a major publishing company, held out well into the 1980s. "I wanted to keep my life simple. I didn't have any credit cards either. I would take my paycheck to the bank, stand in line, and cash it. I'd buy three or four money orders—for my landlord, for the telephone company, and maybe for a magazine subscription or something else I needed to order by mail. I put the rest of the money in my underwear drawer. If I saw a blouse I liked on Tuesday, on Wednesday I'd take money out of the drawer to buy it. I didn't have to balance a checkbook, wait to see if a check cleared, or worry about being overdrawn or in debt."

Obliged to open an account when she bought an apartment, she now can't believe she managed without it. These days, she and her husband write approximately twenty-five checks a month, about average for American households.

Unfortunately for the banks, the success with which they marketed checking accounts after midcentury has come back to haunt them. In 1990 there were about 250 billion commercial transactions in America—more than 56 billion of them settled by checks. Each of those checks passed through an average of ten hands between the time it was written and the time it was returned to the writer, canceled, as part of the monthly bank statement. Moving each check through the system cost about seventy-nine cents, adding up to a total annual burden to the banks of about $45 billion.

Since the 1970s banks have been trying to persuade customers to let them transfer funds electronically or truncate the procedure that sends a check on its cumbersome round from payer to payee, to payee's bank, to payer's bank, and finally back home. When customers authorize the bank to pay their mortgage, car payment, or utility bills, no checks are drawn, and the transaction takes place as an electronic data transfer. The Social Security Administration deposits 345 million payments directly into clients' bank accounts. Large corporations and financial institutions clear their transactions with each other by computer. In 1992 a New York bank advertised, "You can pay gas companies, mortgages, cable TV . . . dry cleaners and doctors, family and friends, all with just one phone call." In that year, one in twenty American households authorized a bank to pay some of their bills electronically. Once a month they received a printout with the name of the person or company to whom funds were sent.

Truncation is the industry's term for a modified version of electronic transfer. After a check is deposited the first time, it ceases to move physically. All the subsequent stages of the transaction are handled by computer. The banks save about two-thirds of the cost of old-fashioned processing—for one thing they no longer have to pay postage on those bulky monthly statements filled with canceled checks.

16

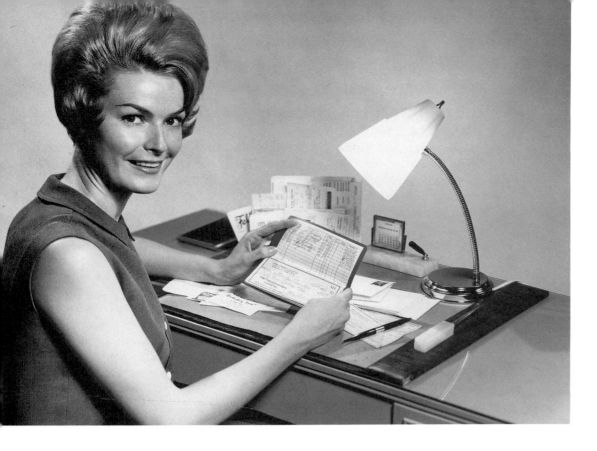

Customers have to be educated to accept a printed statement or images of their checks as their monthly statement rather than the physical return of their canceled checks. Some people are afraid they will have difficulty proving they've paid a bill. However, the Internal Revenue Service and most large financial institutions already accept images as proof of payment, and merchants are coming around. One selling point is that imaging will simplify people's "bookkeeping"—which usually consists of stuffing records into shopping bags or old shoe boxes. One satisfied user, admittedly a banker, reports, "I can put into a narrow three-ring binder the complete history of every payment I've made in the last two years."

Consumers aren't knocking on the door to ask for these services. It's a hard sell driven by the banks' desire to cut costs. But automatic teller machines also began as an economizing measure rather than as a response to consumer demand, and now they're tremendously popular.

The banks are also expanding their traditional credit card business and trying to interest customers in a new piece of plastic—the debit card—which replaces cash, checks, or a traditional charge card at restaurants and stores. Bankers hope that debit cards will appeal to people who don't want to run up credit and don't like to carry cash. The debit card withdraws the amount of a purchase from the customer's checking account immediately. There's no way to bounce a check or play the float. No longer will a customer be able to write a check for $150 to buy a new pair of suede shoes on Friday and rush to the bank after payday the next Monday to cover it, or charge tickets to Tahiti on a credit card and pay later.

Consultants to the banking industry predicted in 1989 that writing checks would peak in the early 1990s and then begin to decline. They believe debit cards and even traditional credit cards that allow customers to pay for many transactions with just one check are better than the glut of paper they're struggling with now. But it may be well into the twenty-first century before checks completely disappear. ☐

In 1957, after Mickey Mantle's second consecutive season as the Most Valuable Player in the American League, the Yankees tried to cut his salary of about $60,000 because his statistics weren't as good as they had been the year before. Mantle finally negotiated a raise to about $75,000. But during his entire eighteen-year career—in fact at any point from 1885 until after Mantle retired in 1969—baseball players were at a distinct disadvantage in all their salary negotiations, because a clause in the standard big league contract prevented them from setting up competitive bidding among several clubs for their services. The so-called reserve clause bound players to negotiate only with the organization they had played for the previous year.

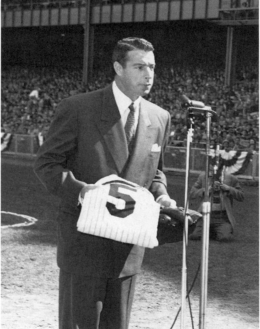

Teams could and did trade players—fewer than half the players on 1965 rosters were with the same clubs in 1970—but most trades affected rookies or over-the-hill veterans. The core of most ball clubs remained fairly stable. Fans memorized the names and statistics of every member of their favorite teams. They also knew who was waiting in the minors to replace an aging third baseman or solve a chronic problem in left field. Few stars changed teams at the height of their careers. All the wheeling and dealing was done by management. The players had no right to undertake such deals for their own advantage. If a ballplayer was traded to a team he didn't like, his only recourse was to sit out the season without contract or salary.

The reserve clause was probably a violation of the country's antitrust laws. The complicity of the team owners in preventing the players from negotiating freely would seem to have met the legal definition of a trust—essentially, any combination of similar businesses colluding to reduce competition. However, those few challenges to the system that were taken to court were settled in favor of the owners, usually on technical grounds. In 1949, dissenting from a majority decision upholding the reserve system, Judge Jerome Frank of the United States Court of Appeals wrote that the players were "quasi-peons" held in "virtual slavery." Nevertheless, it would take twenty more years for the slaves to revolt.

In October 1969, just after his twelfth season as an outstanding center fielder for the St. Louis Cardinals, Curt Flood was traded to the Philadelphia Phillies. Flood decided not to accept the trade. As he later explained, "It violated the logic and integrity of my existence. I was not a consignment of goods. I was a man, the rightful proprietor of my own person and my own talents."

Augustus Busch, proprietor of the Cardinals, said that Flood's behavior, like campus unrest and Vietnam War protests, was a sign of the collapse of American values. Baseball Commissioner Bowie Kuhn said that an end to the reserve clause would be "the end of baseball as we know it." What they failed to say was that every aspect of major league baseball *except* the reserve clause had been changed significantly since the structure of the game was formalized early in the century.

It was the owners who were transforming the game. Corporate interests replaced many of the original family-based managements. Some teams moved from old downtown ballparks to shiny new taxpayer-subsidized stadiums in the suburbs. Others relocated to new cities in search of bigger crowds. By 1969, the American and National leagues together had added eight franchises to their original sixteen. Two more were created in 1977, and two more began operations in 1993. During the first phases of expansion, player salaries remained quite low.

Curt Flood sat out the 1970 season—passing up the Phillies' contract offer of $100,000, though he desperately needed the money. After being assured that his case would not be prejudiced by his decision to come back and play, Flood accepted a trade to the Washington Senators the following year. His challenge to the reserve clause came to trial in March 1970. The United States District Court for the Southern District of New York ruled in favor of the owners (a decision eventually sustained by the Supreme Court). The players and their new union realized they needed to try a different tack.

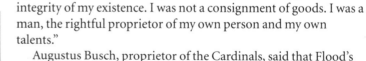

Baseball
Players
Who Stay
With One
Team

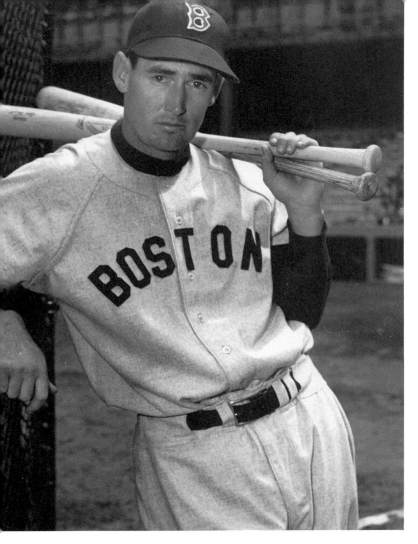

In 1975, two star pitchers, Andy Messersmith of the Los Angeles Dodgers and Dave McNally of the Montreal Expos, played the entire season without contracts. They contended that the basic agreement between management and players governing the format of all contracts implied that if they played for a full year after their contracts ended, they had no further connection to the club. They argued that they could then sign with any team at whatever salary they could command. Management countered that players who had played during this so-called option year were still bound by customary practice, if not formal language, to negotiate only with their former team.

In December 1975, the three-man arbitration panel set up by the baseball establishment and the Players Association to handle labor-management disputes decided that Messersmith and McNally were right. The stunned owners tried unsuccessfully to get the courts to overthrow the arbitration ruling. They also fired the arbitrator who wrote the decision, locked out the players for half of the 1976 spring training period, and tried to convince the press and the public that the players were to blame.

Their strategy, characterized by sportswriter Roger Angell as "paternalistic" and "insensitive," was also unsuccessful. The season, after a short spring, opened on schedule. McNally retired because of an injured arm, but Messersmith signed with the Atlanta Braves for more than twice as much money as the Dodgers had paid him. Other superstars soon renegotiated better contracts with their teams.

In July 1976, the players and management signed a revised basic agreement. It permitted any player to become a free agent after six years in the majors and allowed players with at least two years service to take salary disputes to arbitration.

What the owners had always feared finally came to pass: there was a sudden escalation of superstar salaries, and a subsequent climb in the wage scale of rookies and journeyman players. In 1975, only three players earned more than $200,000 a year. The next year, Reggie Jackson signed a five-year contract with the New York Yankees for nearly $3 million.

By 1992, the *average* salary of major leaguers was over $1 million a year. At least twenty-three players had contracts worth more than $4 million for a single season. Fewer than half were playing for the teams that had brought them to the big leagues. ☐

Some Loyal Old-timers:

Player	Length of Service	Retired
Henry Aaron	22 years with Milwaukee/ Atlanta Braves	1976
Ernie Banks	19 years with Chicago Cubs	1971
Johnny Bench	17 years with Cincinnati Reds	1979
Joe DiMaggio	16 years with New York Yankees	1951
Bob Gibson	16 years with St. Louis Cardinals	1975
Al Kaline	22 years with Detroit Tigers	1974
Willie Mays	22 years with New York/ San Francisco Giants	1972
Stan Musial	22 years with St. Louis Cardinals	1963
Carl Yastrzemski	23 years with Boston Red Sox	1983

The first movies ever made were shot on black-and-white stock. Some of the most vivid images that Hollywood engraved on the world's consciousness were in shades of gray. Yet films like *Citizen Kane, The Informer, All About Eve, Casablanca, Top Hat, Pride of the Yankees,* and *High Noon* are anything but colorless. Conditioned by newspaper halftones and family snapshot albums and manipulated by the subtle arts of cimematographers, audiences accepted the convention of black-and-white images as an approximation of reality.

But right from the start, the film industry tried to get closer to reality by adding color to developed black-and-white film. Many one- and two-reelers were hand-colored frame by frame. As films got longer, hand-coloring became too expensive. Instead, producers began tinting their films. Developed black-and-white stock was immersed in a dye bath, so that entire scenes were washed in a single hue. Sometimes the choice of tint was functional: yellow for daylight, blue for night. Sometimes it was expressive: red for jealousy, green for envy. In the first western, *The Great Train Robbery* (1903), yellow was used for the dance-hall interior, and blue-green for the countryside. A more elaborate chemical process, called toning, made it possible to add a second, or even a third, color to specific scenes. D. W. Griffith's *Way Down East* (1920) combined hand-painting, tinted stock, and toning in some sequences.

The arrival of talking pictures represented a setback for color effects because the toning process interfered with the clarity of the soundtrack. Several companies had attempted unsuccessfully to record images directly onto color negative stocks, and finally the Technicolor Corporation developed a three-strip process that was the first practical system to record "natural" color on film.

Becky Sharp (1935), the first feature shot in Technicolor, was a hit. To get audiences used to color, the director of the film, Rouben Mamoulian, built up color intensities slowly. His opening scenes were pastel; midway through the film the colors become more flamboyant. For the climactic ball on the eve of the Battle of Waterloo, Mamoulian has written, he pulled out all stops and presented a "great color smash." One unconvinced critic said, "The total impression is one of a brass band in color rather than a well-modulated symphony." He concluded, "As long as color in film has the quality of a gaudy calendar lithograph, there is no future for it, artistically, except in the embellishment of . . . the animated cartoon."

Producers were more enthusiastic. In 1936 Walter Wanger said, "Color is just as inevitable as speech. I don't believe that one black-and-white picture will be produced four years hence." A year later Samuel Goldwyn announced that from then on all his pictures would be made in Technicolor, predicting that "black and whites soon would be as rare as silent films."

Just as sound destroyed some stars' careers because their voices lacked timbre, color was expected to threaten others. *The New York Post* warned, "Bleached blonds will never succeed in the new medium. A brown-eyed peroxide blonde may look all right in black and white, and she may even appear all right in life. But, magnified tenfold in natural colors on the screen, she appears definitely unreal." Male stars with heavy beards were also in for a hard time— they would find "their hours of usefulness on a set shortened" unless they faced the reality of shaving several times a day.

Technicolor was a highly complicated process. Part of the difficulty was technical: It was "slower" than black and white; that is, it needed brighter lights to expose an image properly. It had a narrow margin for error: shadow areas were more liable to turn murky and bright areas to burn out. It was much more expensive: It took three times as much film stock to shoot in Technicolor as it did in black and white.

In addition, the Technicolor Corporation controlled all stages of production. The company leased cameras to film producers and developed all the film. Technicolor also had the right to supervise the choice of colors for sets and costumes, a practice which sometimes had surprising repercussions. In 1938 makeup artist Buddy Westmore became furious during the filming of *Kentucky*. The Technicolor expert assigned to the movie felt that Loretta Young's favorite horse didn't match the color

My two black-and-white films, *The Elephant Man* and *Eraserhead*, were shot specifically in those tones to communicate a feeling. You see things differently in black and white, you tend to look at it more closely; it's dreamlike, not reality, and both these films would be ruined in color. — David Lynch, director, quoted in *American Film*, January/February 1987

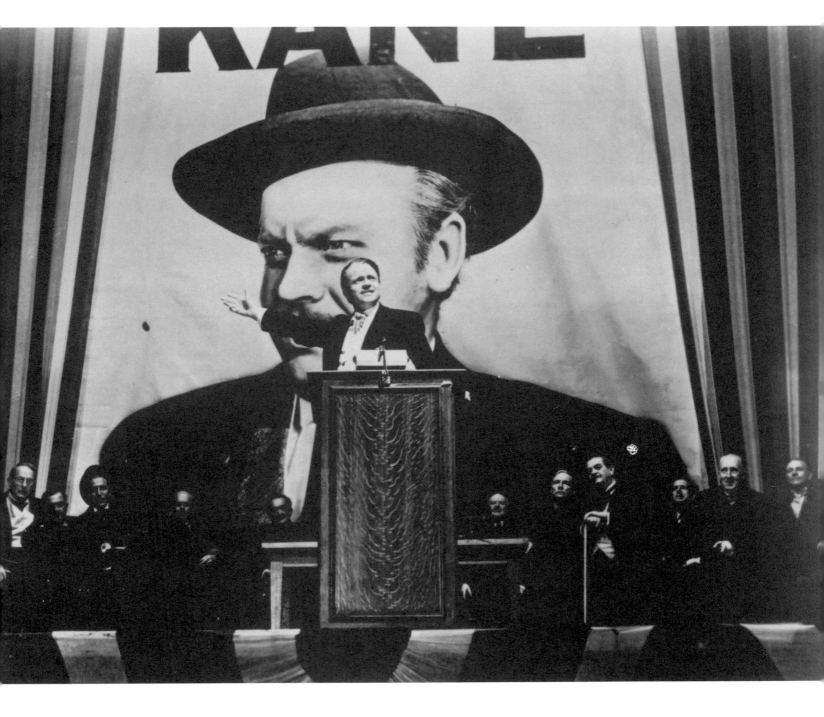

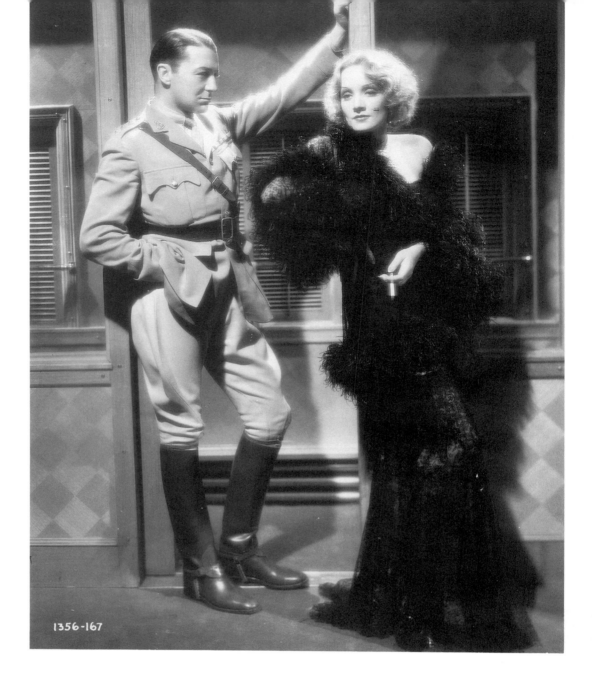

1356-167

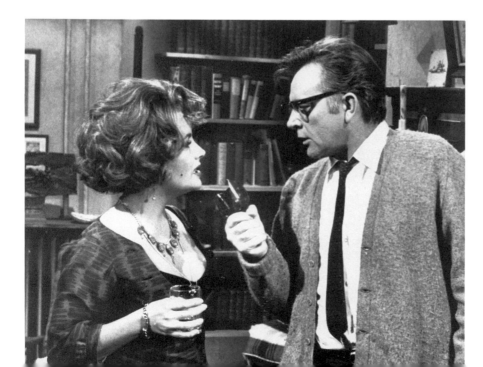

motifs of her riding habit. Westmore was summarily instructed to bleach the horse's mane and tail.

Budget-conscious filmmakers made a virtue of necessity—they convinced themselves and the public that black and white was grittier, more realistic, more serious than color. In an intense story like *The Informer*, "clashing colors . . . would be destructive," wrote one critic in 1935. "The sombre, brooding tragedy of *The Informer* in its grey and purple mantle of night seems eminently more suited to the grey and black shadows of conventional photography." Influenced by German expressionist films from the 1920s, cinematographers had created ways of lighting black-and-white films to enhance the emotional impact of the action. Three Academy Award nominees released in one year, 1940, exhibited the range of technical solutions to narrative problems. Deep shadows conveyed a foreboding dramatic mood in *The Long Voyage Home*. Harsh contrasts with soft shadows, strong highlights, and stark silhouettes underscored the melodrama surrounding Joan Fontaine in *Rebecca*. The brilliant lighting and crisp definition of *The Philadelphia Story* suggested a more carefree mood.

As long as Technicolor continued to pose problems, and the audience accepted the sophisticated conventions that directors and cinematographers had devised for black and white, the two formats existed side by side. Studios used color for musicals and outdoor adventures; black and white was for drama, domestic comedies, and film noir.

Technicolor's monopoly lasted until 1949, when it was challenged by Eastmancolor, which could be used in any camera, could be processed at any lab, and was much less expensive. At first the result was inferior to Technicolor. Alfred Hitchcock's *To Catch a Thief*, shot in Eastmancolor, won an Oscar in 1954 for color cinematography, although the color recording was often coarse.

As costs declined and location shooting increased, directors used color more and more. In the 1960s, films like Fellini's *8 1/2*, Resnais's *Muriel*, and Antonioni's *Red Desert* undermined the classic assumptions about color; they were as immediate and sensuous as any movie in black and white. In 1966, a Hollywood columnist wrote, "The black-and-white film is becoming as extinct as the nickel cup of coffee." Of all the movies that major studios had in release or in production at the time, only six were

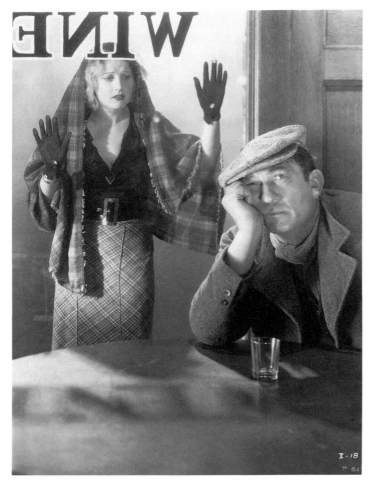

shot in black and white. It was taken for granted that in the future only idiosyncratic and low-budget projects would not be in color.

Television finished off black and white. By the mid-1960s, all three networks broadcast in color; movies supplied hours of entertainment. If motion picture producers wanted to sell their product to TV, it would have to be in color. Even abroad, color films rented for more money than those in black and white.

Some filmmakers held out. Producer Ernest Lehman chose to shoot one of the most dramatic films of 1966, *Who's Afraid of Virginia Woolf?*, in black and white because he thought it captured emotional tones that were lost in color. Woody Allen made black-and-white films into the 1990s. Allen's cinematographer, Gordon Willis, said their films were "designed physically and emotionally for black and white." Some directors and critics agreed that the old dichotomy held up: color focused the eye on the ephemeral and superficial; black and white revealed the essential and profound.

In 1987 the Turner Broadcasting System syndicated "colorized" black-and-white film classics like *It's a Wonderful Life* and *Miracle on 34th Street*. Colorizers either electronically re-create the actual colors used on the set of the original film or arbitrarily assign new ones. An estimated sixteen thousand black-and-white feature films could presumably be colorized and rereleased for a wider audience.

Many filmmakers and film buffs believe that colorizing will destroy the artifacts created by one of America's unique industries. Director Francis Ford Coppola said, "If one doesn't feel that culture and art are more important than commerce, then anyone can buy a Picasso painting and cut it in half because they figure they can sell it as two." Though the original black-and-white versions will be kept in vaults, as time goes by, fewer and fewer people will be able to see them. □

Pittsburgh was the hub of America's industrial heartland. Steel from Pittsburgh's mills was used to make the nation's railroads, cars, and air-planes, hold up its skyscrapers, and support its subway tunnels. In the industry's heyday, over a dozen huge plants up and down the Monongahela Valley pumped out a steady stream of black smoke—visible particles of ash and other residues of imperfect combustion—that polluted the city's air and made it seem to one British observer like "hell with the lid off."

The sky was always orange. Streetlights sometimes went on at noon. Art Rooney, patriarch of the family that owned the Pittsburgh Steelers, recalled that, in his youth, "we'd leave for school in the morning with clean clothes and get there covered with soot." When a blast furnace "slipped," tons of grime would be blown out the top of the furnace, and a dark blizzard would descend. Laundry drying on the line, fresh paint on a front porch, even the newspaper spread open on a desk turned black in an instant.

In 1948, a terrible five-day smog darkened the skies of Donora, a small town up the valley. Families huddled in their homes, afraid to go outside where they could not catch their breath. Half the town's population was stricken with respiratory disease, and five people died before the winds changed and cleared the air.

By the time of the Donora tragedy, efforts that would eventually clean up the mess were already under way. In 1946, Richard K. Mellon, the head of his family's vast banking and corporate holdings, attended a party with his wife in downtown Pittsburgh. When they were unable to see the lights of the Mellon National Bank half a block away, Mrs. Mellon supposedly made her husband promise to save their city from asphyxiation.

Under Mellon's leadership, a group of business and civic leaders undertook what they proudly called the Pittsburgh Renaissance. The railroads, which had brought more than seventy coal-burning locomotives chugging into downtown Pittsburgh every day, were forced to switch to diesel fuel, and the train yards were relocated on the outskirts of town. All coal-burning furnaces were converted to natural gas.

Black Smoke

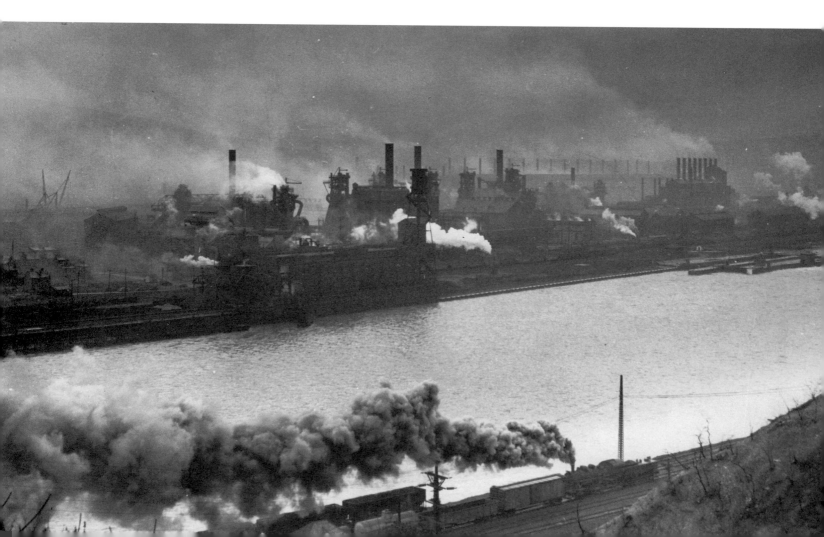

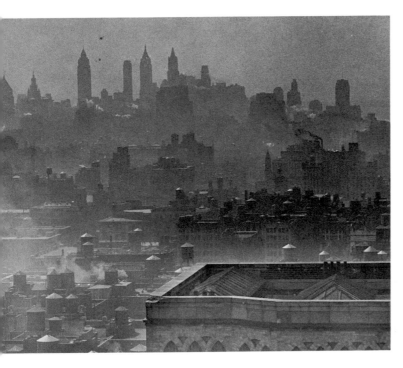

In 1985, Pittsburgh was named the most livable city in America by Rand McNally. Much of the steel industry was long gone from the valley, and the few plants that remained operated under stringent pollution controls. The transformation of the air over Pittsburgh has been a model for the rest of the country.

For several decades, people have been protesting against factories, incinerators, power plants, motor vehicles, construction projects, and heating systems that pollute the air, endanger their health, and make their communities grimy and unpleasant. A number of laws, including the Clean Air Acts of 1963, 1970, and 1990, have created standards for measuring air quality and guidelines for getting rid of pollution. The laws have forced heavy industry, homeowners, oil companies, and public utilities to clean up their act. As a result, air quality in much of the U.S. has improved steadily since the late 1960s.

Many cities have shut down huge municipal incinerators or insisted that they be fitted with filters to catch most of the large ash particles that coat a city with grime. Public utilities and the owners of individual buildings are often required to generate heat by burning low-sulphur oil or natural gas rather than coal. The transformation of American industry from blue- to white-collar operations has helped too. In many cities, old-fashioned blast furnaces and other industrial polluters have closed for good. A resident of Gary, Indiana, said, "It's a mixed blessing. I'm out of work, but I can breathe deeper."

For all these reasons, the amount of measurable suspended particles in the nation's air dropped by sixty-two percent between 1970 and 1990. Cars on the street don't get filthy overnight; it takes more time for black soot to pile up on the windowsills; and people are less vulnerable to upper respiratory infections, cardiovascular disease, and some kinds of cancer.

Industrial exhaust has been reduced so much that, in many communities, wood smoke from fireplaces and stoves is now the leading cause of air pollution. Fireplaces were a particular curse in the West, where they gave a kind of back-to-nature flavor to vacation homes. An editor at the *Aspen Times* remembers when ski lodges had fireplaces in every room. "You saw a huge cloud of smoke on the side of town where condos have been built."

Consequently the town of Aspen forbade the construction of new fireplaces. Everyone who already had them—except those people who gathered wood to heat their homes—was required to burn gas logs. In the early 1990s, similar laws were considered in other Colorado communities including Denver, where fireplaces cause as much as thirty-five percent of the city's serious pollution. Missoula, Montana, which is hemmed in on all sides by the Rockies, used to suffer from noxious air more than one hundred days a year. After a city ordinance outlawed fireplaces in new homes and required anyone who used wood for heat to get a special permit, the number of days of unacceptable air quality dropped to two.

Many communities in northern California impose strict standards on wood-burning stoves and limit the number of working fireplaces in new homes. In the greater Los Angeles area, presoaked briquettes and fire-starting fluids may not be used for backyard barbecues. Some activists wanted to get rid of chain saws and gas-powered lawn mowers, which do not have to comply with emission standards.

Most areas of the country now surpass federal requirements for getting visible particles out of the air. Nearly three-quarters of all Americans live in counties where the level of particle emission is acceptable by federal standards. Invisible pollution, however, continues to produce problems. Sulphur dioxide causes acid rain, and volatile organic compounds, baked by sunlight, can cause ground-level ozone, which is the new definition of smog. Sometimes the smog in Los Angeles is so dense it fills the sky with a murky golden haze.

Although virtually every community in the country meets sulphur dioxide and lead emissions standards, clean air remains an elusive goal in places like southern California and Denver, where mountains prevent the free circulation of air. But in most of the U.S., after three decades of pollution controls, on a clear day you can breathe deeply and enjoy the view. □

Remember the Sabbath day, to keep it holy. . . . The seventh day is the sabbath of the Lord thy God; in it thou shalt not do any work, thou, nor thy son, nor thy daughter, thy manservant, nor thy maidservant, nor thy cattle, nor thy stranger that is within thy gates. —Exodus 20:8, 10

Blue Laws

In New York City, as recently as the early 1970s, you were out of luck if you needed to buy a quart of milk on Sunday. Supermarkets and neighborhood delis alike closed all day, as did banks, department stores, and almost every other commercial establishment except restaurants and a few convenience stores. You could buy razor blades but not a razor; you could buy girlie magazines because newsstands were open, but not a Bible because bookstores were closed. The streets were quiet, the sidewalks still. The Reverend Billy Graham reminded his fellow Americans in 1974 that the "first priority in your Sabbath observance must be attendance at the church of your choice."

Laws to protect the Sabbath were brought to the American colonies from England. The term *blue laws* dates from the seventeenth century when ordinances governing Sunday behavior in the New Haven colony were printed on blue paper. Offenders were whipped, fined, put in the stocks, or caged on the village green. A random sample of arrests in Arkansas in about 1800 shows miscreants apprehended and fined for digging potatoes, shooting squirrels, gathering early peaches, and

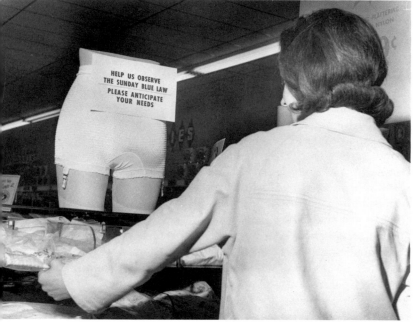

clearing land. Well into the twentieth century, Sabbath legislation remained most extensive in the original thirteen states because of colonial precedents and in the South because of the strength of the Baptist church.

From the start, blue laws caused controversy. Some members of the community, frequently Jews or Seventh-Day Adventists, objected to the choice of Sunday as the Sabbath (a complaint that would be revived by Muslims in the 1980s). Secularists complained that any Sabbath laws broke down the wall between church and state. However, most people—whatever their religious beliefs— had some residue of feeling that Sunday was special. Ernest Hemingway, for one, believed it was bad luck to work on Sunday.

A typical American family in the 1940s probably attended church and Sunday school. Certainly the children spent part of the morning pouring over the funnies. Dressed in their Sunday best, everyone sat down to a big dinner at noon. Men worked a six-day week, so their wives fussed for them on their day off. Then came the Sunday drive. The whole family piled into the car. Maybe they took a picnic; maybe they went to a cousin's house or an ice-cream parlor. Sometimes they took flowers to the cemetery. Togetherness was important.

Imperceptibly, the Sunday drive began to change. The most likely destination became the new shopping strips flanking the new divided highway at the edge of town. The malls offered a wide range of merchandise and the chance for a growing family to buy in bulk. Because husbands took the car to work all week, Sunday was the only time it could be used for heavy-duty shopping. The mall stores did thirty to forty percent of their business on Sunday. Small stores in residential neighborhoods were forced to stay open to keep up with the competition.

At first chain stores and downtown merchants opposed Sunday openings, under the guise of concern for the Sabbath, but really because they wanted to avoid the cost of staffing their stores seven days a week. They often offered financial support to religious leaders who voiced the more traditional objection to Sunday business. Too many Americans "have begun to stamp the Lord's day with the dollar mark," wrote one Catholic editorialist.

The sale of goods on Sunday is a violation of law. . . . It offends the eye of the public, in evincing a disregard for the solemnity of the day, which is set apart by law for rest, quiet and religious worship. — George Harris, member of the Washington, D.C., bar, *A Treatise on Sunday Laws*, 1892

From time to time, a store owner who was fined for opening on Sunday challenged the validity of the laws in court. Finally, in 1961 the U.S. Supreme Court agreed for the first time in the twentieth century to hear arguments on the issue. In the case of *McGowan v. Maryland*, Chief Justice Earl Warren, writing for the majority, said that blue laws weren't religious in nature and that any community had the right to enforce a day or period of quiet. "Insuring the public welfare through a common day of rest is a legitimate interest of government."

Public demand for Sunday shopping, however, persisted as more women joined the work force. Eventually, big stores at the mall and even the old downtown stores switched sides. Local officials usually looked the other way. Enlightened church leaders bowed to the inevitable. One clergyman in Maryland said, "A day of rest? Who is kidding whom? . . . Most Sunday laws do not guarantee a man Sunday rest. They only ensure that he cannot sell certain items on Sunday."

In 1976 the New York Court of Appeals issued an influential ruling in response to a number of challenges to the constitutionality of local and statewide blue laws. The court noted that many of these ordinances were unenforceable or contradictory. Discount stores and food shops routinely flouted the law. There were laws permitting

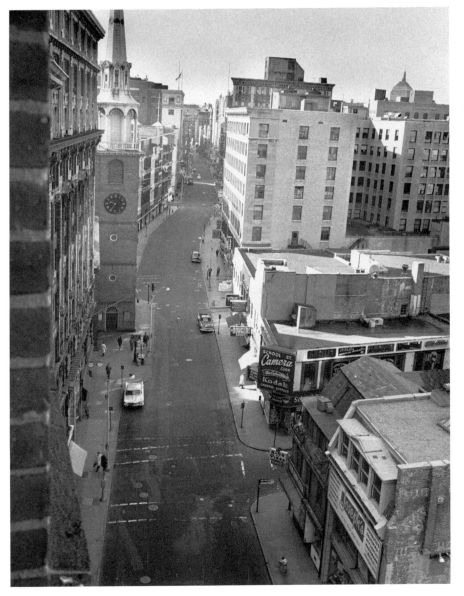

"emergency repairs," but who defined emergency? Drinks could be sold in a restaurant but not in a bar. Christmas tree ornaments could be sold on Sundays, but trees could not. Some communities allowed the sale of fresh produce but not of packaged food. The court found the jumble unacceptable and ruled out the lot, stating that the "gallimaufry of exceptions" had wiped out any connection between intent and practice and that the inequalities of enforcement deprived many store owners of equal protection before the law.

By late 1980s, only thirteen states still had any general laws on the books. Even in the 1990s, various communities around the country retain local ordinances and statutes that forbid selling alcohol, hunting, barbering, playing bingo, bowling, dancing, digging clams or oysters, selling cars or wholesale tobacco products, or playing polo. Except for limitations on the sale of alcohol, hardly anyone enforces the laws, and hardly anyone cares. Customers are used to the convenience of Sunday shopping, and government officials like the sales tax revenues. Most consumers, except those who may live on a busy, noisy street, want everything open all the time. □

In the October 13, 1957, *New York Times*, a reporter characterized the social life of middle-class American couples: "The Smiths have the Browns to dinner and then the Browns have the Smiths to dinner. After they eat, they must do something. Television is hardly social; conversation is a lost art; cards are an acceptable solution." So the Smiths and the Browns played a few hands of bridge—"the top of the heap of social games."

Mrs. Smith and Mrs. Brown also got together with six other housewives from the neighborhood for a Thursday afternoon bridge party. On Mrs. Smith's day to entertain, she set up two folding bridge tables in her living room and laid out her pink linen bridge cloths and napkins. After a glass of Dubonnet and a lunch of chicken à la king and peas, the "girls," as they called themselves, settled down to play. The winner could clear five dollars at the end of the day. Sometimes the girls put all their winnings into a kitty, which they spent on an annual dinner party for their husbands—"the men."

Mrs. Smith's daughter, Jane, came home from school just before the party broke up. She was eager to decipher the rules of bidding, the private language of "finesse" and "renege," and the ritual exclamations, like "very pretty!" when the "dummy" hand was revealed on the table. She believed that playing bridge was a sign and a privilege of adulthood, like smoking or driving a car. After Jane had gained some experience in family games, she was allowed to sit in for a hand or two at the Thursday afternoon parties. When she went off to college, she found several regular foursomes in her dorm. Bridge sometimes seemed second only to boys, and way ahead of books, as a topic of interest to the coeds.

At any time from the 1930s through the 1950s, there were as many as forty million bridge players in the U.S. Bridge was the most popular card game, and card games were among the most common entertainments in the pretelevision age. In 1961, Charles Goren, a great teacher and promoter of bridge, called it a "social necessity."

Not for long. In the late 1960s, when Jane Smith graduated from college, she and other young brides took jobs outside their homes. When couples got together in the evening, they went out to dinner so no one had to cook. They might also go to a movie or, in later years, rent a video. They weren't likely to play cards. By 1990, only ten or twelve million social bridge players were active in the U.S. Most of them were middle-aged or older; the mean age of the two hundred thousand or so Americans who considered themselves competitive players was fifty-seven. A survey of college students revealed that most young people considered bridge players to be old, fat, and dull.

Nevertheless, the game retains considerable appeal for those who welcome it as an intellectual challenge, and competitive bridge still has serious adherents. Many of America's top CEOs claim that bridge games provide a social setting in which to make business connections—or pick up petty cash. Some well-heeled and highly competitive executives have been known to wager $20,000 or so on a single rubber (the best of three games).

More than four thousand clubs across the country sponsor regular evenings of duplicate bridge, a game in which members of every team play the same series of predealt hands and vie to outscore the opposition. Competitive players may also try their luck in the thousand or so tournaments sanctioned each year by the American Contract Bridge League. The ACBL has begun promoting a simpler, shorter version of duplicate bridge and has increased support to bridge clubs on college campuses, hoping to encourage a new generation of enthusiasts.

Yet it's unlikely that social bridge will ever revive. Women continue to work outside the home. Except when a fad like Trivial Pursuits sweeps the country, friends seldom get together to play sedentary games. Young people prefer physical activity. In 1988, two hundred thousand students were asked about their leisure-time habits. Fewer students played bridge than swam or jogged regularly. Even among those looking for intellectual activity, bridge had lost its appeal. At least eight times as many students played chess as those who sat down to an occasional hand of bridge. In the early 1990s, there were probably no more than five or six hundred serious college-age bridge players in the United States.

Bridge Parties

I would have children taught bridge. It will be useful in the end. When all else fails—sports, love, ambition—bridge remains a solace and an entertainment. — Somerset Maugham

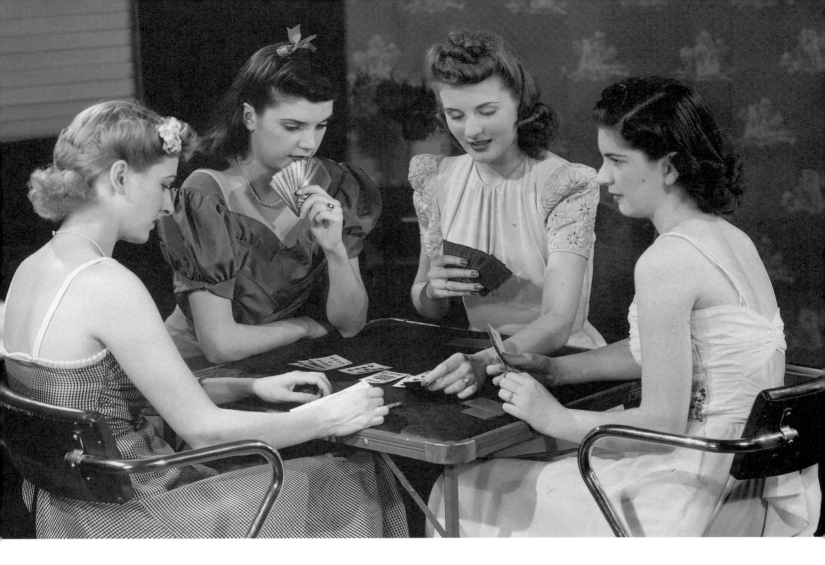

Elsewhere, the game is not totally out of fashion. Several European countries devote the same effort to recruiting potential bridge champions as they do to nurturing chess prodigies. Long anathematized as a capitalist game by the former Soviet Union, bridge is growing in popularity in the free-thinking Russian confederation. The fact that Communist leader Deng Xiaoping loves the game may be one reason for its recent growth in China. Maybe bridge is catching on because it's something new, something Western. Or maybe because it's cheap: investing in a deck of cards hardly makes a dent in hard-currency reserves. ☐

A Book of Bridge Rules underneath the Bough,
A Score Card, Two New Packs of Cards, and Thou
With Two Good Players sitting opposite,
Oh, Wilderness were Paradise enouw!

I sometimes think there's never such Tirade
As where some Bridge Game has been badly Played.
When Some One thinks you should have made No Trump
And you have thriftily declared a Spade!

We are no other than a Moving Row
Of Major Dummy Hands that Come and Go.
Played to the Last Trump by the Hand of Fate
By Whom our Hearts are Shuffled To and Fro.

— Carolyn Wells, *The Rubaiyat of Bridge*, 1909

Carbon Paper

A secretary who worked at *Time* magazine in the early 1960s remembers typing an urgent memo her boss wanted delivered to the chairman of the board and each member of his staff. She took eight sheets of typing paper and interleaved them with seven sheets of carbon paper, inserted the whole batch into her typewriter, and began to type. Then she made a mistake. She started over—more typing paper, more carbon sheets. Halfway down the page, another mistake: m instead of n. She rolled the paper back, erased the error on the top sheet with a strip of Ko-Rec-Type, and banged the required n in its place. She lifted each carbon sheet to assess the damage: black smudges on one copy, and on another a letter above the level of the rest of the line. When she tried to erase the smudge, she poked a hole in the paper. She pulled out the pages and started again.

Like inked typewriter ribbons, carbon paper was a by-product of the growing typewriter industry early in the twentieth century. Carbon paper was a high-quality paper coated on one side with special ink. The paper itself had to be as thin as tissue yet strong enough to withstand the hammering of typewriter keys. Manufacturers experimented to find a happy medium between ink that rubbed off too easily, leaving smudges on the copies, and ink that was too hard, producing little impression at all. To accommodate a wide variation of touch among typists, carbon papers were developed with different weights and finishes. A secretary who struck the typewriter keys heavily required carbon paper with a hard finish that didn't release its ink too easily. A typist with a light touch needed carbon paper with a softer coating.

Secretaries complained chronically about carbon copies. They were too black or too light, they were full of smudges, or they were hard to read. Within a single word, some letters were nearly invisible while others were so dark they blurred together. The carbon paper itself wrinkled easily, it curled, it tore. It left greasy dark stains on hands and clothing.

For decades inventors had been trying to find a cheap, fast way to eliminate carbon paper. A patent attorney named Chester Carlson, working in a makeshift laboratory in Queens, New York, finally did the job. As a boy, Carlson was fascinated with the graphic arts and with chemistry. He supported his ailing parents by working for a local printer.

Carlson graduated from the California Institute of Technology with a degree in physics. He got a job in the patent department of an electronics firm and went to law school at night. On the job, he noticed that there were never enough carbon copies of patent specifications to go around and there was no quick, practical way of getting more. He had no money to buy his lawbooks, so he copied out cases by hand at the public library. He became obsessed with trying to invent a machine that would copy a document in seconds.

Carlson studied up on printing, photographing, the offset process, the chemical treatment of paper, photostating, and other imaging processes. He concentrated on the little-known field of photoconductivity and learned that when light strikes a photoconductive material the electrical conductivity of that material is increased. He experimented with what he called electrophotography in a small lab in Astoria, Queens. On October 22, 1938, he and his assistant printed on a glass microscope slide the notation "10-22-38 ASTORIA." They darkened the room and created an electrostatic charge by rubbing a cotton handkerchief over a sulfur-coated zinc plate.

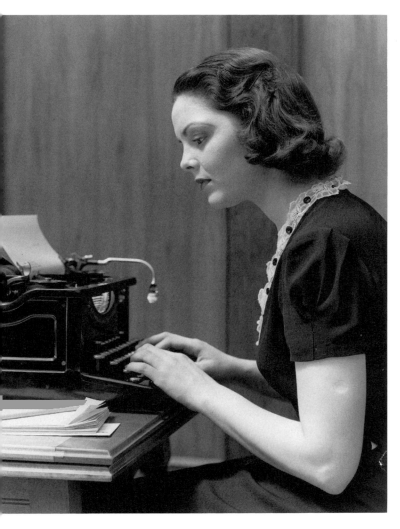

They laid the slide on the plate and lit the apparatus briefly with a bright incandescent bulb. Then they removed the slide, sprinkled a vegetable-based powder on the surface, and blew off the loose powder. There, visible on the metal plate, was a reproduction of the inscription. They made permanent copies of the legend "10-22-38 ASTORIA" by transferring the images to waxed paper and heating the sheets to melt the wax. They went out to lunch to celebrate.

The celebration was a bit premature. During the next ten years, Carlson tried to convince more than twenty companies that his invention was of practical value. The few demonstrations he staged hit all kinds of snags. Sometimes the images were smudged, the paper developed heat blisters, or the edges curled. He later recalled, "How difficult it was to convince anyone that my tiny plates and rough image held the key to a tremendous new industry." Finally, in 1944, Battelle Memorial Institute, a nonprofit research organization, signed a royalty-sharing contract with Carlson and began to develop his electrophotographic process. In 1947 Battelle entered into an agreement with a small photo-paper company called Haloid, which put up $7 million—the equivalent of its annual sales—to acquire rights to the process. Haloid was gambling that this new way of making reproductions without any chemical reaction and by a dry procedure would lead to host of new products. They called the process *xerography*, from the Greek words for *dry* and *writing*.

In 1959 the company marketed the first practical xerographic copier. The 914 (so named because it could copy any document up to nine by fourteen inches) swamped its competitors and was a phenomenal success. It used ordinary paper, required no messy chemicals, and produced uniform, dry, permanent copies at the push of a button. The 914 made seven copies a minute. It could reproduce images from single sheets and bound volumes. The copies were sharp enough to serve as originals from which second- and third- generation copies could be made. Efficiency experts determined that the 914 cost a business about four cents a copy. In contrast, having a secretary type a page cost a minimum of sixty-eight cents.

By the mid-1960s, five hundred thousand copiers, manufactured by some forty different companies, churned out ten billion copies annually—some fifty-two copies of something or other for every man, woman, and child in the country. Files in libraries, offices, hospitals, and schools bulged with duplicate copies. Business costs mounted as office workers used the machines to reproduce everything from chain letters to their children's term papers. Xerox, the name that Haloid eventually adopted, so dominated the market that *to xerox* entered the language as a generic term for copying.

Nowadays there is a copy center on every corner. People wait in line to duplicate income tax returns, drama scripts, bills, and canceled checks. Specialized copiers enlarge or reduce images. They reproduce true color. They copy both sides of a page. They make two perfect copies in one second. They reproduce a multipage document, sort it, insert dividers, and staple or bind it. The price of simple copiers has dropped so dramatically that many people have them in their homes.

Carbon paper still shows up in credit card charge forms. You can dirty your fingers removing the paper, but the bigger problem is liability. Unless the carbon paper is destroyed, someone might steal the credit card numbers imprinted on it. Credit card companies are replacing carbon sets with carbonless paper as fast as they can. Coated with dye that is released on impact, carbonless paper is more practical than photocopying if duplicates of a document must be prepared simultaneously— when, for example, a merchant needs one copy of a sales receipt, and the customer, another. By the year 2000, carbon paper will be very hard to find. The phrase "she's a carbon copy of her mother" may need explaining. □

Card Catalogs

The first library in North America was established in 1638 at Harvard College with an initial collection of 329 religious and philosophical texts. Nearly a century later, Harvard published its first catalog: a bound ledger with the volumes in its growing collection organized according to size, and then, alphabetically, by author. A theologian who wanted to compare several sermons about damnation needed to know the name of every preacher whose words he wanted to study. Since the collection was relatively small, he could find what he wanted rather easily.

As the number of books and pamphlets in print increased and secular subjects attracted more attention, problems of classifying and retrieving library materials got more complex. Libraries tried organizing their catalogues according to donor, date of acquisition, or even the place in the building where the document was stored. In 1830, Benjamin Pierce made a widely acclaimed catalog for Harvard that was alphabetized by author and subject. Other librarians added listings by title and expanded the number of cross-references as well.

To accommodate growing collections, catalogs had to be laboriously recopied and updated. In the 1820s someone at Harvard suggested using loose-leaf sheaves that could be revised more easily, but the idea was discarded as too radical. Several decades later, the notion of cutting up the lists into individual slips and placing them in drawers found more favor. New slips needed only to be dropped into the proper slot as the library expanded. Printed cards were introduced at the Boston Public Library in the 1870s. To keep people from stealing or defacing the cards, they were threaded on a metal rod attached to the drawer.

Individual libraries evolved similar but idiosyncratic cataloging systems. Many problems of cross-referencing remained unsolved until Melville Dewey, an ambitious young undergraduate at Amherst College, volunteered to work in the college library because, as he wrote in his diary, if he could improve libraries he would "exert a very great influence for good." Dewey had a passion for order. He was an advocate of the metric system and of spelling reform. Early in life, he simplified his first name to Melvil, and later, for a time, he signed himself Mel Dui. After thinking about catalog reform for a year, he wrote, "I devysed the Decimal Classifications during a long sermon by President Stearns while I lookt stedfastly at him without hearing a word."

Dewey categorized subjects and assigned each a number: for example, 100 for philosophy, 200 for religion, 500 for natural science, 600 for what he called "useful

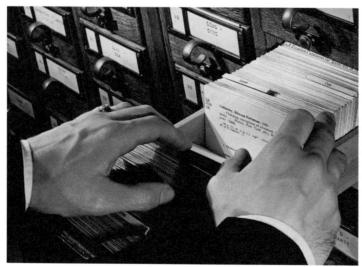

arts" like medicine, engineering, and mechanic trades. Within each larger category, Dewey created subdivisions. Under history (900), general European history was found under 940, Scotland under 941, Ireland under 941.5, England under 942, and Germany, Austria, and their successor states under 943. Numbers to the right of the decimal could be extended without limit when required by the expansion of material within a subject. Second and third lines for author's name, subcategories, and other differentiations were added as needed. Fiction, which Dewey believed to be "the embroidery, not the web," of a collection, was not cross-referenced.

Dewey published *A Classification and Subject Index for Cataloguing and Arranging the Books and Pamphlets of a Library* in 1876, when he was only twenty-five years old. The forty-four-page document appeared at a most propitious time. The amount of printed material and the demands of scholarly and recreational readers were expanding. In the next two decades, Andrew Carnegie made good on his promise to give money to any community that would build a public library. Although some big collections, notably the New York Public Library and the Library of Congress, clung to their own classifications, by 1890 over two hundred new American libraries had installed card catalogs based on the Dewey Decimal System.

Each nonfiction book had at least three cards: one beginning with the author's name, another with the title, and one or more to be filed under the subject—or subjects—of the book. The three-by-five-inch cards—which Dewey, the advocate of

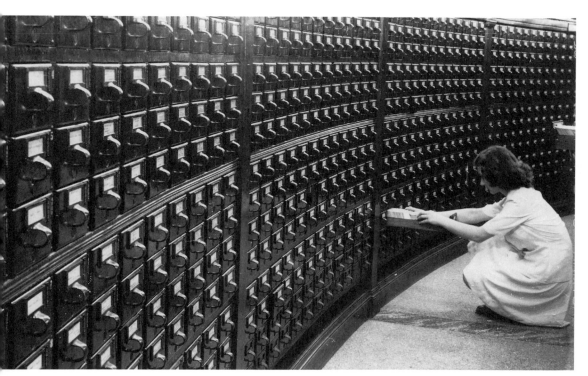

the metric system, always insisted were 75 by 125 millimeters—were stored in long wooden drawers stacked in imposing rows that sometimes filled entire rooms. Readers flicked through the cards—switching back and forth between subject, title, and author drawers, noting any cross-referenced material that might be listed at the bottom of the cards—until they had enough citations to consult the books themselves.

Eventually the flood of printed materials swamped even the most orderly collection. By the early 1980s, the Library of Congress catalog contained over sixty million cards. The main research division of the New York Public Library housed about ten million dog-eared cards in 8,973 oak drawers, the most heavily used catalog in the world. Some cards had not been updated since they were entered in longhand almost a century earlier. A librarian in Illinois lamented that when people couldn't find material in his card catalog, "they assumed we didn't have it, when the truth was they just couldn't find it. "

Computer technology offered a solution. Many libraries began cataloguing every new acquisition in computer-readable form. Much more information could be logged into a computer entry than could be printed on a three-by-five card. In addition, computers had the capacity to search for key words or concepts through an entire database, tracking down in seconds citations someone working back and forth among card catalog drawers would take hours to find. Initially, computerized catalogs were for librarians' use only, while software designers experimented with programs that would be easy for the least computer-literate members of the general public to operate. In 1981 the North-Pulaski branch of the Chicago Public Library became the first in America to replace its card catalog with an on-line computer catalog. Instead of consulting cards in file drawers, readers sat down before a video terminal. A customized program led them through the familiar categories to find the books they wanted. The Library of Congress went on-line later that year. In 1985 the New York Public Library threw a party to celebrate the installation of its on-line catalog. Surrounded by some fifty new computer terminals, historian Barbara Tuchman cut into a cake in the shape of the old file cabinets and said, "The drawers of the card catalog have been a companion of mine throughout life. But high-tech, whether we like it or not, is here to stay."

By 1990, about one-third of the 30,700 libraries in America provided on-line catalogs for their patrons. In professional journals, librarians began to call themselves media specialists, and libraries were referred to as media centers. Computers offered access to databases of general periodicals and specialized publications that contained citations for articles, a summary of their contents, and a printout of the information. Interlibrary loans could be arranged through computers. Some systems indicated if a book had been checked out and when it was due back. The day was coming when anyone with a modem and a PC would have access to an on-line catalog from home or office.

When the New York Public Library discarded the oak drawers from its old card catalog, some were recycled by custom cabinetmakers. Others were rescued by souvenir hunters, sentimental librarians, and clients. One librarian keeps recipes and audiotapes in her salvaged oak drawers. A colleague uses his to serve hors d'oeuvres at cocktail parties. One woman says she stores "useless old elbow-length gloves with fake pearl buttons in an equally useless old oaken drawer." □

Cavities

At the beginning of World War II, dental defects were the most common reason that draftees were turned down for service. Nearly nine percent could not meet the minimum standard of six opposing teeth—three upper and three lower teeth aligned with each other. The armed forces promptly inducted dentists to supply false teeth for recruits who needed them.

American children were not sorry to see their dentists go off to war. Most kids hated and feared the dentist. Every six-month checkup was sure to reveal five or six cavities, requiring the victim to sit tilted back in the dentist's chair while the drill bored relentlessly into rear molars. Novocaine helped—though the shot was as scary as the drilling.

Dental caries—cavities, to the layman—is an infectious disease, transmitted primarily by the microbe *Streptococcus mutans*, which breeds best in deposits of food on the surfaces of teeth. Although dentists trying to reduce cavities urged people to eat less sugar and starch, their campaign didn't work. *S. mutans* is a hardy bug, difficult to kill off with antibiotics. So dentists turned to a chemical that would change the chemistry of teeth.

Enter fluoride, a mineral found in minute amounts in almost all foods and water supplies. At optimum levels, it strengthens the ability of teeth to resist and even reverse some decay. It also helps prevent root caries, which occur in adults as their gums recede.

The detective work that led ultimately to the discovery of fluoride's effects began in 1901. A dentist, Dr. Frederick McKay, was determined to find the cause of a stain on the teeth of adults and children living in and around Colorado Springs, Colorado, where he practiced. Residents told him that the problem, known as "Colorado Brown Stain," came from "something in the water." Children in the area had fewer cavities than children elsewhere, but McKay did not study these implications because his attention was focused on the staining. By 1916 McKay was sure that the water supply was the culprit. It must, he felt, contain something not commonly detected in standard water analyses. In 1925 the residents of Oakley, Idaho, alarmed about their children's discolored teeth, decided to change their water supply. McKay was called in, and although he could not guarantee a positive result, he urged the town to proceed. In 1932 he examined the teeth of children born after the change. None showed signs of mottling. The identity of the waterborne agent, however, was still a mystery.

In 1930 McKay had sent a sample of water from Bauxite, Arkansas, another town with mottling problems, to H. V. Churchill, a chemist at the Aluminum Company of America. ALCOA had a vested interest in solving the mystery: Bauxite supplied the aluminum ore used to make the company's cookware, which was rumored to be poisonous. Churchill's analysis revealed a large amount of fluoride in the town's water. Water from other locations where people had mottled teeth showed the same high fluoride content.

Simultaneously, researchers working with white rats established that mottled enamel was caused by the destructive action of fluoride in drinking water. Other researchers pursued the tantalizing evidence of the low decay rate in discolored teeth. From the mid-1930s to the mid-1940s, they examined many communities where mottling was present and determined that one part per million of fluoride in drinking water sharply reduced tooth decay without causing stains. Strange though it seemed, fluoride in drinking water could both benefit and injure teeth, depending upon its concentration.

Dental epidemiologists advocated adding fluoride to drinking water, and, later, applying it to tooth surfaces in the form of gels, toothpaste, or mouth rinse to enhance the body's capacity to strengthen teeth. The first drop of fluoride was introduced into a public water supply in Grand Rapids, Michigan, in 1945. Crest, the first fluoridated toothpaste, went on the market in 1955. In Crest's advertising, smiling school-children, home from the dentist, yelled, "Look, Mom, no cavities!" It was not an idle claim.

It is more than likely that Johnny will ask sometime before he reaches the dental chair if it is going to hurt him. If he is taken to the dentist when he is the proper age for the first visit, you can be reasonably certain the right answer is "No, Johnny, it won't hurt. It hurts only when you wait too long before going to the dentist. That's why we're going now." But if your child happens to have poor baby teeth and gives evidence of toothaches before his first visit to the dentist, do not lie to him when he asks will it hurt. The correct answer is "Yes, some. But not too much, and it will soon be over." Then immediately divert his thoughts by adding that afterward you will take him for a ride in the park, or perhaps visit Aunt Martha, or do something else he especially likes.
— "Johnny's First Visit to the Dentist," *The American Home*, January 1947

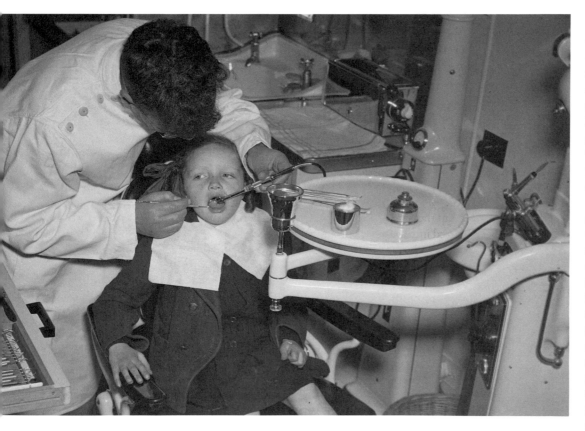

In the early 1970s, seventy-two percent of American children had cavities. By the mid-1980s, almost half of the children in the U.S. aged five to seventeen were cavity-free. Even children who were still getting cavities had fewer of them. The number of cavities in young children continues to decline.

Fluoride in the public water supply now reaches nearly two-thirds of the American people at an annual cost of only fifty-one cents per person. Over ninety percent of the toothpastes and powders available in the U.S. contain fluoride. Though the effects on children are most dramatic, adults who consume fluoridated water also have less tooth decay. They also have fewer dental infections, fewer missing or abscessed teeth, a reduced need for dentures, and fewer working days lost due to dental problems.

From the start, fluoridation had its critics. Libertarians resented any governmental intrusion in their lives. Others believed that fluoridation was part of a Communist plot. The Paul Revere Associated Yeomen Inc. proclaimed in 1965 that "the MAIN communist plots by the internal traitors in the United States are as follows—fluoridation, disarmament of American citizens, federal aid to education." PRAY also charged that fluoridation caused a host of health problems, from cancer to mental retardation.

Medical researchers studied and then rejected claims that fluoridation might be linked to the incidence of cancer, chromosomal abnormalities, Down's syndrome babies, Alzheimer's disease, and mental illness, as well as heart and kidney disease. In the early 1990s, the U.S. Public Health Service reiterated that fluoride was a safe and effective preventative measure against dental caries, with no cancer risk in humans.

Overall, fluoride can be thanked for the remarkable decline in dental caries. However, there may be additional factors at work. The incidence of other streptococcal diseases like scarlet fever and rheumatic fever has fallen over several decades, and no one is sure why. Perhaps infections have been prevented by the antibiotics that are routinely prescribed for many ailments. Children who are exposed to antibiotics over long periods of time have fewer cavities than those who are not.

There may be yet another reason for the decline of caries in children. In the past few decades, the consumption of soft drinks and ice cream has increased proportionately much more than the consumption of other foods. Conventional wisdom would have it that so much sugar is terrible for teeth. However, these foods contain significant amounts of food preservatives, such as benzoate and sorbate, which are potent antibacterial agents in the fight against *S. mutans*.

Although half of America's children are caries-free, fifty percent still have cavities. An even larger number of adults suffer from tooth decay. Will it ever be possible to wipe out this disease? Eradication requires the combination of a weapon (such as fluoride), an intensive public health program, and strong popular support. International campaigns have eliminated smallpox and may yet succeed in getting rid of polio. Since dental caries does not evoke the same terror, an organized crusade against it seems unlikely. ☐

Chop Suey

Chinese food was first served in America to the coolies who came from Canton in the late nineteenth century to build the railroads. Although ingredients in America were not always what the men remembered from the old country, the cooks did what they could. One popular invention—a mix of any vegetables and meat at hand—was called chop suey, probably from the Cantonese words *tsa sui,* meaning "odds and ends." Chow mein—basically chop suey served on fried noodles—also became a staple. *Chow* probably comes from the Mandarin word *ch'ao,* meaning "to cook or fry," and *mein* is Chinese for "noodles."

When the railroads were completed, and the Chinese settled into their own communities, they savored old-country favorites like sharks' fin soup and ducks' feet, but they didn't neglect the dishes developed in the new land. Outsiders who ventured into a Chinese neighborhood looking for a cheap meal were happier with chop suey, chow mein, and egg foo yung than with thousand-year-old eggs. Adventuresome eaters tried shrimp with lobster sauce, barbecued spareribs, or sweet-and-sour pork. In many cases Westerners could only order more exotic creations by pointing to the next table. A traditional specialty like bird's-nest soup was seldom listed on the English language menu. Since the Chinese were often unsure of their proficiency in English, they tried to make their menus as self-explanatory as possible—hence the typical low-priced meal of one dish from column A and one from column B.

The Chinese were among the first non-European immigrants to fan out across America. Many of them opened restaurants. Like their cousins, the laundrymen, they had no historic connection to their trade. They took the classic immigrant path: one entrepreneur started a business, worked hard, prospered, and hired his countrymen. Soon energetic staff members went out on their own. Before long, most medium-sized cities had a Chinese restaurant or two, where the upper classes went slumming on Sunday or Thursday (cook's night out), and ordinary citizens could find a nourishing meal that provided a little more excitement than the fare at the local diner. Chinese restaurateurs, like Italian shoe repairmen and Jewish tailors, had found themselves a niche.

By 1950, there were thirty-one Chinese restaurants in Philadelphia, more than any other ethnic category. Even in the South, where restaurant dining was a rather recent and uncommon experience, and people were especially loyal to their barbecue, greens, and grits, Chinese food caught on. Although there was probably only one Chinese restaurant in all of South Carolina in the early 1930s, by the mid-1980s there were nearly sixty in the state's four leading cities alone. That's more than the number of Italian restaurants, which had been the earlier embodiment of exotic cuisine.

America, the melting pot, has often naturalized the food of its immigrant populations. Italian dishes—which seemed extremely odd to Yankees in the early twentieth century—became blue plate specials. So-called Jewish foods, like bagels, kosher-style pickles, and pastrami, are available in supermarkets all over the country. Ironically, many foods that became most popular were unfamiliar in the old country. Traditional Sicilian cooks never served spaghetti with meatballs. Northern Italians learned to make pizza to satisfy American tourists. Lox was unknown to Jews in the Russian *stetl.* Chili comes from Texas, not Mexico.

As immigrants became more acclimatized, some began to search their own roots for more authentic experiences. Diners from other ethnic backgrounds also became more sophisticated about "foreign" food. Chop suey lost out to twice-cooked pork and General Tsai's chicken. Chili-flavored dishes from Szechuan became the rage. Everyone ate with chopsticks. Diners now expect to use chopsticks in all Asian restaurants, even those serving food from Thailand, where they are not traditional.

In Harrisburg, Pennsylvania, during the 1940s and 1950s, there was one Chinese restaurant, inexplicably named The Tokyo, tucked away on the second floor of an office building in the heart of the business district. The Tokyo offered a menu of chop suey, chow mein, and other staples to government workers and shoppers looking for an uncommon treat. In 1992, Harrisburgers could choose between Mandarin, Cantonese, Szechuan, Hunan, or Southeast Asian Chinese cuisines served at some forty restaurants conveniently located in shopping malls and suburban

CHINESE A LA CARTE MENU

Including Tea

CHOP SUEY

1.	New Year Chop Suey	.65
2.	Fine Cut Chop Suey Rice Shoots	.75
3.	Chicken Chop Suey, Water Chestnuts	.90
4.	Subgum Chop Suey with Almonds, Water Chestnuts, and Mushrooms	.90

CHOW MEIN

5.	Chin's Chow Mein with Noodles	.65
6.	Fine Cut Chow Mein with Noodles	.75
7.	Subgum Chow Mein with Almonds, Water Chestnuts, and Mushrooms	.95
8.	Chicken Mushroom Chow Mein with Water Chestnuts	1.15
9.	Chicken Subgum Chow Mein with Almonds, Water Chestnuts, and Mushrooms	1.15

EGG FOO YONG

10.	Roast Pork Egg Foo Yong (3)	.65
11.	Chicken Egg Foo Yong (3)	.80

DESSERTS

Ice Cream	.10
Home Made Pie	.15
Chinese Preserves	.25
Lichee Nuts	.25
Pie a la Mode	.25

BEVERAGES

Tea or Coffee	.10
Beer (Bottle)	.15 and .20
Ginger Ale	.25

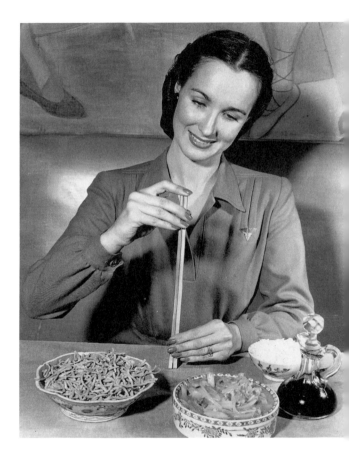

neighborhoods as well as downtown. In fact, nearly twenty different styles of provincial Chinese cooking can now be found in major cities across the country. Although people of Chinese origin comprised only four-tenths of one percent of the nation's ethnically identified population in 1980, thirty percent of the "foreign" restaurants in the U.S. were Chinese.

In the 1990s many immigrants arrived from Hong Kong. Most of these people are originally Cantonese. They eat the less spicy, noodle-based foods that had been popular with the first immigrants, but they want them authentic. Even in America, few Chinese cook or eat chop suey anymore. The dish survives mainly in institutional kitchens, like those of school cafeterias, where the cooks can use up their *tsa sui*, odds and ends, and the clientele is a captive audience. □

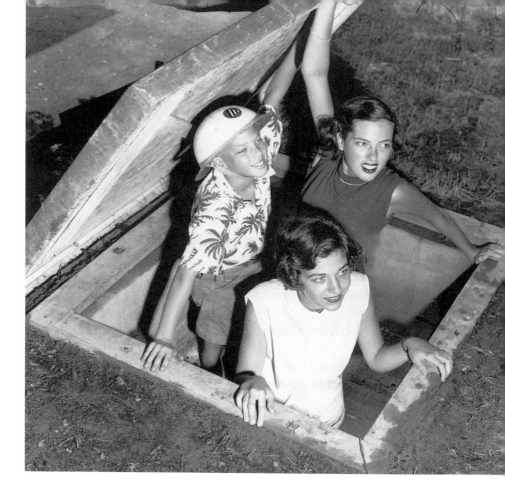

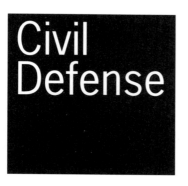

Civil Defense

WHAT YOU SHOULD DO IN CASE OF ATOMIC ATTACK

Keep calm.
If there is time, get to shelter at once.
If no underground shelter is close by, get into the ground
floor of a near-by building or even stand in a doorway if
nothing better is available.
If you see the bomb flash and there is no cover of any kind
within a step or two, drop to the street or gutter, turn away
from the flash, and close eyes tightly. Cover your head, face,
neck, arms and other exposed areas of the body.
If you are indoors, turn off all appliances, such as electric
toasters, irons, stoves, etc. Get into the core of your building
and under a desk or table if there isn't time to get to the
basement. Lie face downward and out of line with windows.
After the burst tie handkerchief over mouth if area is
contaminated.

WHAT YOU SHOULD NOT DO

Don't telephone.
Don't turn on water after blast, unless to fight fire.
Don't eat or drink in a contaminated area.
Don't use metal goods in a contaminated zone.
Don't touch things after ground or water burst.
Don't try to drive your car.
Don't get excited or excite others.

— "You and the Atomic Bomb," New York State Civil Defense
Commission, 1951

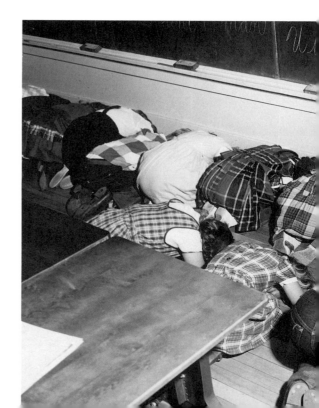

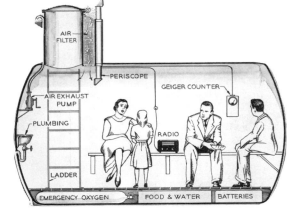

In 1950, the invasion of South Korea by the Communist North Korean army forced Americans to face the possibility of World War III

and total nuclear annihilation. Images of the suffering inflicted five years earlier by the atomic bombs dropped on Hiroshima and Nagasaki were still vivid. The popular press pictured American cities devastated by atomic attack with transportation paralysed, power and food supplies destroyed, hundreds of thousands of casualties, and no way to get help for the sick and dying.

Acknowledging the "grim new reality," President Harry Truman created the Federal Civil Defense Administration in January 1951. Many of the materials it produced were intended to prepare schoolchildren for atomic war, to "alert, not alarm" them. Teachers and parents were urged not to become unduly emotional at the prospect of Russian attack. The national PTA urged a soothing, "positive mental health program" in response to atomic anxiety. The bomb's worst effects, such as traumatic injuries, shock, burns, radiation sickness, and death, were to be played down.

Throughout the 1950s many cities staged regular air-raid drills. Civil defense officials tested all 741 sirens in New York City every month. A one-minute alert was followed by a warbling sound that meant "take cover." Schools, especially in target cities like New York, Los Angeles, Chicago, and Philadelphia, conducted "duck-and-cover" drills. When the teacher suddenly shouted "drop!" all the children would kneel, hands clasped behind their necks and their faces shielded.

The FCDA circulated a comic book featuring Bert the Turtle. Bert said: "You have learned to take care of yourself in many ways—to cross streets safely—and what to do in case of fire. . . . BUT the atomic bomb is a new danger . . . things will get knocked down all over town. . . . You must be ready to protect yourself." Bert warned children to "DUCK to avoid things flying through the air." With his head retracted into his shell, he urged them to "COVER to keep from getting cut or even badly burned."

Many school districts distributed special student identification, modeled after military dog tags. The tags were designed to help civil defense workers identify lost or dead children in event of nuclear attack. By 1952 New York City had issued two and a half million free dog tags to public, parochial, and private schoolchildren.

In 1954 Lewis Strauss, chairman of the Atomic Energy Commission, revealed the existence of a new weapon, the H-bomb, which could incinerate an entire city. The H-bomb made obsolete all previous civil defense plans based on estimates of A-bomb damage. The only response, said one civil defense administrator in 1954, is to "die, dig, or get out." Digging bomb-proof shelters throughout the country would have cost more than the Eisenhower administration was willing to spend, so plans were made to evacuate cities on the basis of a four- to six-hour warning of a bomber attack.

It was later revealed that the federal government was willing to shelter a select few. A secret concrete-and-steel bunker for members of Congress was built in 1958 into a hill adjacent to the luxurious Greenbrier resort in White Sulphur Springs, West Virginia, 250 miles southwest of Washington. The government also built quarters at Mount Weather in Virginia, where the president, members of the Supreme Court, and other top officials could ride out the emergency.

In the late 1950s, intercontinental ballistic missiles armed with nuclear warheads put an end to evacuation planning. ICBMs could cover the five thousand miles between Washington and Moscow in thirty minutes or less, which barely allowed anyone enough time to get out of town or take shelter. "Civil defense is dead, as of right now," declared a writer in the September 28, 1957, issue of the *Nation*. "To all the people who have been worrying because the stumbling procedures of the FCDA left them uncertain and unprepared, the ICBM brings a paradoxical note of cheer: you don't have to worry anymore."

The Rand Corporation, however, predicted that civil defense could limit carnage even in a nuclear exchange. An effective combination of military and civil defense would give half the population a good chance of survival in a thermonuclear war, which, though catastrophic, would not wipe out all life. Rand recommended that people spend one or two hundred dollars of their own money to build a family fallout shelter.

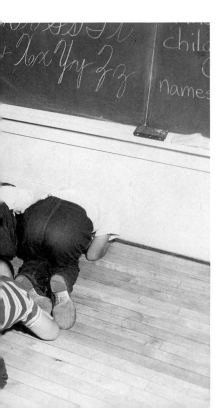

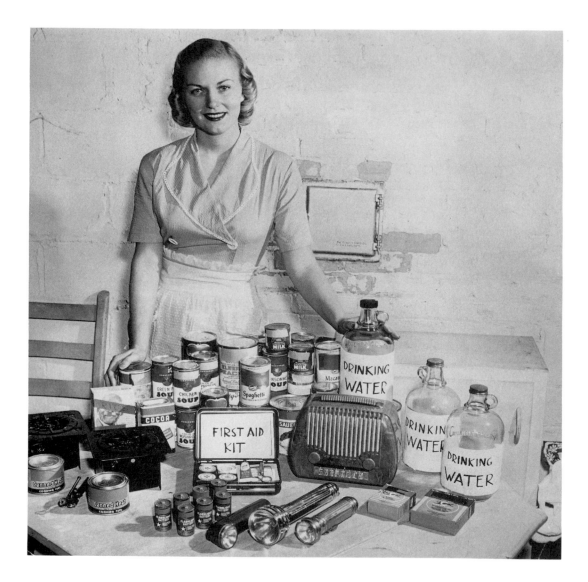

If I lived 15 miles or more from the Capitol in Washington, I would build myself a backyard shelter. If I had the money I would build a place in my backyard that was constructed of concrete reinforced with steel. I'd cover it with three feet of dirt, I'd have filters in my air intakes. I'd put water and foodstuffs and some kind of sanitary facility down there, and a battery-type radio. The reason I say this is that if you have that type of shelter in your backyard, and the Russians came in and attacked the capitol city, you would be absolutely safe against radioactivity. This backyard shelter would give you that. The three feet of dirt would give you that, whether it was reinforced or not. — Val Peterson, head of the Federal Civil Defense Administration, quoted in *U.S. News & World Report*, April 8, 1955

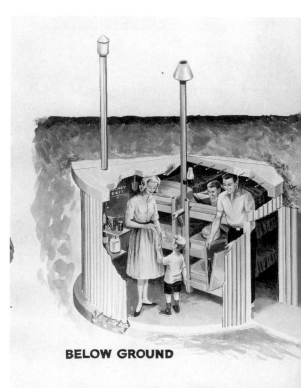

BELOW GROUND

FAMILY FALLOUT SHELTE

In July 1961, with the superpowers facing a showdown over the Berlin Wall, President John F. Kennedy addressed the nation on television. In the event of a Russian attack, he said, "those families which are not hit in a nuclear blast and fire can still be saved—if they can be warned to take shelter and if that shelter is available. We owe that kind of insurance to our families—and to our country. The time to start is now."

Kennedy asked Congress to appropriate millions for civil defense. Shelter space in public buildings was to be identified, marked, and provisioned with a two-week

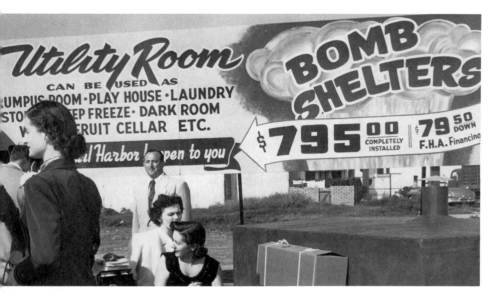

supply of food and water. He asked for money to develop a simple alarm system that could be placed in homes to warn of attack, and later urged families to build their own shelters.

"Fallout shelter fever" hit America. Sporting goods stores did a brisk business in camping equipment for use in basement shelters. The sales pitch at the Prince Georges County Shopping Plaza outside Washington, D.C., was typical. A bass voice over the loudspeaker announced, "This is condition Red." A siren wailed; a bomb exploded. A male voice screamed, "My wife, my children." Pause. "If I'd only listened to Civil Defense, I'd be in a shelter now." This commercial message was designed to attract attention to a closed-circuit TV view of a nine-by-ten-foot cinder-block basement shelter which could protect a family of four for a week before they ran out of supplies.

Life's cover of September 15, 1961, proclaimed that ninety-seven out of a hundred people could be saved if they were in a shelter and offered a special section on how to build one. There were several options, complete with plans, appropriate building materials, and approximate cost. Families could choose to wall off a section of their cellar, sink a reinforced concrete underground bunker in the backyard, or build a double-walled bunker aboveground. A prefab shelter could be assembled in four hours. Loans were available from the Federal Housing Administration for prefab models with no down payment, provided they met civil defense specifications.

No one knows how many shelters were sold—maybe as many as two hundred thousand. But by the end of 1962, the threat of nuclear war eased. One Detroit dealer advertised "Fallout Shelters While They Last" and slashed prices down to $100. He tried to give one away. A writer was willing to use the shelter as a study. A woman wanted it for toolshed. A businessman in Beirut thought it would make a nice beach house. "But almost nobody wanted it as a shelter," the dealer said. A Michigan farmer finally hauled it off, because he thought it might be useful in the event of a tornado.

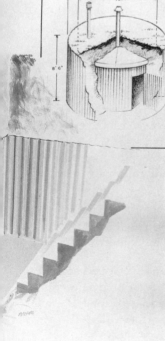

In December 1961 the *Washington Daily News* summed up the state of civil defense in the early 1960s: "C is for confusion; D is for Dilemma." People feared that shelter programs emphasized surviving war rather than averting it. Others complained that the government's every-man-for-himself approach brought out the worst in human nature. There were serious debates about whether or not the head of a household had the right to gun down any outsider who tried to get into the family shelter. The average person couldn't afford to build one and, in any case, thought the nation should be responsible for each citizen's personal defense.

As time passed, speculation centered on the horrors of nuclear winter: subfreezing temperatures, darkness at noon, worldwide fallout, and partial destruction of the ozone layer. As Jonathan Schell wrote in *The Fate of The Earth*, "The vulnerability of the environment is the last word in the argument against the usefulness of shelters: there is no hole big enough to hide all of nature in." Although the preoccupation with nuclear war continued, and national defense remained a major issue, civil defense ceased to be a viable solution. No one wanted to live on in a devastated and radioactive world. □

Remember the old lady who swallowed the fly? Then swallowed a spider to catch the fly, then swallowed a bat to eat the spider, then swallowed

a bird, a cat, and a cow. Then she swallowed a horse. She died of course. A similar succession of unintended consequences makes up the saga of DDT.

In 1940, Paul Müller, a Swiss scientist searching for a chemical to control household moths, unearthed some research done by an obscure Alsatian chemist in the 1870s. The synthetic insecticide Müller rediscovered was a chlorinated hydrocarbon called dichloro-diphenyl-trichloroethane, or DDT. When DDT was sprayed on a surface, any susceptible insect that rested there during the next six months would die. DDT worked either by contact or by ingestion. It attacked the insect's nervous system but caused little discernible harm to humans and other warm-blooded mammals, and it was very inexpensive to manufacture.

DDT was promptly put to use during World War II to kill typhus-bearing lice. Soldiers, refugees, and prisoners were sprayed, to no apparent ill effect then or later, and they were universally grateful to be rid of the plague that had historically been one of the worst torments of people jammed into temporary and unsanitary quarters.

DDT was hailed as a great boon to mankind. Released for civilian use after the war, it was touted as "the atomic bomb of insecticides" and "the killer of killers." It was cheap and easy to use. Housewives were advised to spray their kitchens, bathrooms, and mattresses to eliminate cockroaches and bedbugs, and to douse the family dog to get rid of ticks.

International health officials allowed themselves to hope that DDT would prove to be a powerful weapon against malaria, one of the worst plagues the world has ever known. Most residents of tropical or underdeveloped nations were weakened by chronic infection with the disease. In 1940, a typical year, there were an estimated three hundred million new cases of malaria worldwide, and three million deaths. During the 1930s and early 1940s, as many as four million Americans got sick and between four and five thousand died, even though many spawning grounds of the insect that spread the disease had already been eliminated.

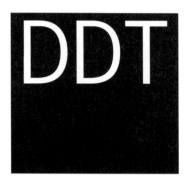

DDT will be to preventive medicine what Lister's discovery of antiseptic was to surgery. — U.S. Surgeon General's Office, June 1944

DDT turned out to be an extremely effective killer of the anopheles mosquito, which carried malaria to its human victims. An early field trial of the insecticide was conducted in the late 1930s in the Tennessee Valley, where large bodies of standing water created by the new flood-control dams provided attractive habitats for the pests. Within a year or two after the lakes and swamps were sprayed with DDT, malaria was gone from the valley. In the immediate postwar years, successful malaria control programs were carried out in Cyprus, Greece, and Central and South America. Paul Müller won a Nobel prize in 1948. A few years later ambitious schemes to wipe out malaria worldwide were under way. Even in what had been some of the most afflicted areas—the Indian subcontinent, West Africa, and Southeast Asia—the disease began to disappear.

During the 1950s and 1960s, DDT was one of the most world's extensively used chemicals. But wherever the insecticide was introduced, it caused unexpected results. Entire ecosystems were disrupted. In the jungles of Malaysia, the mosquitoes disappeared after the first few seasons of spraying, and for the first time in memory, there were no new cases of malaria. Nonetheless, health workers were soon unwelcome in the villages, because the local people noticed that shortly after their huts were sprayed, the roofs collapsed. Investigations revealed that the roofs were made of palm fronds, which were the favorite food of a local caterpillar. A species of wasp normally ate enough caterpillars to keep their numbers low, but when DDT killed off the wasps, the caterpillars multiplied and ate so many of the palm fronds that the roofs fell in.

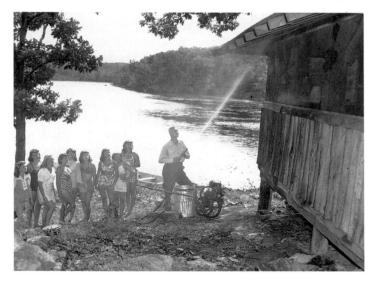

Distressing results were also noticed soon after farmers began routinely dusting crops with the insecticide to kill off a variety of pests. There were few guidelines for how much—or how little—of the chemical was necessary. When initial spraying with DDT proved to be ineffective against certain pests, farmers sometimes

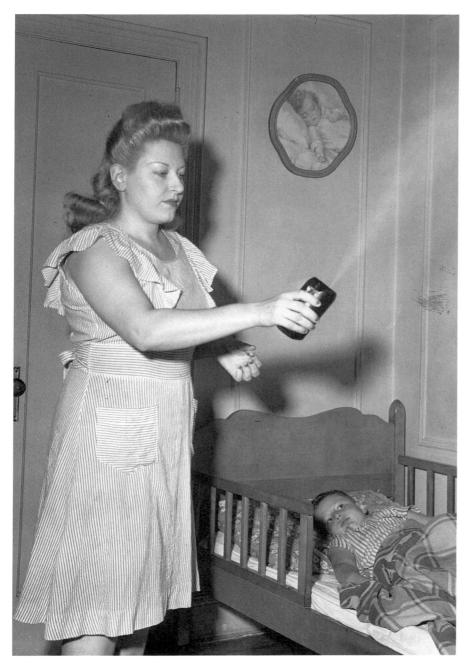

upped the amount and sprayed again in vain efforts to get results. Rivers, lakes, and streams were frequently contaminated by regular water runoff from sprayed fields. Left around in bags in barnyards and garages, DDT often got mixed into animal feed and dumped into water supplies.

Accumulations of DDT were found in the tissues of some animals. The chemical also caused fatal weakness in the eggshells of many kinds of birds, which prevented these species from reproducing successfully. In North America alone, many raptors, notably peregrine falcons and ospreys, virtually disappeared. Similarly decimated were shorebirds, whose diet depended on smaller creatures raised in contaminated waters draining from farmlands that had been saturated with pesticide.

In 1962, Rachel Carson published *Silent Spring* to warn the general public of a future in which no eagles would soar above the plains and no songbirds greet the dawn. Intensive DDT spraying of blighted Dutch elm trees in the Midwest (which turned out to be of no help to the elms) was killing off robins, cardinals, chickadees, and other familiar nesting birds by the hundreds. Carson pointed out that natural insect control was dependent on predatory insects and birds, which DDT killed as well, making the original problem all the worse.

Carson also raised alarms about infants poisoned by their mothers' milk and adults imperiled by the buildup of DDT residues in their bodies. But, until the early 1990s, scientists could not find significant evidence linking human illness to the use of DDT. Then, in April 1993, researchers reported a correlation between the level of a woman's exposure to DDT and her chances of getting breast cancer. The higher the level, the greater the risk. If other studies uncover additional long-term links, Carson's fears may yet be borne out.

In the wake of Carson's crusade, DDT has been banned in North America and Western Europe since the early 1970s, and many bird populations have begun to recover. For a time it was thought that organo-chlorines like DDT could continue to be used in the tropics because they would swiftly decompose in the hot moist climate. Unfortunately, there, too, secondary problems soon affected local animals and migratory birds. Reluctantly, even the less developed countries have joined the ban on DDT.

As an unintended consequence of Carson's campaign, diseases that had been under control are spreading anew. Today malaria is once again the earth's most devastating human ailment. In India, where the incidence of new cases had dropped to about a hundred thousand a year, the number has skyrocketed back to about thirty million. Worldwide, between one hundred and two hundred million cases arise annually, nearly two million people die of the disease, and the most virulent strain is resistant to traditional medication. Elephantiasis and other ghastly parasite-borne diseases are also on the rise.

Alternate means of pest control are in the works. The use of pheromones—chemicals that mimic hormones—may someday be the best way to prevent voracious insects from breeding. At the moment DDT remains the only practical means of widespread protection, but no one wants to take the risks involved in resuming its use. □

The Dining Room

In the dining room of the late 1940s and 1950s, dinner was served promptly at six o'clock, because that's when the man of the house insisted the family assemble. Father sat at one end of the table, mother at the other. The menu never varied: Monday night, meat loaf; Tuesday, chicken; Wednesday, steak; Thursday, spaghetti; Friday, roast beef.

For decades the dining room was the setting for holiday rituals and family celebrations. In Norman Rockwell's vision of middle-class perfection, three generations gathered around the dining room table waiting for grandfather to carve the Thanksgiving turkey. In countless snapshots of a child's party, six or seven kids in paper hats sit at the table and watch expectantly while the birthday girl blows out the candles on her cake. In the dining room, young women told their parents they were getting married, or presented their fiancés for approval. Dining room deportment is the metaphor for family values in *Annie Hall*. Director Woody Allen parodies both Annie's Waspy relatives and the hero's Jewish clan by contrasting scenes of the formal, circumspect Halls seated around their dining table in Chippewa Falls, Wisconsin, and the boisterous, emotional Singers crammed together in their small dining room in Brooklyn.

The dining room was often the shrine to a family's level of affluence. Crystal goblets, silver candlesticks, bone china cups and saucers, napkin rings, and even finger bowls were proudly displayed behind the glass doors of the breakfront. Grandma's old linen tablecloths were lovingly folded between layers of tissue paper and stored in the bottom drawer of the sideboard. It was the one room in the house where the art of conversation flourished. Family and friends might linger over dessert served on the "good" dishes or argue into the night until the last drop of brandy was gone.

The American dining room as a separate unit dates only from the mid-nineteenth century. In simple colonial houses, people ate in the kitchen. Before 1800 wealthy families had so-called eating rooms, which also doubled as sitting rooms. Only the most elaborate homes, like southern plantations or prosperous merchant's houses in the North, had a separate room commodious enough to seat at least two dozen people. Inevitably, the growing middle class also wanted dining rooms as an amenity in their homes.

No American room has been more transformed by changing tastes, fashions, and economic climates. In the twentieth century, the dining room has shrunk from being a spacious and self-contained unit to a "dining area" in the far corner of an L-shaped living room. It was briefly restored to its prior status during the Reagan years of studied formality and conspicuous consumption. But the traditional dining room is headed toward extinction. The grand, formal dining room of an earlier era no longer suits a casual life-style. When couples build a new house, they want the interior to be "open." The living room, dining room, and kitchen are planned as one interconnected flowing space.

People who buy an old house will break up the dining room because a large space devoted only to eating seems a waste. Or they come up with ingenious ways to salvage their white elephant. How about a library/dining room? Or an entertainment center/dining room? Instead of carrying trays into the living room to eat in front of the TV, they put a television set in the dining room and eat at the table.

The biggest change in the American home in the last twenty-five years has been the shift in the center of family life from the dining room to the eat-in kitchen. If there is a dining room, it sits, unused, like a strange vestigial organ. Just as new diets are touted each month in women's magazines, so are ideas for eat-in kitchens: tips on how to build banquettes, counters, and islands for the quick, casual meal that "today's busy families" grab on the run. In its August 1989 issue, *Better Homes and Gardens* reported on the dilemma of Janet and Bob Mincer of San Diego. "Four children and dual careers were creating rush-hour gridlock" in their sixty-year-old kitchen. "Traffic bottlenecked in the cramped 9 X 11 foot space." The Mincers solved their problem by annexing a laundry room and closet to create a "comfy banquette dining nook" that satisfies their needs.

There is something about the traditional dining room that conveys a feeling of family solidarity, permanence and security, so essential especially these days to the proper development of the younger generation.
— "What Women Want in their Dining Rooms of Tomorrow," a report by *McCall's*, 1944

44

Old things mean much to me and in such a room my mother's silver and demurely sprigged china would feel at home. . . . In such an atmosphere the young fry could not help but absorb some of those refinements which today so many sadly lack, a better background, poise, and an appreciation of things that endure. — "What Women Want in their Dining Rooms of Tomorrow," a report by *McCall's*, 1944

The disappearing dining room is a symptom of changing family life. Families seldom sit down to eat together. The very nature of the family has changed; mothers aren't home all day slaving over the stove, and fathers may or may not be there at all. Meals are often ordered in or microwaved for quick consumption. In his play *The Dining Room*, A. R. Gurney writes, "Nowadays people eat in kitchens, or in living rooms, standing around, balancing their plates like jugglers. Soon they'll be eating in bathrooms. Well why not? Simplify the process considerably." □

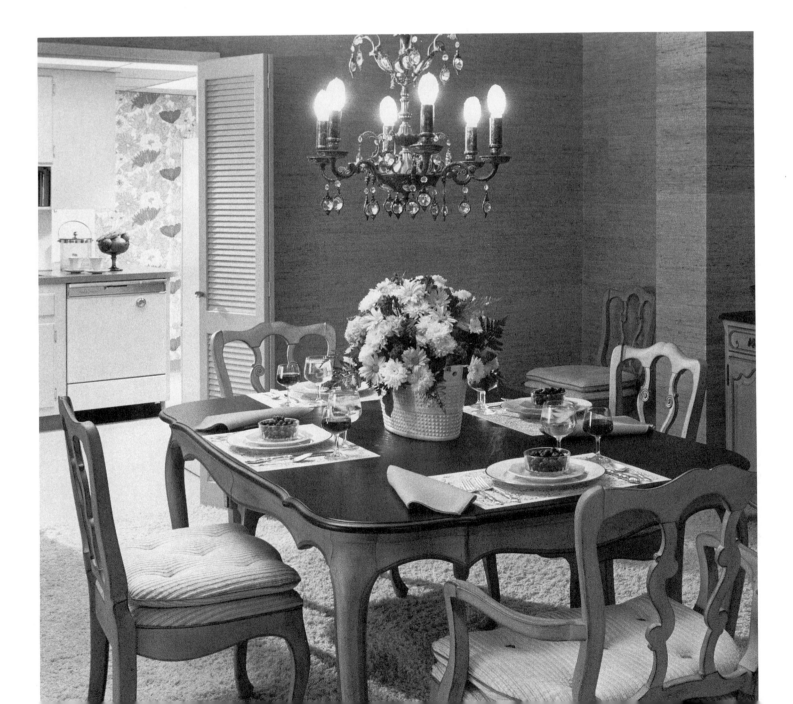

The Draft

A month after the United States entered World War I in April 1917, President Woodrow Wilson signed a law authorizing a draft. The country had a small standing army of fewer than one hundred thousand professional soldiers, not nearly enough men to help the European Allies. The new law required every man between twenty-one and thirty to register. In communities all across America, young men arrived at city hall prepared to do their bit for their country. Leading citizens were there to greet them. Schoolchildren cheered as they marched in an impromptu parade down Main Street. Before the war ended, nearly twenty-five million men registered, and nearly three million were drafted.

It was the third draft in the country's history and the first that was at all popular. During the American Revolution and the Civil War, draftees were reluctant to serve for more than a few months, and the desertion rate was high. Men drafted into the Union Army could buy an exemption for three hundred dollars or hire a substitute, practices that prompted critics to say that the Civil War was fought with "rich man's money and poor man's blood." Nearly a thousand people were killed during riots in protest against the disparity between who got drafted and who actually served. Determined to prevent the same thing from happening in 1917, the government decreed that no one could buy an exemption or hire a substitute.

After the Armistice in 1918, the draft lapsed. During the next two decades, the armed forces shrank to about half a million men. In September 1940, the Roosevelt administration, anticipating that the United States would have to fight Germany and Japan, urged Congress to authorize the nation's first peacetime draft. Nearly seventeen million men showed up to register, including heavyweight champ Joe Louis and two sons of the president. Every man filled out a short form with his name and address. Five days later he received in the mail a number based on the order in which he had

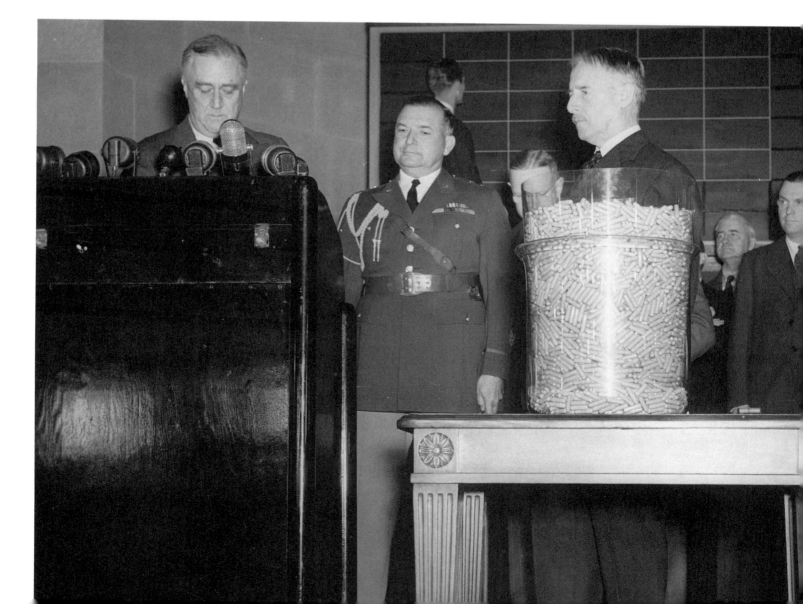

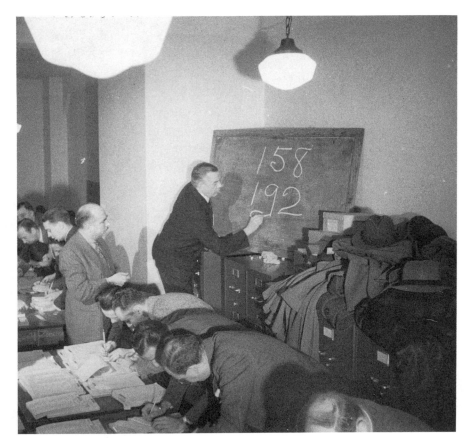

registered. Two weeks later, at a public ceremony in Washington, D.C., government officials took turns pulling nine thousand numbered blue capsules from a drum to determine the sequence in which men would be called up.

Number 158, the first chosen, was held by 6,175 young men around the country. Along with other men at the top of the list, they reported back to their local draft boards and filled out a longer questionnaire—on the basis of which they were declared eligible, unfit, or deferred because of their job or family situation. Men who were 1A got their affairs in order and awaited induction.

By the end of the war, nearly fifty million men between the ages of eighteen and sixty-five signed up. Few challenged their classification, although one New Yorker tried to get an exemption because he was a corset maker, arguing that he worked in a vital industry essential to the well-being of American women. About half the men failed their physicals, mostly for bad teeth. "Only once in a while do we find a boy who's glad his defects kept him out of the Army," said a draft board doctor. "Most of those rejected are depressed and disappointed." Many tried to enlist in other units.

Hollywood stars like Clark Gable, Jimmy Stewart, Robert Taylor, and Henry Fonda enlisted, inaugurating a national debate, which many people took quite seriously, about where they were most needed. The January 9, 1943, issue of *Colliers* magazine complained that too many "stars and technicians are marching off to war instead of making films essential to the war effort. Result: America faces the loss of its most valuable single morale weapon—the movies."

After World War II, the draft was retained because of the Cold War. Although all young men between eighteen and a half and twenty-one were required to register, no one was actually called up because the threat of conscription encouraged enough men to volunteer. Volunteers could choose their branch of service and had some control over when they were inducted.

The armed forces resumed the draft after the Korean War broke out in June 1950. For the first time since the Civil War, large numbers of Americans opposed the government's policy, and many young men did not want to serve. "Everyone wants out; no one wants in," said Maj. Gen. Lewis Hershey, head of the Selective Service System.

Greeting:

Having submitted yourself to a Local Board composed of your neighbors for the purpose of determining your availability for service in the armed forces of the United States, you are hereby ordered to report to [your] Local Board . . . for forwarding to an induction station.

This Local Board will furnish transportation to the induction station where you will be examined, and, if accepted for service, you will then be inducted into a branch of the armed forces. — Selective Service System, Order to Report for Induction, 1948

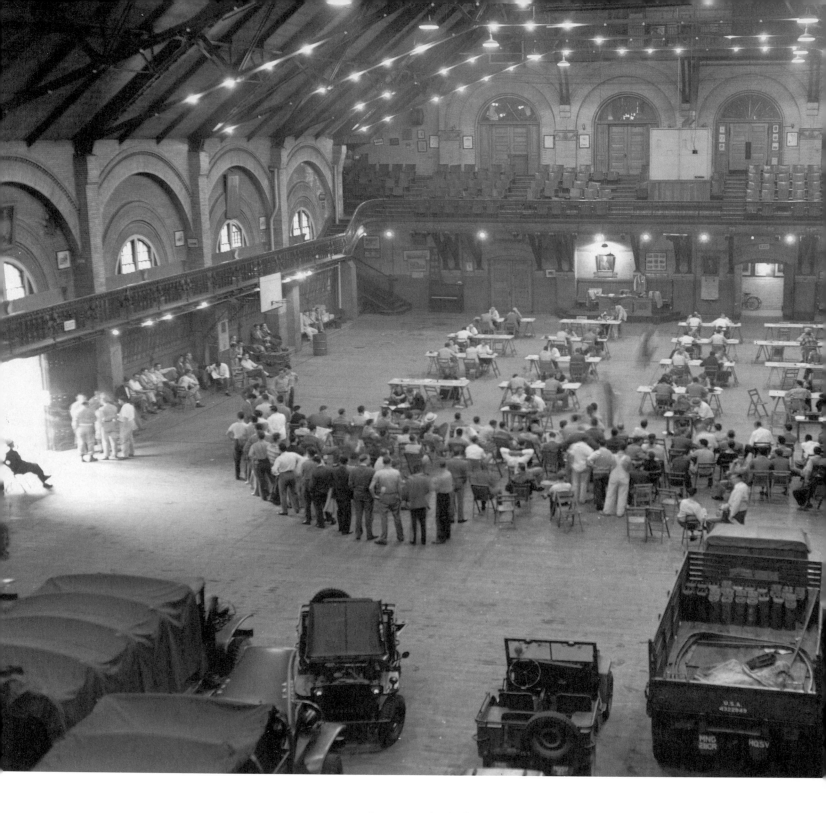

After Korea, the draft continued. Failure to register or show up for induction could lead to five years in prison and/or a ten thousand dollar fine. Young men were forced to make personal and career choices based on their military obligation. Many chose to serve a brief tour on active duty followed by six to eight years in the National Guard or reserves. A few regulars were deployed in an obscure corner of Southeast Asia to advise the army of South Vietnam.

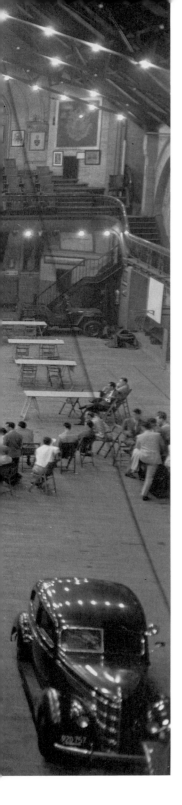

As America got more deeply involved in Vietnam, about one hundred thousand men a year were drafted. But in the mid-1960s, draft calls shot up to three hundred thousand annually, and opposition to the war, and to conscription, crystallized. Young men scrambled to enroll in college and graduate school, get a place in the National Guard, or marry. Exemptions and deferment enabled many sons of the middle and upper classes to avoid being drafted; the poor were more likely to serve.

Opponents of the war burned their draft cards on college campuses, chanting "Hell no! We won't go!" in full view of network television cameras. One son of a career navy officer dropped out of college to end his exemption, then searched his soul for the best way to dramatize his defiance. "Shall I burn my card? Apply for conscientious objector status? Ask for asylum in Cuba? Go to Canada?" Eventually he went to jail. After Muhammad Ali, the heavyweight champion, became a Black Muslim, he applied for conscientious objector status. His draft board turned him down, and the World Boxing Association stripped him of his title.

In 1969 the draft was revised. The Selective Service replaced a system that had kept young men in limbo until their twenty-seventh birthday with a national lottery for nineteen year olds. Men with high numbers knew they would get through the year without being called and would not be vulnerable again. Men with low numbers scurried for places in the National Guard or went off to war. The rest played lottery roulette: Should they gamble on being exposed for a year? Or should they enroll in school, knowing they would go back into the pool when they graduated, but hoping the war would be over before that day came?

The bitterness of the Vietnam years led to the end of the draft in 1973. Registration was eliminated two years later. It was resumed in 1980 in response to the Russian invasion of Afghanistan and remains in effect in the 1990s. Young men must register within thirty days of their eighteenth birthday. Ninety percent eventually do. The few who do not are seldom prosecuted unless they draw attention to themselves. However, unregistered students cannot get federal loans, and some states will not employ anyone who has not signed up.

The armed forces have no desire to reinstate the draft. Only in the unlikely event of a long land war might they change their position. "Be all that you can be," the army tells potential volunteers, enticing them with technical training, money for education, and a great credit on a resume. The quality and morale of the all-volunteer armed forces in the early 1990s are considered the best in decades. For the foreseeable future, the military is happy with the highly motivated, highly skilled force of men and women who choose to serve. □

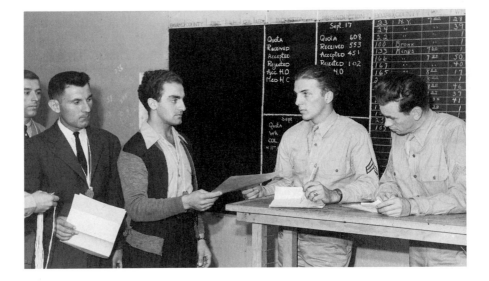

Drive-In Movies

In 1991, New Jersey, the birthplace of the drive-in, lost its last outdoor movie when the Route 35 Drive-In went dark. Closing night was like a New Orleans funeral: sad but celebratory. As its final bill, the theater showed a movie from the year it opened, the 1956 film *The Girl Can't Help It,* starring Jayne Mansfield and featuring Fats Domino, Little Richard, and the Platters. Also playing was the 1958 version of *The Fly* starring Vincent Price, a drive-in classic. Admission was ten dollars a carload. Before the last picture show, ground was broken for a new twelve-screen indoor multiplex on the site.

In 1956 America had 5,000 drive-ins, up from 743 less than a decade earlier. The drive-in—or "ozoner" as it was known in the trade—was the brainchild of a south Jersey man named Richard Hollingshead, Jr. Hollingshead put up a motion picture screen in front of his garage, mounted a 16-millimeter projector on the roof of his car, and sat back in the front seat to watch home movies. In 1933 he patented a ramp system that permitted passengers in cars to see over the cars in front of them.

Shortly afterward Hollingshead opened the world's first drive-in on Admiral Wilson Boulevard in Camden, in a parking lot big enough for four hundred cars. One month later he added a snack bar. People who lived in the area protested that the high-volume loudspeakers blasted sound into their bedrooms. Soon that problem was solved with an RCA invention—a small speaker attached to posts between the parked cars which could be hung inside the car window.

In the years that followed, Americans by the millions steered into outdoor movies. They maneuvered their tail-finned Chevies, DeSotos, and Fords close to the speaker post and waited for the sun to set. Latecomers glided in silently, except for the sound of gravel crunching beneath their tires.

Going to the drive-in was cheaper than hiring a babysitter. Mom and dad sat in the front seat, and two or three kids, already in their pj's, bickered in the back. With any luck, the parents got to see the opening credits before having to take a child to the bathroom or to the concession stand. With even better luck, the kids were asleep before the second feature began.

Summer nights and drive-ins: images of Sandra Dee and Tab Hunter three or four stories high; *The Blob* or *Beach Blanket Bingo* under a crescent moon; the headlights of late arrivals; lawn chairs, six-packs, and portable barbecues set up for picnics before the show.

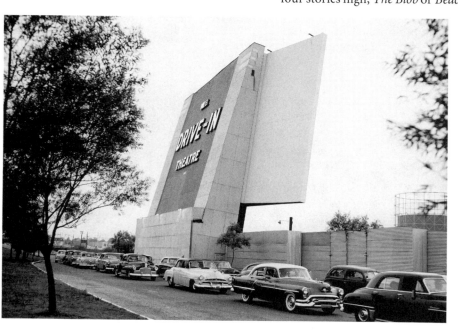

Double and even triple bills were the usual fare. At intermission everyone headed for the concession stand. "The longer the program, the more often they eat," one drive-in owner explained. Milk shakes, pizza pies, grinders, and hamburgers were hauled back to the car and devoured before the lights dimmed once again. As the closing credits rolled, an announcement over the PA system reminded customers to remove the speaker from the car window so they wouldn't drive away and rip it from its stand.

Drive-ins were a magnet for teenagers on a night out with the family car. Six high school buddies might pool their resources for four admissions and try to sneak past the gate with two of their gang hiding in the trunk. Couples going steady parked in the back rows, as far from the lights of the concession stand as possible, so they could neck in private while Cochise and his braves bushwhacked the cavalry on the screen. Sometimes employees knocked on the windows if no heads were visible. Drive-ins were condemned from pulpits and editorial pages as "passion pits." "If you went to one with a boy, your reputation was ruined with your friends," recalls a middle-aged woman from Morris County, New Jersey.

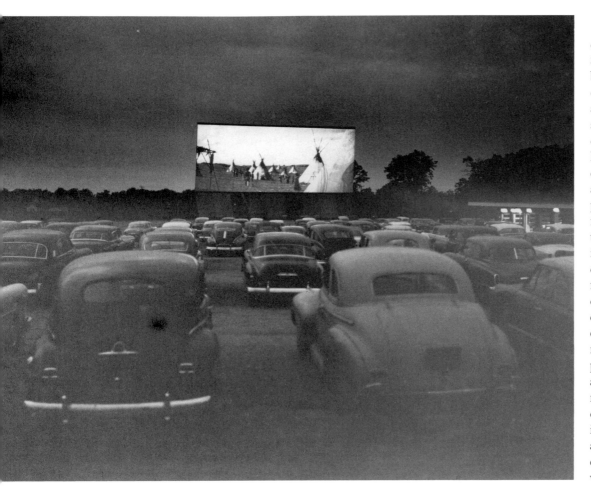

Drive-ins offered all kinds of come-ons to attract customers. Some Texas theaters had a rail behind the back ramp where a cowpoke could tether his horse and watch the movie in the saddle. Naturally they were called gallop-ins. Others offered laundry service; a housewife dropped off clothes at the gate as her family entered and picked them up clean and folded when she left. At one theater the price of admission included free milk and fresh diapers for babies, a kiddieland for small fry, a miniature golf course, a driving range, and dancing under the stars. To stay open in winter, some owners in northern states offered premiums—electric heaters or a free gallon of gas to keep the motor idling so the car heater could run. One theater owner issued "fog checks"—good for admission on another evening—when sleet cut down visibility to zero.

The number of drive-ins in America reached an all-time high of six thousand in 1961. Thirty years later, only nine hundred were in business. They continued to thrive in the Sun Belt, where any activity that keeps people outside is popular. Elsewhere the value of their underlying real estate did them in. The vast majority of drive-ins opened in the decade after World War II. They were often built on undeveloped stretches of highway at the edge of town. In the 1960s and 1970s, cities expanded, and suburban real estate prices soared. All that asphalt-covered acreage became too valuable to devote to a business that functioned only after dark and mostly in warm weather. Theater owners found themselves sitting on prime commercial space coveted by developers of industrial parks, tract housing, and shopping malls—which would eventually have their own indoor multiplexes.

**The drive-in movie is the answer to the sitter problem, and to the downtown parking problem. It's the answer to the young family night out. It's the neighborhood theater of the future.
— Bob Lippert, theater chain owner, quoted in the *Saturday Evening Post*, September 15, 1956**

There were other, less obvious reasons for the decline of drive-ins. One was daylight saving time, which became standardized in most of the nation by the late 1960s. Theaters had to synchronize their first show with the setting sun. During daylight saving, they couldn't get started until nine o'clock—too late for families that had to get up early the next morning.

Maybe moviegoers got too sophisticated for the less than state-of-the-art outdoor projection and sound. Perhaps parents were unwilling to expose their kids to the increasingly violent and sexually explicit movies that were the only ones drive-in operators could afford to book as attendance waned. The sexual revolution of the 1960s may have been the last straw. Drive-ins were no longer the only place where teenagers could park and pet.

Whatever else was going on, there was also a correlation in the 1980s between the rise of VCRs and the decline of drive-ins. During the same decade, the number of people who subscribed to pay cable services offering first-run movies doubled. One of the main attractions of drive-ins used to be that the whole family could pile into the car and see a movie with all the comforts of home—blankets, pillows, snacks, and privacy. Watching cable or renting a video meant you didn't even have to leave the house. ☐

Enclosed Telephone Booths

Chicago, 1935. Ann Dvorak dashes into a phone booth, pulls a dime from her raincoat pocket, and frantically dials the number of James Cagney, the lawyer-turned-govenment-agent hero of Warner Brothers' movie *G-Men*. Before Dvorak can blow the whistle on the mob, her gangster husband, Barton MacLane, closes in. A burst of tommy-gun fire shatters the glass windows of Dvorak's phone booth. Her lifeless body pushes against the door and falls to the pavement.

For Hollywood screenwriters from the 1930s through the late 1960s, an enclosed phone booth was a convenient setting for advancing the plot. What better metaphor for peril and vulnerability than a character trapped inside a box with the evocative shape of an upended coffin. Conversely, what safer haven for a hero patching things up with his girl, or an ingenue landing her first job, than a phone booth that shut out eavesdropping neighbors and the tumult of the street.

Privacy was an objective of Thomas Watson, Alexander Graham Bell's assistant, who is credited with designing the first telephone booth. Because his landlady complained about the racket he made when he shouted into the phone, Watson draped blankets over his furniture and crawled inside the makeshift enclosure to make his calls. By 1883 Watson had devised a wooden booth with a domed top, ventilator, screened windows, and a writing desk.

Many early booths had silk-curtained windows with tiny panes and opaque colored glass in the door. Hotel guests sometimes mistook them for elevators. Most booths were outfitted with rugs and upholstered chairs. An attendant collected change. One inventor designed an unattended booth with a door which locked behind callers when they stepped inside and released them when they deposited a coin in the locked door.

In 1905 the Bell System installed the first outdoor public pay phone in Cincinnati, Ohio. Before placing their calls, customers dropped coins directly into the phone, which sat on top of a metal stanchion located on a busy downtown street. Callers

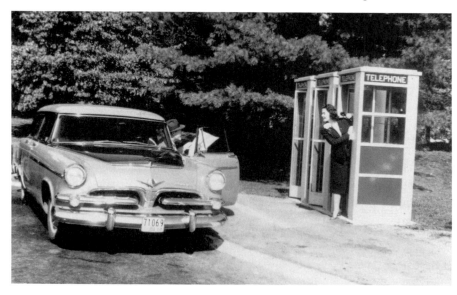

complained about traffic noise and the lack of privacy; the service was a failure.

To overcome public resistance, Western Electric (the manufacturing division of the Bell System) introduced its No. 1 type telephone booth in 1912. This wood-and-glass booth with a hinged door remained the standard design for forty years, though in time the cabinet was enlarged to accommodate a man about six feet four inches tall, with a shoulder width of twenty inches, even though ninety-seven percent of the population was not that big. Advertisements promised cleanliness, attractive colors, and convenient locations. Booths were available in walnut, oak, mahogany, and birch, with harmonizing interior colors. Swivel chairs, armrests, ashtrays, writing ledges—many features could be added to enhance customers' comfort and satisfaction.

The phone company bragged about its sanitary standards. In the early 1940s, an historian of the Bell System wrote that "experience with millions of telephones used each day for many millions of conversations . . . has failed to produce an authenticated case of disease transmission by use of the telephone." Cleaning services did their job well. In Chicago and New York, scientists cultured bacteria from mouthpieces. Ninety percent of the germs died in the open air within minutes, and "none of them could jump from their resting place into a talking mouth."

Bell System designers and engineers sought perfection in maintenance and client satisfaction. They tested hundreds of ventilation methods, frequently adjusting the size of the blow-through openings at the bottom of the booth and the exhausts at the top. In the early 1970s, they produced a hands-free booth featuring a microphone in front of the caller and a loudspeaker in the ceiling. Unfortunately, because people shouted at the ceiling, the model was withdrawn from the market.

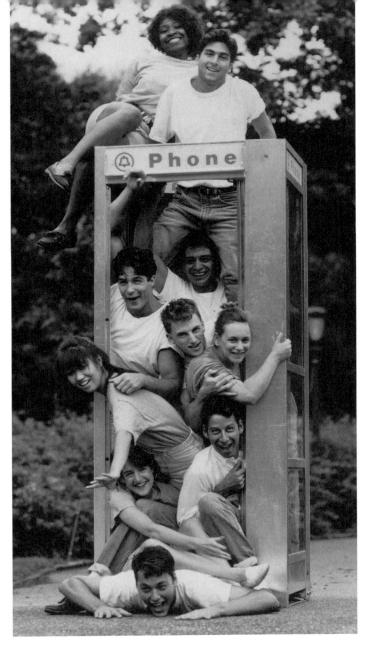

AT&T worried constantly about wear and tear: "When his call is finished, the customer typically pivots on his right foot to leave the booth; this region of a booth floor is thus subject to unusually severe wear conditions. . . . Synthetic rubber stands up best under such hard wear." A press release hailed the advent of an improved shatterproof glass, which, if someone succeeded in smashing it, broke into tiny pieces without jagged edges.

Shatterproof glass signaled AT&T's acknowledgment that the phone booth wasn't everyone's home away from home. From the early 1970s, the prevention of vandalism dominated every effort by the company to maintain pay phone service. The language of advertising and public relations no longer assumed that all sectors of the public shared a social contract with large corporations. Gone were words like *trust* and *convenience* and selling points like "striking color motifs in special exterior finishes." The new vocabulary got right to the point. In 1971 the Bell System announced the availability of an "armored pay phone—a new phone with a cable sheathed in steel. That way it's harder to cut. The dial is recessed and made of virtually unbreakable plastic. The case is heavy-gauge steel. And there's a special anti-theft device to make sure the money you deposit goes for a phone call. Instead of into someone's pocket."

In 1972, thirty-five thousand pay phones were wrecked each month in New York alone, and vandalism cost the company nearly $15 million nationwide. Two years later, AT&T stopped making enclosed phone booths altogether. Designers tried desperately to keep one step ahead of the increasing rage and ingenuity of the booth bashers with a series of open or semienclosed models without tops or floors.

One solution was a "vandal resistant walk-up enclosure." The phone was mounted in a small box attached to a hollow steel post, the base of which was embedded in concrete. It was anchored to the post by fasteners inserted from within the instrument and was thus "hidden and protected from all unauthorized access." The 1990 sales brochure offered the newest models: "Designed to be rugged and versatile, AT&T Public Telephone Enclosures require little maintenance. They provide a secure environment and are maintenance-free, scratch-resistant, durable, sturdy and dependable, minimizing vandalism and fraud."

Early in the century, when the Bell System introduced the first outdoor pay phone, people spurned it because they valued the privacy that an enclosed booth guaranteed. Ninety years later, privacy was a barely noted casualty of the public phone wars.

There were other casualties as well. In the 1978 movie, *Superman*, Clark Kent rushes to transform himself into his alter ego in order to save Lois Lane, who clings to the runner of a crashed helicopter dangling from the ledge of the Daily Planet building fifty stories above the street. Frantically seeking a phone booth—his customary changing room—Kent finds only a new "walk-up enclosure." Barely breaking stride, he turns instead toward the revolving door of a nearby building. Modern Superman may still be more powerful than a speeding locomotive, but even he can't bring back the past. □

LIKE A LIGHTHOUSE ON THE HIGHWAY . . . Lighted outdoor telephone booths are multiplying along America's highways. . . . A thoughtful husband, hurrying home, phones to reassure his wife. A young family calls ahead to make reservations for the night. A vacationing couple enjoys a telephone visit with old friends off their route. A sputtering car coasts to a stop and two grateful women phone for road service. . . . There's always a public phone handy to help you.
— Bell Telephone System ad, 1959

There is in all the world no finer figure than a sturdy farmer standing, his feet well planted in the earth, looking over his rich fields and his beautiful shiny cattle. He has a security and an independence unknown to any other member of society. — Louis Bromfield, *Out of the Earth*, 1950

Family Farms

A woman who lives in Minneapolis grew up in the 1950s on a farm in South Dakota that her dad inherited from his father. The family thought of farm life as a "high calling." She and her sister weeded the vegetable garden; their brother drove the grain truck during the harvest. She remembers that her mother came home from the hospital after the birth of another baby, rolled up her sleeves, and fixed lunch and dinner for a crew of workmen building a new milk house. In summer the women took cold water and iced tea to the high school boys who hired on for several weeks to bale hay in the hot sun. In autumn her mother put up mason jars full of tomatoes, pickles, green beans, and corn for the winter. Farm life was hard but satisfying work. It was also productive—for the farmers and for the nation.

Too productive, in fact. Throughout the twentieth century, American farmers have raised more food than the country needed. Even in the midst of the Depression, while destitute families went hungry in the cities and Dust Bowl farmers lost their land, the U.S. Department of Agriculture advised farmers to destroy one-third of their bumper crop of baby pigs, in a vain effort to prop up farm prices by restricting supply. For the next fifty years, national politics was dominated by the catchwords *surplus*, *parity*, *price supports*, and *soil banks*, as successive administrations tried, and often failed, to cap agricultural production and stabilize what farmers earned.

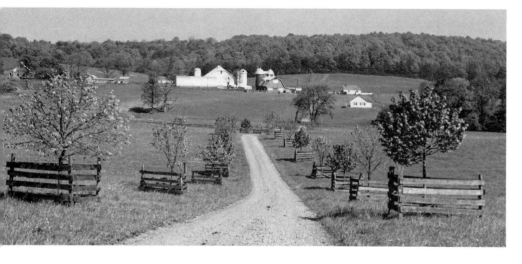

For a brief period during and after World War II, the world needed everything the American granary produced. Farmers were exempted from military service to grow the food that fueled the Allied war effort and fed starving refugees. They made enough during the crisis to buy better machines, better seeds, and better fertilizer—and therefore to raise more than ever.

The boom continued through the 1950s, which was probably the last golden age of the family farm. The January 3, 1955, issue of *Life* magazine celebrated the abundance of American agriculture: a portfolio of photographs by Margaret Bourke-White captured contoured grain fields in Iowa, a well-kept clapboard homestead on a Wisconsin dairy farm, and red barns with hex signs in prosperous Pennsylvania Dutch country. Grain elevators in the Midwest were filled almost to bursting, and the mothballed naval fleet that was rusting in rivers and harbors from the Hudson to Puget Sound was pressed into service as unlikely storage space for surplus wheat.

Even in good times, farmers worried about prices and the weather. In the 1970s they had to cope with the consequences of an unexpected windfall—the rising value of their land. Real estate developers, gentlemen farmers, and corporations looking for rural factory sites bid up the cost of open tracts. The value of agricultural land rose from an average of $300 an acre in 1970 to $1,700 in 1981.

Farmers used this boost in their assets to finance expensive new machinery—specialized tractors and combines, specialized milking sheds, specialized buildings for managing livestock. With their overvalued land as collateral, farmers burdened

54

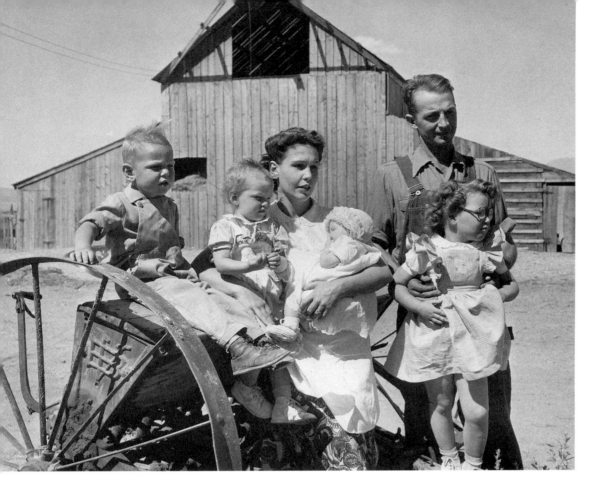

themselves with a total debt that rose from less than $50 billion in 1970 to $190 billion in 1990. Yet it seemed inconceivable that the agonies of the 1930s—sheriffs' sales and foreclosures—could come again.

By the early 1980s, individual farmers found their cash income dropping and their loan payments harder and harder to meet. The local banker changed overnight from the farmer's friend to his worst enemy. Banks foreclosed mortgages without attempting to find a way to refinance. Ignoring bankruptcy orders, some bankers sent their agents on midnight raids to carry off valuable assets like machinery and livestock.

Farmers became suicidal. Banks went under. Drugstores, clothing stores, restaurants, and five-and-dimes closed their doors. Schools consolidated. Whole rural communities began to die. Willie Nelson, who had been a member of the Future Farmers of America in high school, organized a Farm Aid concert in 1985 to dramatize the agricultural crisis. Farm Aid raised more than $50 million, which was used to help set up support services for bankrupt farmers. It was only a drop in the bucket. "Willie can sing and pluck all night," one farmer said. "But he's not going to make too much headway with farm debt. We're in too deep."

At the height of the catastrophe, an Iowa farm wife said, "When people talk about losing the farm, they think just of a farmer losing his job, and they say 'He can get another job.' But it's not just that. It's losing your life-style and everything you and your kin have worked for. It's comparable to a death in the family."

Those family farms that survived the financial crisis of the 1980s faced an even more insidious problem in the 1990s. The average age of farmers in 1990 was fifty-plus. Their kids preferred the regular hours and steady income of town jobs. About thirty-four thousand farms were abandoned each year, leaving just over two million in the whole country by 1993. Fewer than five million Americans lived on the land, the lowest number since the Civil War.

Corporate farms, run by white-collar executives rather than blue-denim dirt farmers, accountable to stockholders rather than the family roundtable, now dominate the production of citrus fruits, vegetables, and beef cattle. They're the folks that brought America a mixed bounty: cartons of fresh orange juice, "lite" beef, prepackaged poultry, and the tasteless tomato.

Some innovative family farmers have identified crops that agribusiness ignores and that restaurants, ethnic markets, or fancy grocers will pay a premium for. Successful farmers in New England produce goat cheese, hand-pressed cider, stone-ground flours, free-range chickens, pheasant, and quail. Truck farmers sell salad greens like arugula, radicchio, and red leaf that were unknown a decade ago. One ranch family in Montana made enough money raising marijuana to repurchase land that had been sold to pay back taxes. Once out of debt, they returned to cattle grazing. □

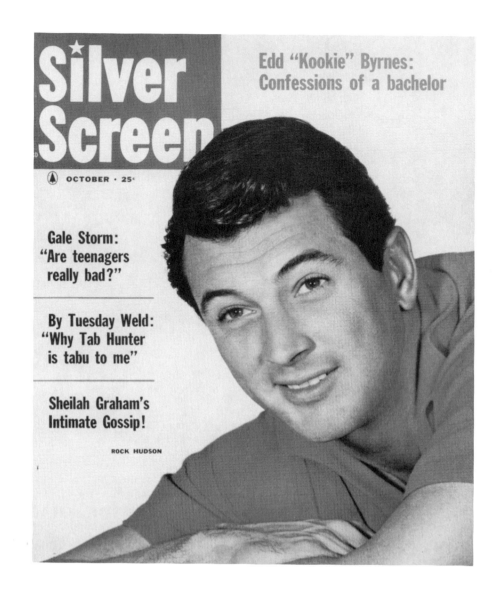

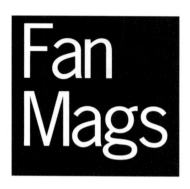

Just ten years into the twentieth century, Americans flocked to movie theaters in such numbers that motion pictures quickly became the country's fifth largest industry. Moviegoers idolized the leading players. They collected their press clippings and mobbed their personal appearances.

The studios responded by issuing magazines about the stars. But the prose, stiff as an official press release, made fans clamor for more personal information. An alert publisher, James Quirk, sensed the potential of the new kind of magazine. With the studios' blessings and a little bit of pizzazz, it could be transformed to give fans an intimate look at the stars and make them think that the writers were privy to the most telling details of the stars' lives. Quirk's magazine, inaugurated in 1911, was called *Photoplay*. His first reporter, Adela Rogers St. Johns, moved to Hollywood to write the kind of gossipy tidbits about her neighbors and close friends that became the staple of *Photoplay's* pages and of the competitors that followed.

The fan mags of the day were filled with stories about Hollywood's ingenues—Mary Pickford, Mabel Normand, the Talmadge sisters, and Lillian Gish. Entire pages were devoted to portraits of the stars. Since everybody wanted to be in movies, there were stories about how to be "discovered" and how to write a script. Occasionally there was a feature on Theda Bara, Hollywood's resident "vamp." When Charlie

Jane Peters is Carole Lombard. That's her real name; Carole Lombard is just something a numerologist gave her. And The Moose is her pet name for Clark Gable, the guy she's in love with, and vice-versa. That is, she calls him "the moose" when she's talking about him with others. When she talks with him, she just calls him "Poppy." And he calls her "Ma."

That's how it is with Clark and the Lombard. That's how it's been for more months than cynical Hollywood ever believed it possible for two people to be as deliriously, insanely, happily head-over-heels in love with each other in movie-land.
— "Will Clark Gable Ever Marry Carole Lombard?"
Motion Picture, February 1939

Chaplin married Mildred Harris, *Photoplay* was privileged to interview "the most fortunate young woman in the world." When Mary Pickford had breakfast with her "Mumsey," *Motion Picture* readers were there to share it.

During the 1920s, the fan books wrestled with the changes in morality that were sweeping America. Sex appeal nudged aside innocence. There were inside scoops about Clara Bow, Ramon Novarro, Gloria Swanson, and a newcomer, Gary Cooper. In an article called "Woman and Love," Rudolph Valentino confided to *Photoplay* readers, "One can always be kind to a woman one cares nothing about." However, when scandals struck stars like Fatty Arbuckle and Mabel Normand, the magazines treated their difficulties sympathetically, more as grand tragedy than dirt.

The years between the Depression and World War II represented the apogee of fan literature. Luscious pictures with folksy captions were interspersed with saccharine love stories dished up by the all-controlling film studios. America's favorite stars were presented as "the folks next door," as people who baked brownies, played with their pets, and found Love. They may have been famous, but as the magazines assured readers, they had problems, too, just like you and me. In pages of *Photoplay, Silver Screen, Modern Screen*, and *Motion Picture*, fans learned "The High Price of Screen Love-Making," "The Tragic Truth about John Gilbert's Death," "Why Movie Stars Can't Stay in Love," and "The Truth Behind the Stanwyck Court Case: Barbara Stanwyck fights to give her adopted son, Dion, the Happiness and Security she missed in Childhood."

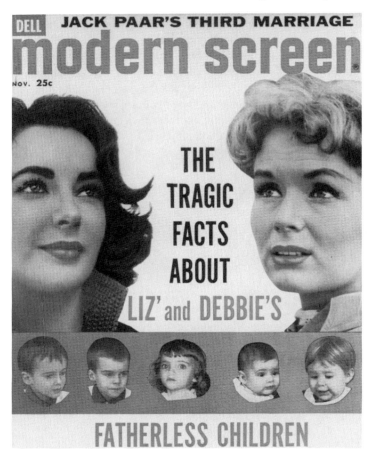

The fan mags of the 1940s introduced America to new male heartthrobs like Van Johnson and Frank Sinatra. They glorified the pinup, with dazzling portraits of Rita Hayworth, Bette Grable, and Veronica Lake. As the "Red Scare" swept Hollywood, Humphrey Bogart assured *Photoplay* fans, in headline-size type, "I'M NO COMMUNIST."

In 1951 *Photoplay* boasted of a 1.2 million monthly circulation, a figure that put it ahead of its twenty-nine other competitors. Twelve million teenage girls and middle-aged women paid twenty cents a month to read about the latest romances and heartbreaks of their friends, the stars. Even sophisticates who wouldn't dream of buying fan mags avidly read them under the dryer at their hairdressers. The women of America loved being in on a typical night at home with Rock Hudson and his wife. ("'How did things go today?' Phyllis will ask, when Rock limps in after a rugged day on the set, and it pleases him that she will inquire.")

During the 1950s, the studios were shaken by the impact of television. By the end of the decade, the artificial world of the movie magazines had collapsed as well. For forty years, their success had been based on mutuality of interest among the studios, their stars, and the journalists. In return for controlled access, fan mags presented the stars in the most flattering light—even if gossip columnists Hedda Hopper, Sheilah Graham, Dorothy Kilgallen, and Louella Parsons occasionally gave them demerits for unseemly behavior.

In 1952 a new magazine called *Confidential* hit the newsstands. *Confidential* raised the stakes on scandal; its formula of sex and sin attracted readers away from the syrupy fan mags. Soon it spawned dozens of clones: *Behind the Scene, Exposed, Hush-Hush, Inside Story, The Lowdown,* and *Uncensored.* To compete, the fan magazines in the late 1950s began printing more sensational stories, thereby breaking the pact they had with the industry. Traditional headlines like "Hollywood's Most Successful Human Beings" gave way to "Five Stars Boldly Admit: 'I had a Love Baby!'"; "Husband Says: Leslie Caron Admits Adultery!"; and "We Have Court Records—Ryan O'Neal has Two Wives." Elizabeth Taylor provided grist for the rumor mill almost every month: "Liz Taunts Burton: 'Have an Affair—I Dare You!'"; "Liz's Bodyguard Betrays her Secrets"; and "Neither Love nor Liquor Can Help Liz Now."

Confidential went out of business after losing a series of libel suits, but its place was more than filled by the supermarket tabloids. In the early 1970s the owners of Time Inc. spotted a market for a more upscale celebrity magazine. They launched *People* in 1974. *People* was different from the traditional fan mags. It covered all kinds of famous people, not just movie stars. Though it took readers into the homes of the rich and famous, it claimed to report with "wry detachment," and an attitude that was "perhaps a little skeptical."

Most of the fan magazines had died out by the time *People* appeared. The monthly edition of *Photoplay* limped along until 1980. The overwhelming success of a special edition in 1977 when Elvis died suggested that the publishers could keep their title alive by producing other occasional one-shots. In the years that followed, *Photoplay* reappeared to commemorate events like John Lennon's death or Michael Jackson mania.

People was the first of many magazine and television programs to capitalize on the fact that famous faces still bring in the audience. The public today has more interest in the lives of its favorite celebrities than ever, and almost anything goes. Stars talk about their sex lives on late-night television. When Ingrid Bergman left her husband in 1948 and had a child out of wedlock, her career was finished. Now when stars have children without getting married, the public can't wait for pictures of the baby. Celebrities are still the embodiment of their fans' hopes and dreams. But that complicity in innocence, the worshipful view of stars as gods and goddesses, and the intimacy that movie magazines led readers to believe they shared are gone forever. □

A year ago Lana wouldn't have understood or appreciated Tony Martin; wouldn't have found pleasure in the simple pastimes, the love of sports and easy laughter that are a part of Tony. Recently Lana was scheduled to do a benefit. . . . But when the day came she was feeling desperately tired from her work at the studio. She consulted Tony.

"Don't go," he advised. "You've got to think of your health and your work."

"Can you imagine me?" Lana said afterwards, "eating milk toast in bed and going to sleep at nine o'clock with a new dress hanging in the closet?"

Whatever comes to pass, Tony Martin will remain an important milestone in Lana's life; for even greater than love right now is the new Lana Turner, the girl who has found herself.

— "No More Divorces!: The New-Fashioned Love affair of Lana Turner and Tony Martin," *Photoplay*, March 1941

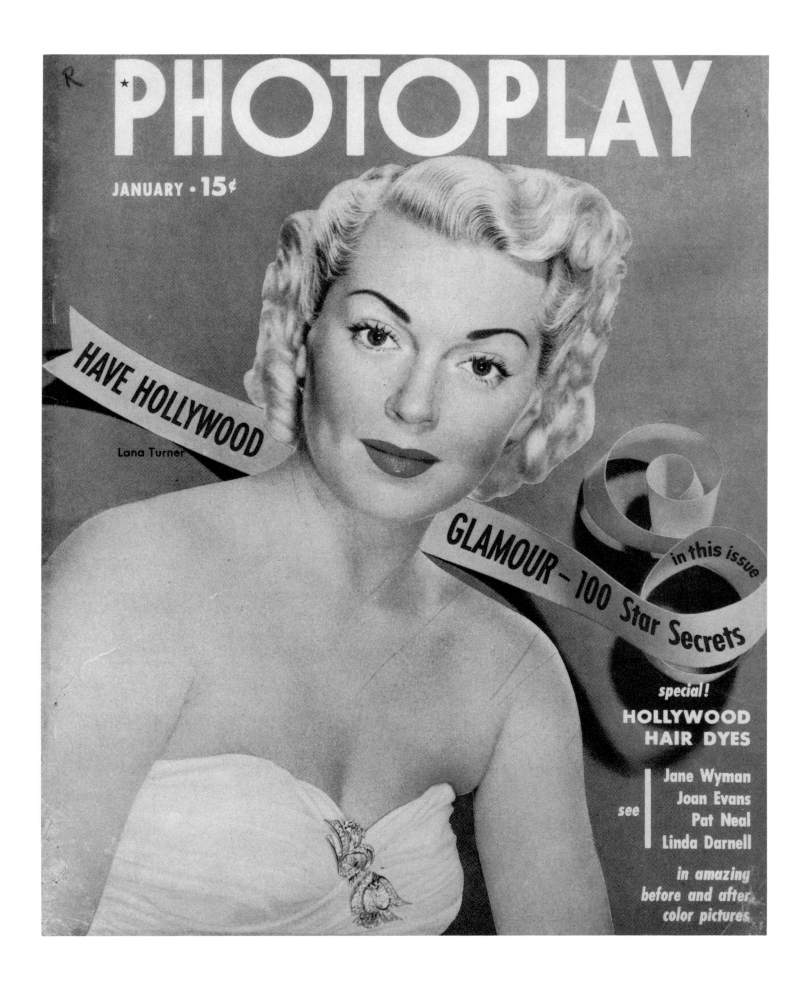

PHOTOPLAY

JANUARY · 15¢

Lana Turner

HAVE HOLLYWOOD

GLAMOUR – 100 Star Secrets

in this issue

special!

HOLLYWOOD HAIR DYES

see

Jane Wyman
Joan Evans
Pat Neal
Linda Darnell

in amazing before and after color pictures

Fire Escapes

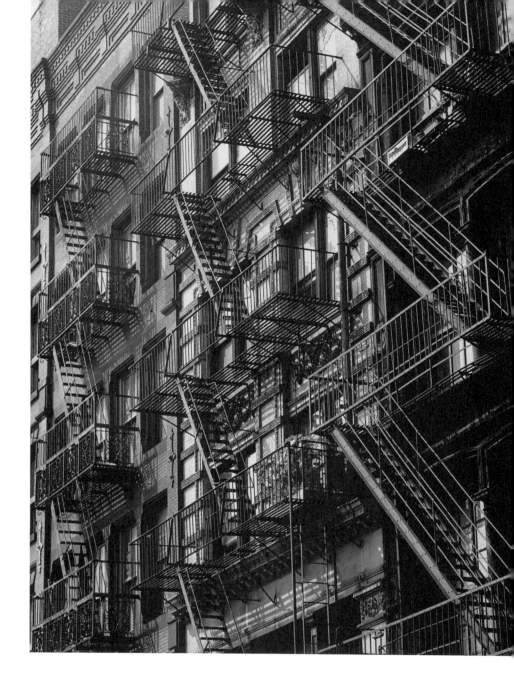

On February 2, 1860, a blaze destroyed a six-story tenement on Elm Street in lower Manhattan. Twenty people either perished in the flames or jumped to their deaths. The Common Council of New York immediately passed an act requiring that all new buildings designed to house eight or more families have fireproof stairs attached to the exterior walls. The city's first comprehensive housing law, the Tenement House Act of 1867, made fire escapes mandatory for all existing tenements and those on the drawing boards.

Enforcement of the act, however, was another matter. In the four decades before 1860, four million immigrants had entered America, primarily through the port of New York, and nearly four hundred thousand of them had settled in the city. By 1865, half a million people—seventy percent of the total population— were crammed into fifteen thousand five- or six-story tenements. Conditions were appalling: Six or seven people often slept in one small room, sometimes in the coal cellar below the street level. There was no cross-ventilation, only one toilet to a floor (and those were often broken and overflowing), no effective garbage collection, and often no running water.

Come over here. Step carefully over this baby—it is a baby, spite of its rags and dirt, under these iron bridges called fire escapes, but loaded down, despite the incessant watchfulness of the firemen, with broken household goods, with washtubs and barrels, over which no man could climb from a fire. — Jacob Riis, *How the Other Half Lives*, 1890

60

The problem of substandard housing and fire hazard was nationwide. A Chicago fire department official described his city's great fire in October 1871 as being "without a parallel in the history of the world, if we except the sacking of Moscow." The fire, which started in a planing mill, spread unchecked across the city for three days. By the time it ended, twenty-three hundred acres were swept bare, eighteen thousand buildings destroyed, and one hundred thousand people left homeless. "Nearly the whole territory was covered with tenement houses," the official said, "and so swift was their destruction that it became necessary, in order to rescue human life, to throw women and children out of windows upon beds."

By 1900 more than eighty thousand tenements in New York City housed two-thirds of the city's total population. Despite forty years of legislation, a substantial number of people still lived in buildings that had no fire escapes at all. "A fire in the night in one of those human beehives, with its terror and woe, is one of the things that live in the recollection ever after as a terrible nightmare," wrote Jacob Riis, the social critic and photographer.

Continued agitation for reform led to the Tenement House Act of 1901, commonly called the "New Law," which set the national standard for tenement legislation. To comply with the New Law, every room in a tenement apartment had to have some means of escape in case of fire, and interior stairs and halls in larger buildings had to be entirely fireproof to retard the spread of flames between floors. New nonfireproof tenement houses could be built no higher than six stories. New fire escapes were required to have slanting stairways, instead of unsafe vertical ladders, and iron balconies three feet wide at each sill level. Fire escapes could not be erected in air shafts.

Despite the legislation, the Tenement House Department of the City of New York reported with dismay in late 1902 that thousands of tenement houses were still lacking fire escapes. Thousands of others had absolutely useless fire escapes or dangerous ones. More than ten thousand fire escapes had balconies with floors made of wood instead of iron. Many others were located in narrow enclosed air shafts that, during a blaze, would form "a veritable furnace from which there was no escape." Some fire escapes at the rear of buildings landed people in tiny courtyards with no exit to the street. "A more perfect form of fire trap could scarcely be conceived."

Every point the Tenement House Department raised was bitterly contested by the landlords, who did not want to put fire escapes on fronts of buildings because they lowered property values. Nonetheless, the owners were forced to comply. By the early 1920s, most low-rise multiple dwellings in the city without interior fireproof

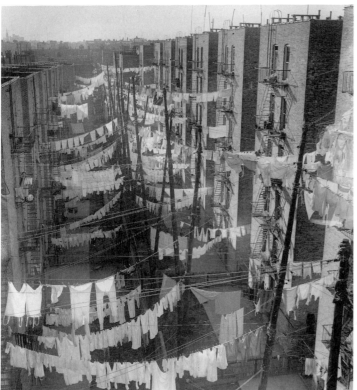

stairways were equipped with exterior fire escapes.

Undoubtedly, fire escapes saved countless lives, but no one ever thought they were the best way to get out of a burning building. Unless a landlord kept them well maintained, they could rust and possibly collapse. People afraid of heights were terrified to use them. Their narrow treads and tiny landings made them daunting for all but the most agile to descend. Fire escapes were especially treacherous if the stairs were covered with snow and ice, or if flames and smoke poured out from open windows on the lower stories as people tried to reach the ground. Since the stairs were made of iron, which heated rapidly in the fire, people often burned their hands. Landings were sometimes blocked by iceboxes and flowerpots which tenants illegally kept outside their cramped apartments. Architects and urban planners objected to fire escapes because they ruined the design of a building. Nonetheless, fire escapes were permitted on new low-rise residential buildings until the 1970s.

After 1975 the rules changed. For safety and aesthetic reasons, fire escapes were effectively banned on all new buildings. Most American cities continue to allow them only on existing structures that otherwise conform to fire safety laws or in special cases when there is no other way occupants can get out of a building in an emergency. The remaining fire escapes must be periodically inspected and properly maintained. Though they impart a distinctive look to many older urban neighborhoods, they will gradually disappear as new buildings replace the old. ☐

Fur Coats

Fur was man's first status symbol. At some un-recorded moment in a Neanderthal village, the chief appropriated the skin of a cave bear for himself, and the race was on. Wearing costly and desirable animal pelts became at least as much about showing off as it was about keeping warm.

From the Middle Ages through the sixteenth century, sumptuary laws established class distinctions in dress by spelling out who could wear which furs and who could not. Nobles were allowed to parade about with costly furs like ermine- and sable-lined cloaks and stoles. Merchants and tradesmen were limited to cheap skins like weasel, while their wives had to settle for squirrel. Peasants could wear only lamb or sheep.

By the seventeenth century, the sumptuary laws were gone. Demand had depleted the resources of the forests of Britain and Europe, and desirable pelts were becoming scarce. Fortunately for fashion, the opening up of North America led to new supplies and revived the passion for furs of all types. The French and Indian War of the mid-1700s was fought for control of the fur trade.

During the mid-nineteenth century, illustrations in the new women's magazines introduced an innovation: a garment not just lined or trimmed with pelts but made entirely of animal skins—the first modern fur coat. It was not surprising that Victorian women should start wearing coats with the fur outside. For the newly prosperous middle class, flaunting furs was a way to advertise wealth. The expensively dressed woman and, by extension, her family were claiming their place in a hierarchical society which increasingly equated money with social status.

By the latter part of the century, decorative furs verged on the perverse. Cats' heads and tiny monkeys adorned bonnets, and stuffed mice perched on the shoulders of evening gowns. Victorians were so fond of dead animals that they used them in their homes. Visitors to the royal family's estate at Sandringham, England, were greeted by a stuffed bear with a card tray in its paw. Leopard pelts were made into chair backs, and Sarah Bernhardt proudly displayed a lion's hide in her study in Paris.

The Edwardians were mad for chinchilla, ermine, and, above all, sable. A leading fashion emporium in Edinburgh had eleven departments devoted to fur apparel, including ladies' coats and wraps, boas, gentlemen's fur-lined coats, hats, capes, and foot muffs, as well as fur floor rugs, carriage throws, and traveling blankets. The store even sold fur stoles to wear with summer dresses.

Motoring was another excuse to wear furs, especially the new, hard-wearing, sporty kinds that could stand up to the elements. Men and women took to the road in bear, goat, and wolf. Nothing summons up the 1920s better than a flapper in a raccoon coat, waving a college pennant in one hand and a cigarette in the other.

Between the wars, young "career girls" bought inexpensive coats and jackets of rabbit, muskrat, and moleskin. Stern Brothers advertised "the evening wrap fashion of the year"—a lapin cape, on sale for $34.75: "It checks with Paris on every fashion point . . . a neckline that snuggles close to the throat, satin bow that gleams under the chin, soft low shoulders, tubular willowy lines. Even Dad will weaken when he sees its loveliness, its quality, its low price."

Introducing—Genuine Baby Sealskin! When a woman of today goes shopping for a fur coat—what does she ask the furrier? "What is new? What is unusual? What is smart?" The answer is waiting . . . GENUINE BABY SEALSKIN! Sleek and brown, a soft pliant pelt . . . GENUINE BABY SEALSKIN will appeal to every woman because it is ideally suited for "sports" and general wear. Wonderfully luxurious, with the durability expected from furs, it is molded with ease into flattering supple lines. — Newspaper advertisement, mid-1920s

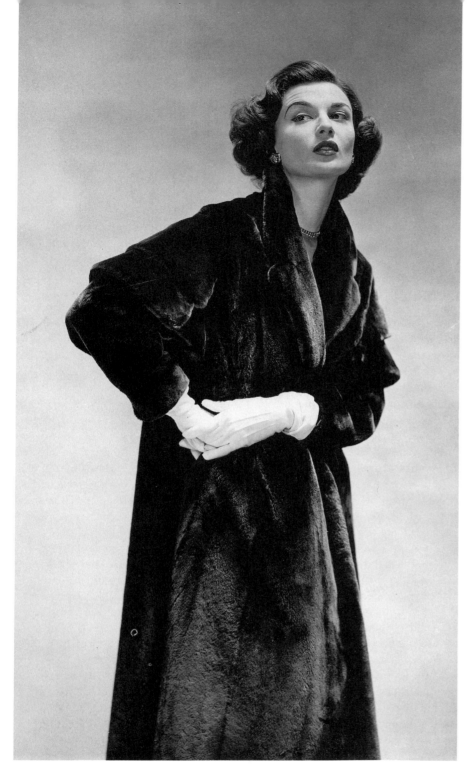

Girls may have worn rabbit, but they coveted silver fox. A fashion historian has said that for stylish women in the 1920s and 1930s, "to be bereft of fox was almost to be naked." The whole animal, complete with lifelike head and beady eyes, tail and paws, could be slung round the shoulders.

After World War II the mink coat became *the* international status symbol. Young women who couldn't afford mink started out with "fun furs"—trendier cuts in less expensive pelts. By the 1980s, working women were buying their own furs, and they wore them every day rather than only on special occasions.

Yet an increasingly vocal constituency of people opposed the very idea of fur coats. Influenced by the ecological consciousness of the 1960s, they wanted to preserve endangered fur-bearing species, especially the spotted cats, and they deplored the way all animals were trapped or killed. In 1973 Congress passed the Endangered Species Act, which banned trade in endangered wildlife. Despite mounting opposition, the industry stayed on a roll until 1987, when the combination of a recession and animal rights advocacy started it on a downward spiral which seems irreversible.

Animal rights activists stopped the bludgeoning of baby harp seals. They've set their sights on breeders who raise fur-bearing animals and then brutally kill them for their pelts. Campaigning against the steel-jaw leg-hold trap used to snare animals in the wild, a Canadian group coined the slogan, "Get the feel of fur—slam your hand in a car door." Abashed, and sometimes intimidated, many women turned to down coats or synthetic furs, which are just as warm.

In the early 1990s, the number of trappers, the number of trapped animals, the price of pelts, and the sales of fur garments in the United States all dropped off sharply. More than two hundred independent furriers went out of business. The largest fur company in America closed thirty-four department store salons. Another large chain liquidated merchandise from seven stores, at prices seventy to eighty percent off the original prices.

Fashion models refused to walk down runways in fur. Protestors disrupted a New York fur show in the spring of 1991. Dressed only in flesh-colored underwear, they carried a sign saying, "We'd rather go naked than wear fur!"

Furriers fought back, sometimes taking the high ground by defending freedom of choice. Ads for the Fur Information Council of America asked, "Aren't you tired of animal activists telling you what you can't wear and eat?" The industry, which blamed its decline on the recession and mild weather, was sure that an upturn in the economy would bring back sybaritic customers. But antifur organizations claimed credit for the effectiveness of their campaigns. "Fur is no longer fashionable to people who have any kind of a heart," said a spokesperson for the Fund for Animals. "We foresee the end of the fur industry in ten years." ☐

Gas Station Attendants

The Majerus gas station was the unofficial community center of Bellchester, Minnesota. Farmers sat on benches outside the service department, killing time while their grain was being ground at the mill. Teenagers came by after a day's work on the farm to buy fifty cents worth of gas so they could cruise around for the evening. Customers drank a soda, complained about the weather, and traded local gossip with Jim Majerus and his sons.

The Majerus family serviced tractors, pickups, and cars for Bellchester's 150 inhabitants. In the late 1950s and 1960s, the station sold Pure Oil gas. The boys wore snappy blue caps with the red company logo. Their dad made sure they greeted every customer by name, washed the windshield, checked the oil and water, measured the pressure in the tires, and inspected the fan belt for wear and tear. When business was slow, they brushed out the carpeting inside the customer's car.

Gas station attendants were the front-line salesmen for the oil companies and independent filling station owners that competed for the patronage of Americans on the road. Their ads featured cheerful professionals in crisp white uniforms, even though, in reality, the attendant was more likely to be a grease-stained kid who had to be reminded to wipe the back window.

The 1950s and 1960s were boom years for gas stations and the men who worked in them. The expanding Interstate Highway System enabled more people to take a family car trip for their summer vacation or drive longer distances to work. Detroit bragged about increased horsepower under the hood, and the bigger the cars, the more they guzzled gas.

In the late 1950s, there were about 215,000 filling stations in America. Sometimes four of them shared a busy intersection. Profit margins on gas were low, but station owners made up for that by doing auto repairs and selling tires, seat covers, batteries, and other accessories. Since gas doesn't vary much from brand to brand, oil companies and station owners tried to build customer loyalty with good service and giveaways: free maps, balloons for the kids, or, as a summer-long come-on, a set of glasses honoring the American presidents doled out six at a time over the course of the season.

A profile in the July 14, 1956, *Saturday Evening Post* spotlighted "The Men Behind the Gas Pump." The owner of an Esso station in South Carolina proudly reported that he sent new employees to classes run by the oil company where they learned how to greet customers and how to push motor oil and filters. He and his attendants were occasionally bothered by tourists who asked directions, filled their tires with air, and used the restrooms, but didn't buy gas. They called them IWWs—Information, Wind, and Water cheapskates.

In the 1960s, chains specializing in auto service or parts began to cut into gas station business. Firms that repaired mufflers, brakes, or transmissions attracted customers who used to have their cars tuned and repaired at the local filling station. During the oil crisis of the early 1970s, the Organization of Petroleum Exporting Countries and U.S. government price controls drove up the price of gasoline to nearly a dollar per gallon. Car manufacturers responded with compact cars and energy efficiency in all their models. As a result, the market for motor fuel went flat. Tires, batteries, and brake parts were built to last longer, and the recommended oil change cycle in American cars increased from every three months or five thousand miles in 1973 to every six months or seventy-five hundred miles in 1987. Finally, during the same period, station owners had to invest in expensive double-walled gasoline tanks, lead-monitoring equipment, and vapor-recovery nozzles to meet environmental protection regulations.

The rising cost of labor in the tight job market of the late 1970s and early 1980s was the final straw. It was harder to find employees willing to pump gas out-of-doors in all weather for the minimum wage. Station owners needed to cut costs or go out of business. A lot of stations took a second look at self-service.

Self-service gas stations, which had first appeared in California in the late 1940s, offered people who pumped their own gas a discount of twenty or twenty-five percent. Before long, full-service stations were forced to drop their rates in retaliation. The October 31, 1953, *Business Week* reported that customers had abandoned the do-it-yourself stations, preferring to have an attendant pump their gas if it only cost a penny or two per gallon more. "This rings down the curtain on a

Oh, we're the men of Texaco.
We work from Maine to Mexico.
There's nothing like this Texaco of ours.
Our show tonight is powerful,
We'll wow you with an hour-ful
Of howls from a showerful of stars.
We're the merry Texaco men,
Tonight we may be show men,
Tomorrow we'll be servicing your cars.

I wipe the pipe, I pump the gas,
I rub the hub, I scrub the glass.
I touch the clutch, I mop the top.
I poke the choke, I sell the pop.
I clear the gear, I block the knock.
I jack the back, I set the clock.
So join the ranks of those who know
And fill your tank with Texaco.

— From *Milton Berle's Texaco Star Theatre* theme song, 1948-55

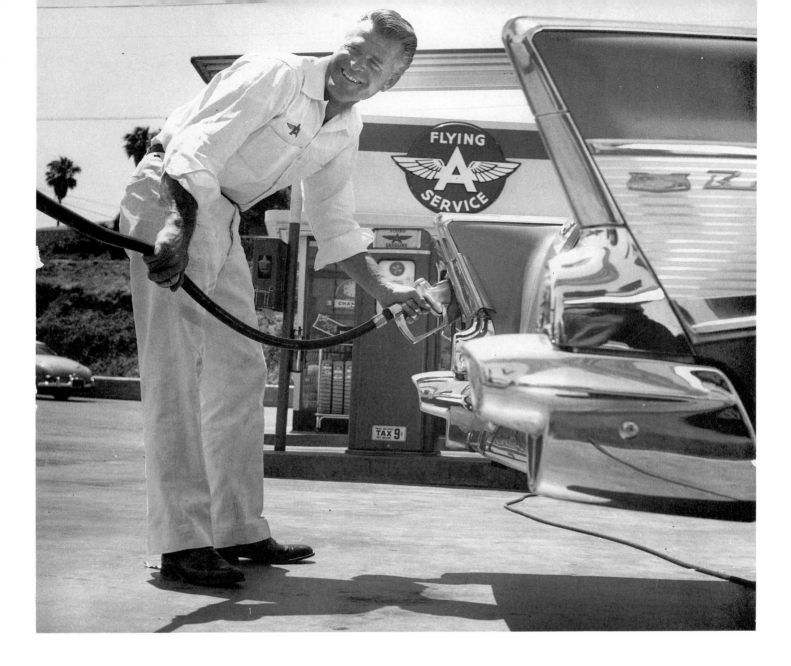

marketing venture," the magazine declared. "People will always prefer service."

To protect themselves in the future, oil companies and station operators lobbied for laws against self-service. Although they were unable to cite actual incidents, industry press releases asserted that "tragedies, especially fires and explosions, could happen when an untrained person operates a gasoline pump." One handout showed a six-year-old boy pumping gas into the family car while a passerby lit a cigarette and tossed the match. By the early 1960s, seventeen states had laws against customers pumping their own gas.

A decade or so later, the threat of bankruptcy forced the owners of surviving stations to make an about-face. They now fought to get anti-self-service laws repealed. They estimated that with their properties reconfigured for self-service, they could sell twice as much gas, while cutting labor costs. One cashier in a glass-enclosed booth was able to monitor a station of twenty pumps by remote control.

Self-service pumps sprang up everywhere. Owners of convenience stores discovered that self-service gas attracted customers who were delighted to refuel at the same place they picked up a six-pack and a loaf of bread. Car washes, multiplex movie theaters at the mall, and even parking lots installed a self-service pump or two. By 1990, filling station attendants pumped only thirty percent of all the gas sold in America.

Customers taught themselves to remember which side of their car the gas tank was on, to release the latch on the pump, and to squeeze the nozzle just enough to maintain a steady flow of fuel. Executives on their way to work topped off their tanks without spilling a drop on their power suits. Everyone learned not just how to unscrew the gas cap but, more important, how to replace it before driving away. ☐

Girdles

For centuries, women have worn undergarments that flattened or distended their bodies—pushing flesh from one spot to another according to the dictates of fashion. Until recently, corsets, girdles, and bras have so disguised the natural shape of the female body that whole generations of men were imprinted with an illusory notion of the female physique. And women bought into the illusion, tolerating cruel compression to disguise reality.

Although women wore various forms of the corset before the sixteenth century, either over or under their clothing, the concept that the human figure could be totally reshaped began in Elizabethan times. Among the most outlandish undergarments of the day was the farthingale, a contraption of whalebone and canvas that tied around the waist and supported layers of petticoats and skirts. As if the farthingale was not enough, the stylish Elizabethan lady also wore a corset-bodice, a device of stiffened canvas reinforced with whalebone that kept her trunk rigid. It was impossible to move normally in such a rig, but fortunately the sixteenth century was an age that prized artificiality.

From the seventeenth century through the early part of the nineteenth, tight-laced corsets emphasized the breasts by pushing them upward. The lacy undergarments were themselves visible under low-cut bodices. Courtesans received callers in a carefully contrived state of near undress. Titillation was the gambit and seduction the goal.

The Victorians changed all that. They retained tight lacing and tight corsetry but covered everything up. Although underwear became invisible, its mystery made it seem even more erotic. Voyeurism and fetishism were the unacknowledged dark side of prudery. Proper Victorian gentlemen in the privacy of their diaries revealed the delicious pleasure they took in watching a woman unlace her corsets, roll down her black silk stockings, and step out of her delicate underthings.

Bell-shaped skirts and a shapely bosom emphasized the mania of the time—the tiny waist. Pillars of the medical profession pronounced that tight corsets were orthopedically useful. Others said they were dangerous and injurious to the skeleton. The swoon became fashionable; "loosen her stays!" was the remedy.

Although women seemed to accept the acute discomfort of laced-up undergarments, a revolt was brewing against this British version of foot-binding. William Morris and his acolytes in the Aesthetic Movement rejected artificiality; the pre-Raphaelites popularized loose flowing gowns and natural waists, which meant liberation from women's body armor. Dress reform was part of the women's emancipation platform. In 1880 the Rational Dress Society denounced garments that cramped movement. Corsets were omitted from its list of approved underwear, which, the society specified, should not weigh more than seven pounds. Most women, however, remained strapped in.

It took French couturier Paul Poiret to loosen their stays. In the early years of the twentieth century, Poiret designed a long, slim silhouette that needed a long look underneath. Although he was unable to do away with corsets altogether, his designs did inspire the first undergarment that left the waist unconstricted, and the hips and, eventually, the bust unexaggerated. For the first time, stylish women stood upright and breathed deeply.

World War I brought abrupt changes in fashion. Women involved in war-related activities needed and demanded more freedom of movement. The corset suddenly split at the waist: its elements became the girdle and the forerunner of the bra. The girdle served primarily to constrain the abdomen and hips; it ran from waist to groin

All emphasis is on the extended waist. Girdles rise five inches above the normal waistline. Fabric boning, new-fashioned lacings, and godets of elastic hold the high waists in place. Bias and zigzag bands swathe the sides of girdles for extra control, and front panels are shaped to grasp the waistline. — *Harper's Bazaar*, January 1939

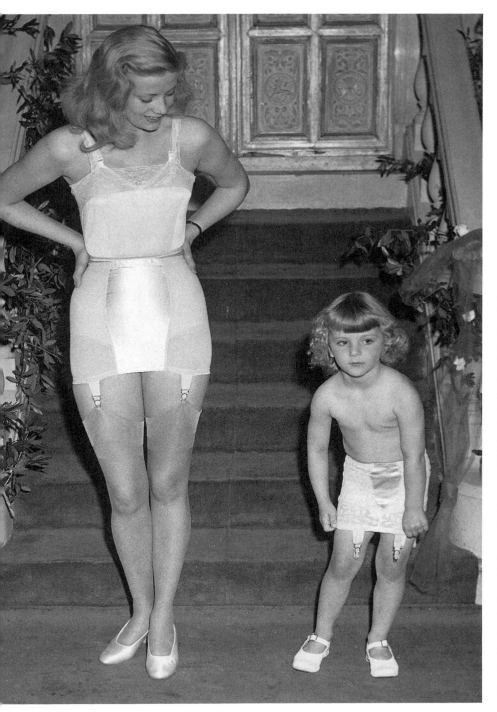

and was anchored by garters to hold up stockings. Slim young flappers who affected a boyish look dispensed with their corsets altogether.

When curves returned to the silhouette at the end of the Jazz Age, corsets made a comeback too, but this time with an emphasis on suppleness: a new version had elastic panels and was boned only at the sides, giving a smooth look to the hipline. The more natural look reflected the changing status of women, who demanded ease and comfort in their clothes. In 1935 *Vogue* touted a garment that weighed only "two and a half ounces. . . . No more, in fact, than your pearls." Girdles were now made entirely of elastic fibers for two-way stretch. The "roll-on," the most famous girdle of its time, was a seamless tube of circular-knit elastic that young women adored because of its light control. It fit the body accurately, without tight laces or hooks. After World War II, elasticized cotton and rayon were replaced by nylon—perhaps the greatest innovation in the history of underwear.

The youth revolution of the 1960s extended to underwear: women of all ages insisted on lightweight, uncluttered, comfortable undergarments. Girdles and pantie-girdles in new man-made fibers like Lycra spandex revealed and enhanced the body's natural shape. A bra-less, girdle-less, "nothing-on-underneath" look was even acceptable. Newly invented pantyhose became, with bras and briefs, the only underwear that most young women would tolerate. The girdle was left with a bad reputation that it never shed.

Between 1968 and 1975 girdle sales dropped ten percent per year. More than half the women under thirty-four spurned them altogether. Research showed that women had never liked girdles but felt forced to wear them because they had no other means to hold their stockings up and their stomachs in. They thought wearing foundations harmed their circulation or was a sign of getting old. They believed that girdles conned men into thinking you were something you weren't.

Most of all, women hated the names: foundations, corsets, girdles. So manufacturers invented new ones: intimate apparel, bodysuits, body fashions, pants smoothers. They produced seamless, one-piece garments, which were invisible under clothes but still offered support. What the industry calls "bodyshapers" come in bright colors and are even sexy. They are lightweight—"whisper-thin" in ad-speak—and move with the body. Given the vagaries of fashion and the cult of youth, bodyshapers may be here to stay, but the unlamented girdle—with stays, bones, heavy reinforced panels, and cinching devices—seems gone for good. □

In one of his verses, the Roman poet Catullus pleads with a friend to return his handkerchief. A *sudarium* (from *sudor,* "sweat"), the word

Catullus chose, was used to wipe perspiration off one's face or to cover one's mouth against infectious disease or inclement weather. Nero used a *sudarium* to mop his brow. He might have kept one handy in the folds of his toga, since pockets didn't exist. Patrician women waved *mappae* to greet each other or to signal applause at the theater or the games. These small, decorated cloths, usually white, were associated with the ruling classes. Made of linen—a very expensive fabric—they were a sign of rank and high office.

For a thousand years, handkerchiefs continued to be a showy accessory confined to the privileged classes. Finely worked handkerchiefs were a part of the marriage dowry in fourteenth century Italy. White oblongs of silk and linen were incorporated into church ritual as part of the priest's vestments. Use of a handkerchieflike cloth in England was first mentioned in the late fourteenth century during the reign of King Richard II. Referred to as "hand cloths" or "hand-coverchiefs," they allowed the king "to wipe and cleanse his nose."

The designation *handkerchief* first appeared during the sixteenth century, when Venetian lace makers exported decorative handkerchiefs all over the world. Men and women of the Renaissance perfumed their handkerchiefs (and their gloves), which they carried, waved, and demurely dropped in the intricate rituals of flirtation. Some silk- and gold-threaded handkerchiefs were so costly they were singled out in wills. In Elizabethan England, highborn men and women gave handkerchiefs as New Year's gifts to the court, and young ladies gave them to their suitors as tokens of love.

Handkerchiefs of drawn-thread work, cambric, silk, or lace were carried mainly by the upper classes. The lower classes used their fingers to blow their noses, or a

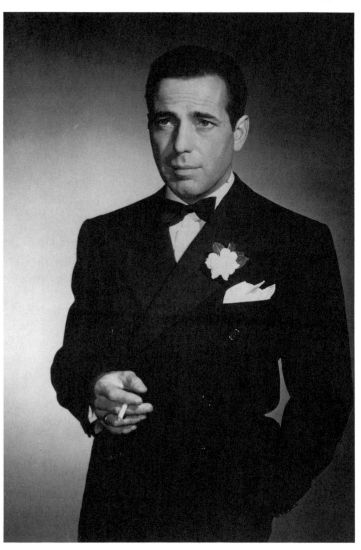

sleeve to wipe them clean. Admonitions against these practices began to appear in sixteenth century etiquette books, at the same time that handkerchiefs became more common.

By the mid-seventeenth century, handkerchiefs had become indispensable to the middle classes. They were carried conspicuously to be seen and admired, and inconspicuously to be used. Ladies and gentlemen, meanwhile, found a new task for the decorative accessory. The fad of taking snuff—the "devilish fashion disease" sweeping England and the Continent—turned everyone's nostrils a dirty brown color. Those who wanted to indulge needed to use a handkerchief, preferably a large colored square, which disguised tobacco stains.

On June 2, 1785, handkerchiefs became the subject of law. Responding to Marie Antoinette's opinion that they came in too many sizes and shapes, Louis XVI issued an edict that "the length of the handkerchief shall equal its width throughout the kingdom." The small square has since that time been the standard form of the handkerchief.

Throughout the nineteenth century, printed handkerchiefs, many of them mass-produced, were the rage. Improved printing technology enabled manufacturers to respond quickly to contemporary trends: social events, maps charting the expanse of empires, and commemorative and satirical pictures of politicians like Disraeli and popular actresses like Ellen Terry were rushed to market each season.

Gentlemen and ladies continued to use white linen handkerchiefs, often monogrammed at the corner. Middle-class women were never without them, whether cycling, motoring, or just sipping tea. Balzac, the exhaustive chronicler of nineteenth century mores, considered writing about the psychology of women based on "how they hold their handkerchiefs."

In the first half of the twentieth century, the handkerchief remained an indispensable fashion accessory, though it was not displayed as ostentatiously as before. Men's handkerchiefs settled

Handkerchiefs

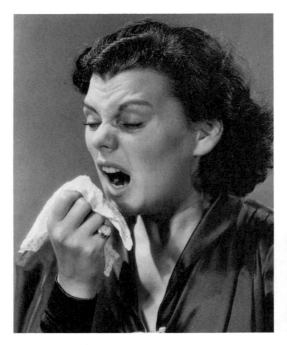

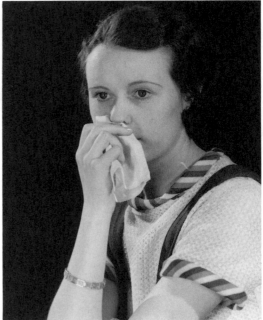

To wipe your nose on your cap or your sleeve is boorish; it may be all right for pastry-cooks to wipe their noses on their arm or their elbow; to blow your nose in your hand and then, as if by chance, wipe it on your clothes, shows not much better manners. But to receive the secretion of your nose in your handkerchief, at the same time turning slightly away from persons of rank, is a highly respectable matter.
— Erasmus, *De Civilitate Morum Puerilium*, 1530

into a standard form: approximately eighteen inches square, with a simple hemstitched edge, sometimes monogrammed. Women's were usually daintier in size and embroidered or trimmed with lace. So fundamental were handkerchiefs to one's toilet and to fashion that in 1929, 350 million were sold in the United States.

The beginning of the end came in 1924 when Kimberly-Clark introduced an innovative paper product—Kleenex Facial Tissue, a "scientific way to remove cold cream." A package of one hundred of these disposable substitutes for face towels sold for sixty-five cents. Early advertisements showing Hollywood makeup studios featured endorsements by stars like Helen Hayes, Gertrude Lawrence and Ronald Coleman. In 1929 the POP-UP box was added, as were tissues in colors.

Much to the manufacturer's amazement, a survey of consumers in 1930 showed that more than sixty percent of the people buying Kleenex tissues used them as disposable handkerchiefs. Advertising was changed to emphasize this unexpected application, and sales doubled within a year.

Today most people blow their noses into paper tissues—190 billion of them a year. As an executive of a major handkerchief company observes, "Once an artificial item is introduced, only the fashion end of the business is left." Well-dressed men still display decorative handkerchiefs in their jacket breast pocket or keep plain ones for functional use in their trousers pocket. Women have all but ceased to carry them. A paper tissue—in a choice of designer colors—takes care of hygiene, and a decorator scarf makes the fashion statement. ☐

In the 1960s, it seemed as if half of America was on the road. From coast to coast young people held up destination signs: "Berkeley," "Chicago," "San Francisco—or New York." With sleeping bags and knapsacks slung over their shoulders, they were rejecting everything that stood for the establishment: material possessions, the Vietnam War, legislated morality. They shared a sense of community—a belief in helping one's brothers and sisters—and they sometimes shared drugs. A veteran traveler remembered, "When you could walk out on the road, stick out your thumb, and immediately receive a ride, a smile, and a lit joint, there was litle reason to go any other way."

Thumbing a lift was as American as apple pie. It was a by-product of America's passion for automobiles, a national wanderlust, and the vast distances that people wanted to cover cheaply. After Henry Ford began mass-producing cars, people discovered that hailing a ride was easier than jumping on and off freight trains.

During the 1920s, hitchhikers were a familiar sight on the American road. These were years of adventure, when young people took off to find someplace new or to meet people different from the ones back home. They were just like other travelers— except they had next to no money and felt little pressure to get to their destinations.

By the end of the decade, there were twenty-six million cars on the road. Children hitched rides. So did college students. Some young men wore beanies and covered their suitcases with fraternity insignia, implying that collegiate status was a character reference, even if they weren't undergraduates at all. Girls hitched, especially during summers. In 1928 the *Saturday Evening Post* ran a series of short stories about two waitresses who thumbed rides up and down the coast between New York and Florida looking for jobs.

Hitchhiking

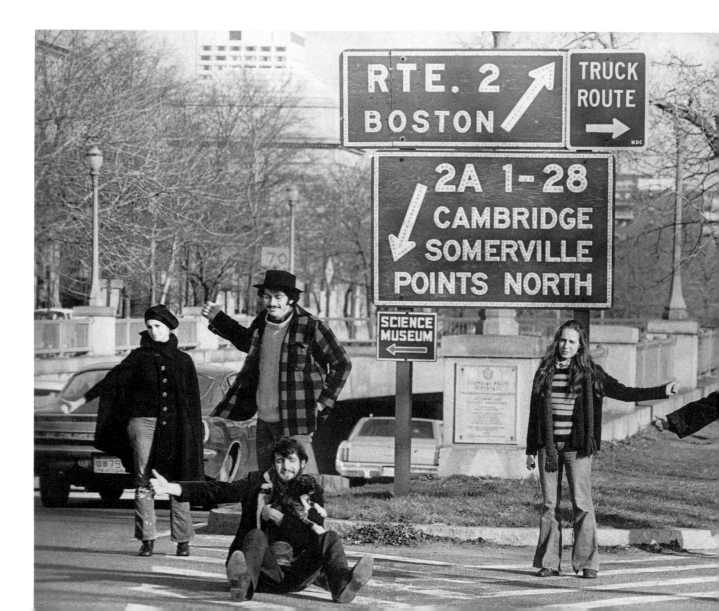

During the Depression, the nature of hitchhiking changed. People hit the roads because they had no place to stay and no money to spend. Young boys left home to seek jobs in the cities; dispossessed farmers headed west. Female hitchhikers—small girls, teens, even grandmothers—haunted the highways. One eighteen-year-old girl thumbed around the country for three years and managed to survive by staying in jails. In the movie *It Happened One Night* (1934), driver after driver passed up Clark Gable, but when Claudette Colbert bared her leg, the next car stopped on a dime.

With so many people on the move, there was an inevitable increase in highway crime. The September 14, 1932, *Nation* reported: "A lonely pedestrian on a country road is no longer a weary ploughman who on being invited to ride will pay his way in homely country epigrams. He is, instead, a gangster from Chicago, who is expert himself at taking people for a ride." Pretty Boy Floyd, who escaped from the police on the way to prison, hitchhiked by night through the back roads of Ohio, Indiana, Illinois, and Missouri while on the lam.

Because of crimes against motorists, states passed laws prohibiting hitchhiking, but they were hard to enforce. Most people saw vagabonds as victims of the Depression. Transient bureaus ran centers where people could stay the night, eat a nourishing supper, and get information about jobs.

During World War II, when gas was rationed, and the country's transportation system deteriorated, hitchhiking became almost patriotic. Although it had started because so many people owned cars, now it continued because so few drivers were on the road. Emily Post said it was acceptable for girls who had jobs in defense plants to thumb rides to work. Employees hitched to and from the office, and soldiers thumbed rides back to the base. Ralph Schimpf, a fugitive from the Ohio State Penitentury, was apprehended in Nebraska. Schimpf was allowed to hitch back to Ohio on his own because neither state could provide transportation. "We all got to do our bit at a time like this," he said.

When Jack Kerouac's *On the Road* was published in 1956, it became a bible for the beatnik generation. A decade later, the hippies heeded Kerouac's call to get out and experience America. One young nomad summed up their restlessness. "I just want to move, man. And I don't want to worry about money or wearing the right clothes or any of that trash."

By the 1970s, hitchhikers were everywhere—you could hardly drive into or out of Cambridge, Massachusetts; Austin, Texas; or Madison, Wisconsin, without a beaded, bearded stranger in your backseat. They stood at the entrance ramp to the highway with guitar cases bigger than their backpacks. They came from all classes, almost all were young, and nearly half were women. They saw America on less than five dollars a day. Tom Grimm, who wrote a hitchhikers' handbook, once traveled from Chicago to Canada to California to Texas, and than back to Chicago. He covered ten thousand miles in two and a half months and spent $120.

With the soaring popularity of hitchhiking for both males and females, what the February 19, 1973, issue of *Newsweek* labeled a "new and still unofficial category of crime" was perhaps inevitable. "The old order of highway violence has been stood on its head. Instead of the driver fearing the pickup it is now the hitchhiker herself who runs by far the greater risk of being robbed, assaulted, abducted, murdered—or, most likely of all, raped."

In one year, Boulder, Colorado, reported 120 cases of sexual assault, almost half of them against hitchhikers. In the Boston area, eight young women, most of them college students thumbing rides, were strangled. Five coeds at the University of San Francisco believed to have hitchhiked between their homes and the campus were brutally murdered, and another two were missing. *Good Housekeeping* and *Seventeen* published psychological profiles of driver-rapists, urged girls not to hitch, and, if they refused to be prudent, supplied advice on how to get out of a car unmolested.

By the 1980s, hitchhiking was on the wane. More and more kids had cars, for one thing. Yuppie values were very different from those of their idealistic predecessors: why hitch a ride if you could afford a BMW? Then, too, the romance of the open road had cooled. Voluntary vagabonds were lumped with the homeless and undesirable. Above all, hitchhiking was no longer safe, for the driver or the person thumbing a ride. □

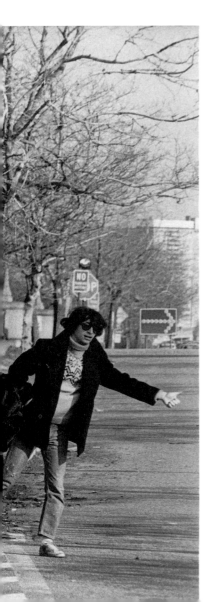

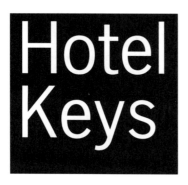

Hotel Keys

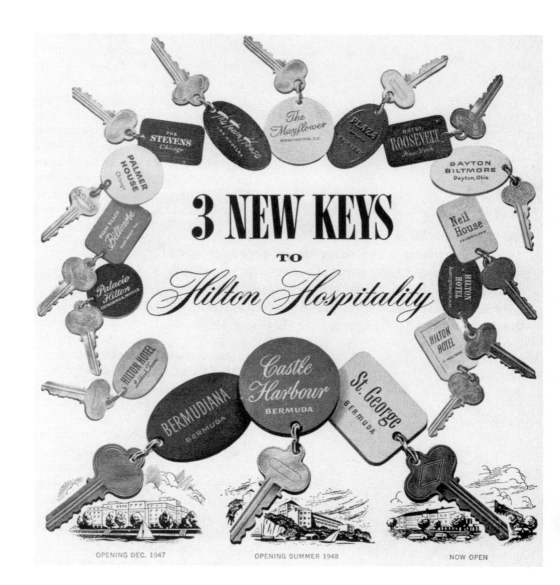

Until November 1987, Wayne Schrimp, the locksmith for the San Diego Marriott Hotel & Marina, spent most of his time replacing locks or keys for the lodging's 682 rooms. Sometimes he had to rekey forty to sixty rooms a day. If a guest lost a key or walked away with it, Schrimp had to reconfigure the room lock, make four copies of the new key, and record the number of each one. If someone made off with a master key which overrode the dead bolt in guestroom doors, Schrimp had to rekey every room. Each new key cost two dollars, but the major expense for the hotel was time. Schrimp usually spent twenty to thirty hours a week on key replacement. A total rekeying took him two weeks.

The typical brass hotel key is designed to include the name of the inn, the room number, and perhaps an address for return through the mail. It is often extremely heavy or attached to a heavy object, so the guest cannot easily carry it off by mistake. Nonetheless, three to five keys per room disappear each month in American hotels and motels. Returning a key through the mail takes time and costs money. And there is no way of knowing if the key has been copied even if it is returned.

Anybody finding a key embossed with identification has an open invitation to enter the room for which the key was made. In 1984, according to an NBC report on hotel crime, each hotel room was broken into four times a year on average. Thefts from hotel guests included $100 to $300 million worth of travelers checks and fraudulent charges on stolen credit cards.

72

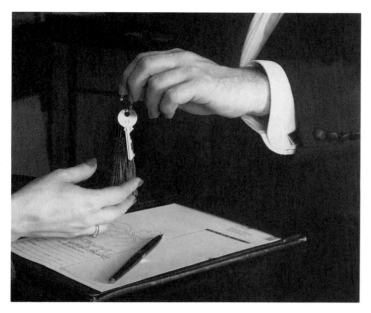

In the early 1980s several victims of hotel room crimes sued for damages, arguing that the lodgings should have provided better protection. In one case, an employee of a motor inn gave a pass key to a man claiming to be a guest who had lost his key. The employee did not ask for identification. The man used the key to enter the plaintiffs' room, where he and an accomplice mugged and robbed them.

In another case, a woman charged that she had been raped in her room at a Las Vegas hotel. There were no signs that the room had been forcibly entered. The rooms in that hotel had not been rekeyed in twenty-five years, although as many as five hundred keys were lost each week. Management could not account for the number of master keys that had been misplaced, nor could it produce records indicating which employees had access to individual rooms. In this and similar cases, the courts ruled that lodgings are liable if harm comes to a guest in a room with a traditional lock fitting because such locks did not provide "that degree of care which a hotelier would use to protect guests from intentional injury caused by a third party."

Because burglary and violent crime are on the rise, hotels have had to pay millions of dollars worth of damages in personal injury suits. Today forty percent of business travelers are unescorted females—prime targets for certain kinds of criminals. To meet the standard of protection defined by the courts, hoteliers have had to upgrade security for guests as well as for their own personnel.

To keep guests safe and costs down, many hotels and motels have installed electronic locksets, which use a keycard instead of a metal key, in guest room doors. Those at the top end are computer-based. In these systems, each lock contains a microprocessor which can read more than 2.4 million combinations. At check-in, a desk clerk gives each guest a keycard with a newly generated, unique code which is also conveyed electronically to a microprocessor in the door lock. When the keycard is inserted in the lock, its code is recognized by the microprocessor and the door opens. The keycard works until a new guest card is inserted in the lock, at which time the previous code is invalidated. Hotels no longer have to rekey, since lost or stolen keycards cannot open the door once a new card is in use.

Electronic keycard systems can build in several levels of protection. Television or telephone repair people can be given a one-time keycard to enter a room for a single service call. Bell staff, room-service waiters, and room attendants can have special cards that permit them to enter specific rooms only at certain times or on certain days. In some systems the door lock retains a memory of all the keycards used to gain entry. In more elaborate versions, a central computer keeps track of each person who enters or leaves the room, noting the time, date, and identity of the card user, thereby preserving an accurate record in the event of a break-in or robbery. An estimated seventy percent of all thefts are inside jobs, and the keycard system makes it much easier to catch the culprit. Since staff members are identified by their cards, the deterrence factor has been considerable—employee theft has been reduced by as much as seventy to eighty percent.

If carried away inadvertently, drop in any mailbox. Return postage guaranteed. — Hotel Westward Ho, Phoenix, Arizona

Several systems on the market allow guests to use a personal credit card as a key. A scanner at the front desk reads the card and sends a magnetic radio transmission to another scanner in the guest room lock. This activates the lock to open when the credit card is inserted. Such a system can also set off an audible alarm in case of fire and can adjust heating and cooling to conserve energy when the room is unoccupied.

Soon guests will be able to check in without ever seeing a desk clerk. The Hilton, Choice, Hyatt, and Marriott chains are testing a self-registration system that allows new arrivals to insert a credit card and a blank keycard into a terminal in the lobby. Within seconds the guest is registered and, encoded card in hand, is on the way to a good night's sleep.

Someday keycards may be replaced in turn by systems that recognize a person by identifying some physical characteristic. A few hotels in the United States are already experimenting with biometric systems that verify the guest by fingerprints, hand geometry, voice, or signature. Retinal eye patterns are also used, but their high reliability can be compromised if the guest has a hangover. □

House Calls

Fifties children were put to bed the minute they got a fever. They were given an extra pillow, an alcohol rub, and permission to listen to Stella Dallas on the radio. They were served milk toast and Jell-O on bed trays. Late in the afternoon the family doctor arrived. He pulled a stethoscope and a tongue depressor from his black satchel and made the patient say *aaah*. He left white pills to be taken three times a day with plenty of fluids.

The doctor made one or two house calls in the late morning before his office hours, then several more on his way home for dinner. He was available on evenings and weekends. He came if his patient had a high fever or was vomiting or to calm parents. Parents tried not to take advantage; they didn't call in the middle of the night unless they thought it was absolutely necessary. Everyone agreed it was better for the doctor, rather than the patient, to travel.

There was a ceremonial quality to the visit. Parents put out fresh soap and a clean towel for the doctor to wash his hands. They offered him coffee and cake after the examination. It was reassuring just to have him there.

Fifties children were the last generation to have the doctor come to their homes. Between the early 1930s and the end of World War II, the percentage of specialists doubled from twenty-five to fifty percent of all doctors. "As 'specialitis' spread," the July 1954 *Cosmopolitan* reported, "it got so that in the better-class suburbs any doctor who called himself a G.P. suffered the pangs of an underfed pocketbook or was reduced to applying Band-Aids and Unguentine." By midcentury, with expanded medical technology available in hospitals and offices, few doctors of any kind were willing to depend only on the resources of their black bags. By 1957 house calls had dropped to eight percent of doctors' visits.

Parents who were upset found partisans in the popular press. An article in the November 1958 *McCall's* was sympathetic. "At any gathering of women in the supermarket or in the playground watching the kids or over coffee in someone's kitchen you may hear talk that makes you wonder. 'That Dr. B. has such a big reputation, but I wouldn't call him again if my child were dying. Jeanie had a temperature of 104 and all he said was, Wrap her up and bring her down to the office. How did he know she wasn't critically ill? How did he know she wasn't contagious?'"

Doctors themselves debated the value of home visits. One pediatrician called them "as outdated as the horse and buggy," because patients often needed to be examined with equipment that was not available in the home. A colleague disagreed: "If more doctors would learn to use their five senses instead of calling for lab tests and consultation, they could do a good job even above the din of the average household. What's more, a doctor can learn a great deal about the patient by observing him in his home."

Dr. Benjamin Spock tried to reconcile both views. He knew the emotional stress a parent felt when bundling a feverish four year old off to the doctor's office, but he conceded that better medicine could be practiced there. He felt certain that within a decade or two parents would no longer expect house calls for children's ordinary infections.

By the mid-1960s the relationship between doctor and patient was so fragmented by specialization that the general practitioner was, according to the *New York Times* of October 16, 1966, "like the bison of the plains, a vanishing phenomenon." People no longer had one regular doctor—they had several, depending on the nature of their complaints. In the course of a year, a patient might see a gynecologist, an allergist, an orthopedist, and an otolaryngologist. In these encounters, the *Times* noted, "The doctor is a stranger, the patient one gall bladder among hundreds." Today, nurse-practitioners, home health attendants, and hard-pressed family members look after most of the needs of the chronically ill.

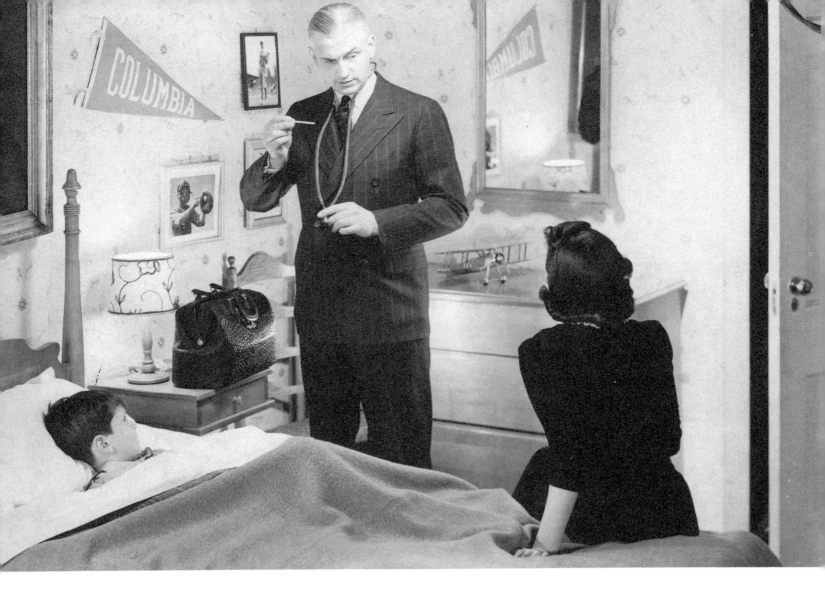

To restore the doctor-patient relationship, medical schools developed a new speciality: family practice—a modern version of the old GP. In the mid-1980s, seven thousand medical residents were training to be family practitioners. In addition, managed health-care programs assigned clients to a primary doctor who tended their routine medical needs. Except for the occasional visit to the infirm, aged, or dying, none of these doctors was expected to make house calls. □

I am a doctor. Not a pediatrician, not a gynecologist, a psychiatrist, internist, ophthalmologist, dermatologist. Just a plain, ordinary, garden variety general practitioner—a family doctor, if you will. . . . When I make a house call, I learn more than just the temperature of the bedridden one. I check up on the health of the whole family. I practice preventative medicine. I may suggest father cut down on his cigar smoking, or content himself with nine holes of golf on Sunday. I might propose we do something about little Judy's excess fat or get to work on young Billy's pimples.
— Francis Hodges, M.D., *Colliers*, August 6, 1954

Landfills

The Fresh Kills landfill in Staten Island, New York, is the largest man-made structure in the world, with a volume greater than that of the Great Wall of China. It covers three thousand acres. Sometime within the next fifteen years, when it is fully packed with New York's garbage, Fresh Kills will be 435 feet high—one of the tallest geographical features on the Atlantic coastline from Maine to Florida. The Durham Road landfill near San Francisco is twice as big as the Pyramid of the Sun in Teotihuacán, Mexico—the largest pre-Columbian structure in the western hemisphere.

Until the 1950s, garbage from American households ended up in town dumps or incinerators, which stank and fouled the air. Coastal cities dumped much of their trash into the sea. As far back as the 1930s, people along the shore began complaining about litter washed up on beaches and polluting the water.

In the decade after World War II, about fifteen hundred American cities, desperate to dispose of growing mounds of garbage, opened sanitary landfills. They picked a low-lying site into which garbage—preferably compacted—was dumped every day and covered over at night with fresh soil. Many cities planned to use the filled site for future real estate development.

When the Fresh Kills landfill was begun in 1951, Robert Moses, who built New York's parkways and created Jones Beach, promised that after the fill operations were complete, Staten Island would be enhanced. Creeks buried under the garbage would reemerge as freshwater lakes and the landfill itself would provide about seven hundred acres of parkland and two thousand acres suitable for residential communities and industrial development. As the garbage scows began dumping on the site, another city official said, "Maybe it *does* smell a little bad, but we're making a lot of nice taxable property for New York City."

By the 1980s, landfills took in two-thirds of all the household waste produced in the country and were filling up faster than anticipated. As it turned out, most were not going to be reusable as housing or recreation sites, because the ground created was too unstable and was possibly contaminated by toxic wastes. By 1990, over fourteen thousand dumps and landfills had reached capacity. Six thousand were still in operation, but their days were numbered.

Coping with mountains of trash was toughest in the Northeast. New Jersey, which had more than three hundred landfills in 1975, was down to about twelve in 1990; over half the state's municipal solid waste was trucked to other parts of the country. Long Island exported about 1,350 tractor-trailer loads of garbage every day. The crisis was dramatized in 1987 by the travails of the Mobro 4000, a barge that left Islip, New York, loaded with 3,168 tons of garbage and spent the next two months trying to find a place to dump it.

People assumed that plastic packaging contributed disproportionately to the garbage glut because they saw so many polystyrene fast-food containers littering street corners and roadsides. The antipolystyrene forces scored a major victory in 1990 when they convinced McDonald's to replace its familiar orange and yellow "clamshell" sandwich packaging with a less bulky paper-and-plastic wrapper. McDonalds' customers tossed out eleven million containers a day; the company said it was abandoning the foam because "our customers just don't feel good about it."

It was a nice gesture but irrelevant. The Garbage Project, a research group started in 1973 by archaeologists at the University of Arizona, has been sifting through landfills and measuring what really fills up the dumps. Over the years, Garbage Project studies have demonstrated, among other things, that our "waste stream" contains less plastic than it used to and that polystyrene makes up only about one percent of the nation's solid waste. The greatest bulk of refuse in landfills comes from construction debris and newspapers. One annual subscription to the *New York Times* adds up to about 520 pounds—the equivalent in weight of fifty thousand Big Mac clamshells.

Project archaeologists found out that in a modern landfill nothing disintegrates, not even food wastes. Whole hot dogs have been found that are several decades old. Newspapers strewn throughout the debris are so perfectly preserved that researchers can distinguish strata of garbage by their datelines. There is not enough oxygen inside a landfill for the bacteria that cause decay to survive. Biodegradable or

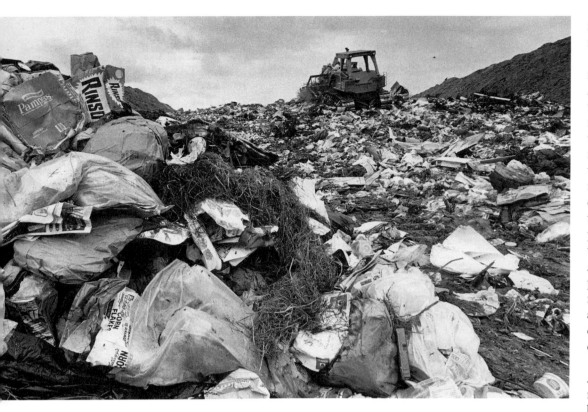

nonbiodegradable is a meaningless distinction.

The two hundred million rubber tires discarded in America every year are the torment of every landfill manager. No matter how well tires are buried, they eventually rise to the top. No one knows why—perhaps because they refill with air after being compressed or, like rocks rising to the surface of a field, they get pushed up by small particles that settle under them. Although demonstration projects suggest that discarded rubber may one day be treated and then burned to produce energy, so far old tires have no economically viable second use.

Aluminum cans recycle best. About two-thirds are currently reused; eventually nearly all will be. Big plastic soda bottles can also have a new life. Polystyrene can be transformed into construction materials, tennis balls, and video cassette cases. Glass can be recycled. So can paper, but more newsprint and phone books are thrown out than the market can absorb. It is cheaper for most paper producers to start from scratch with trees.

In a perfect world, recycling might cut the total amount of garbage by forty percent. At present it barely makes a dent in the total bulk of solid waste. Even if people set aside food scraps and yard clippings for municipal compost heaps, the effort will only help incrementally.

Incinerators, condemned in the past, are now hailed as the hope of the future. The first municipal incinerator, called a "destructor," was installed in Nottingham, England, in 1894. The first one in America, the "cremator," was built on Governors Island, New York, in 1885. Incinerators produced stench, ash, and greasy smoke. By 1970, after decades of support for sanitary landfills and clean air, only about a hundred garbage-burning incinerators were left operating in the United States.

New, squeaky-clean incinerators will cut down on pollution and run on their own fuel, but no one wants one in the neighborhood. Nonetheless, incinerators will have to handle about one-quarter of municipal waste by the year 2000. Faced with the imminent closing of Fresh Kills, New York City approved a huge new incinerator to be built in Brooklyn, scheduled to be in operation by the century's end. ☐

Volume of debris in landfills:

Disposable diapers	2%
Plastic bottles	1%
All other plastic	15%
Large appliances	2%
Newspapers	13%
All other paper	40%
Food and yard waste	7%
Construction debris	12%
Misc. sludge and sewage	8%

— **The Garbage Project, University of Arizona, Tucson**

Leisure Suits

In 1992, "The Prince of Polyester" retired. Delbert Meyer, the chemist who found a way to produce the synthetic fiber easily and cheaply, sparked the polyester revolution in America. The process he developed still supplies more than half the polyester produced in the world. Meyer is justly proud that his work made possible drip-dry underwear, no-iron sheets, inexpensive recording tapes, and soft-drink bottles. But as the New York *Daily News* pointed out in a valedictory tribute on February 14, 1992, without Meyer's work America might have been spared the "clammy shirts, snaggy blouses, shiny ties and slick trousers that took mysterious hold on the public for an embarrassing couple of decades. The disco craze would not have been possible." Above all, we might have escaped the double-knit leisure suit.

Before World War II, men's knitwear consisted mostly of union suits, argyle socks and vests, and cardigan sweaters. The only place a gentleman could wear a complete knit outfit, and not feel like a fool, was on the ski slopes. The booming postwar economy brought more leisure time and a trend toward synthetics—the notion that "wash and wear" meant "modern." As a result, men dressed more comfortably in clothing that would give them greater freedom of movement. During the Eisenhower years, striped or pastel knit sport shirts enlivened golf links and backyard barbecues, but knitwear didn't really take off until the Peacock Revolution of the 1960s.

According to one fashion magazine, the Swinging Sixties was "the age of synthetic double knits." Polyester was the fabric of choice for the unconstructed suits that were all the rage in the last years of the decade: jumpsuits, vest suits, shirt suits, tunic suits, suits with vinyl-trimmed collarless jackets and flared vinyl-trimmed pants. They came in wild colors and in jacquard and tapestry patterns that reflected the most garish pop art styles. Although polyester double knits had their drawbacks—they pulled apart at the seams, bagged out in the knees and seat, snagged easily, and gave the wearer static cling—they charged into the 1970s, reported a trade paper, "with a vigor directly proportional to America's hatred of ironing."

Polyester—a fiber spun from petrochemicals—was invented by British scientists during World War II, but was very expensive and complicated to make. As the original patents were about to expire in the early 1960s, Delbert Meyer, a young chemist at what is now the Amoco Corporation, succeeded in finding a way to process it economically. Subsequent scientific advances improved the wearability and resistance to wrinkling of the finished fabric. Whereas one hundred million pounds of polyester were manufactured in the late 1950s, seven billion pounds were on the market by the mid-1970s.

In October 1970 *Esquire* raved about improved synthetic knits: "The creativity of chemistry has wrought wonder fabrics undreamed of in all the eras of elegance that have gone before. . . . Now that knits are no longer novelties, they are accepted as an integral part of one's wardrobe. Accompanying this tribute were fashion spreads of a double-knit Dacron sports coat, a Dacron blazer suit, and one of the first offerings from the new "Johnny Carson" line—a three-button belted double-knit suit of Celanese Fortrel—"the way to dress for leisure," said Johnny.

Double-knit polyester reached its apotheosis with the invention of the leisure suit: an informal suit whose shirtlike jacket had a convertible collar, "sporty" buttons, and sleeves with no cuffs or with single cuffs. More than any other item, the leisure suit summed up the casual attitude toward dress that began as a political statement in the 1960s but reached the more mature mainstream audience a decade later.

Ads in fashion magazines urged men to lounge around the golf club or marina in a one hundred percent Dacron or Levi's Panatela leisure suit, preferably in lime green or baby blue, coordinated with a full-fashioned Ban-Lon open-collar shirt or Fortrel turtleneck. Delbert Meyer's daughter-in-law remembers being charmed by her husband-to-be in 1973. "I fell in love with him on dates when he was wearing a polyester leisure suit. It was powder blue and had a moon rising out of the sea on the jacket."

During the 1980s, a preference for all things natural, including natural fibers, routed polyester. Innovative knitwear included cotton fleece sweatshirts and pull-on pants, button-front pleated knit trousers, and polo-style Shaker-knit cotton sweaters. By 1990 synthetics had only twenty-two percent of the market, while cotton

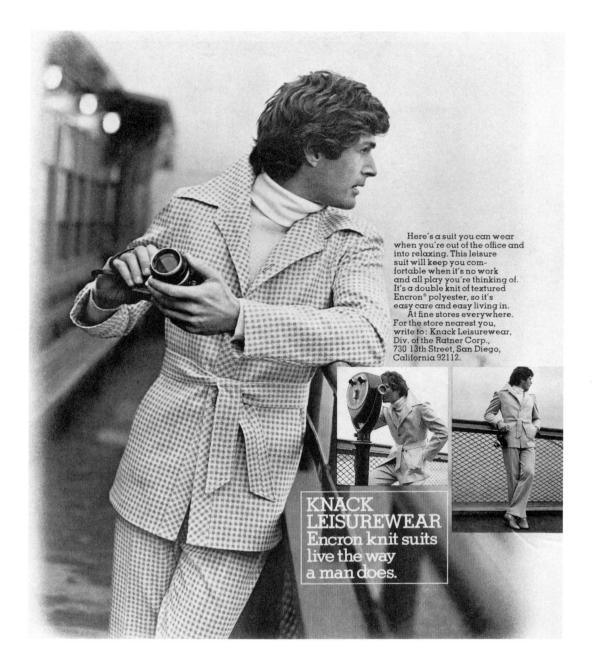

Here's a suit you can wear when you're out of the office and into relaxing. This leisure suit will keep you comfortable when it's no work and all play you're thinking of. It's a double knit of textured Encron® polyester, so it's easy care and easy living in.

At fine stores everywhere. For the store nearest you, write to: Knack Leisurewear, Div. of the Ratner Corp., 730 13th Street, San Diego, California 92112.

KNACK LEISUREWEAR
Encron knit suits live the way a man does.

had fifty-three percent. The polyester leisure suit remained synonymous with the tacky, with bad taste, with visions of overweight men in shiny avocado-colored suits and white shoes.

In the early 1990s, microfiber, a new form of polyester, came on the market. A far cry from the shiny double-knit synthetics of the past, microfiber feels softer, even silky. Manufacturers of the new fiber talk glowingly about a polyester comeback, but the marketing challenge is daunting. As a sales representative said, "There are still parts of the American garment industry where *polyester* is a dirty word."

Not among the fifteen hundred die-hard fans who gathered in Des Moines, Iowa, on March 1992 for the fourth annual International Leisure Suit Convention. The participants danced to the music of the Bee Gees in carefully preserved lemon yellow and mustard polyester outfits. The event was organized by Van Harden, a local talk show host, who said of leisure suits, "I loved them. They were functional, you didn't need a tie, and food slid right off." □

The new double-knits . . . don't pull apart at the seams, they don't bag out in the knees and seat; they stay the same size at the waist and in length as they were when you had them fitted. . . . At one time, if your neighbor's dog jumped into your lap, his claws could be fatal to your knit slacks. These newer double-knits, however, are more tightly knit to protect your clothes from snags, pulls or pills. You may now love dogs again. — GQ, September 1971

Marbles

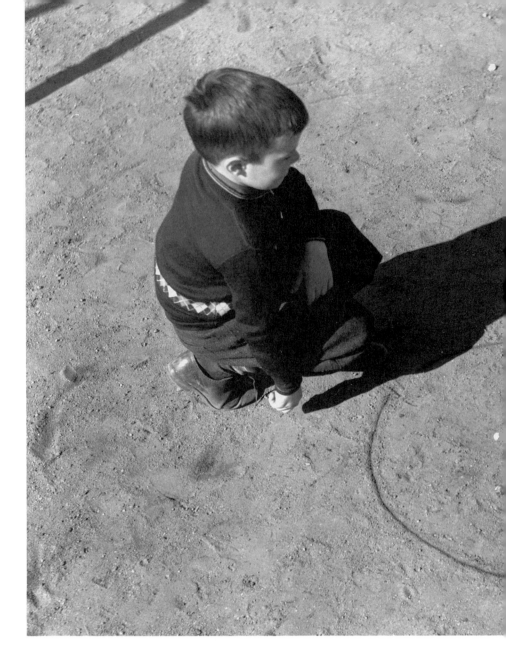

Aggies
Black Beauties
Bumboozers
Chalkies
Clearies
Commies
Glassies
Mibs
Peewees
Shooters

The 1991 National Marbles Tournament was held on the beach in Wildwood, New Jersey, during the third week in June. Seventy-seven contestants ranging in age from nine to fourteen and hailing from fifteen states knuckled down in a series of face-offs on eight concrete playing pads under the watchful eyes of judges and a few supporters. After five days, Dawn Lancaster from Cumberland, Maryland, and Brian Shellenberger from Reading, Pennsylvania, were crowned the best "Ringer" players in the land.

Ringer, one of several versions of marbles, is played in a ring ten feet in diameter, in the center of which thirteen target marbles have been arranged in the shape of a cross. The players take turns "knuckling down" outside the ring, then propelling their "shooters" with just the right amount of force and backspin to knock the target marbles out of the ring. The first player to knock seven marbles out wins the game, and the best of twenty-one games wins the match. The games are played "for fair"— the winner does not walk off with all the loser's marbles.

Once upon a time it would not have been necessary to describe the game in such detail. Marbles, a staple of American childhood, were among the few toys that were cheap and easily obtained, even on the frontier. Legend has it that as a boy in Pigeon

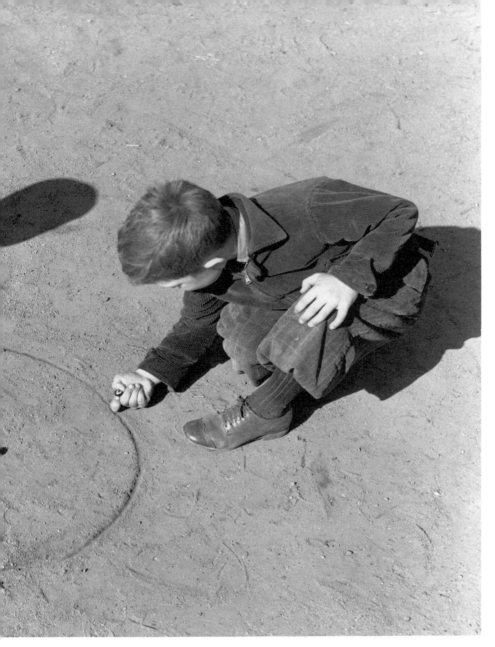

Creek, Indiana, Abe Lincoln played with marbles his father had shaped in clay and baked in a bullet mold.

Until the mid-1950s, the kids of America gathered every spring in vacant lots, backyards, and playgrounds. They scratched a circle in the dirt, spit on their favorite shooters for luck, and knelt down to knock their opponents' marbles out of the ring. In addition to Ringer, they might have played Potty, Hot Scramble, Spanish Bowl, or Old Bowler (reputedly Lincoln's favorite game), and all sorts of local variations on the basic theme of displacing marbles in a target. Within weeks, the most confident players sported blisters or calluses on the knuckles of their shooting hands and bags of captured marbles as trophies. The game rewarded skill rather than strength; a little kid could beat the biggest boy on the block, and sisters played on even terms with their brothers.

Marble playing began to decline in the late 1950s because of the popularity of organized activities like Little League baseball and after-school sports programs, summer camps, television, and video games. There are fewer vacant lots to play in, and those in cities are often filled with garbage. Many local tournaments have disappeared. Sports and hobby shops seldom stock marbles. They're easier to find in gift shops or at antique fairs, where a rare glass marble from the nineteenth century might be priced at more than $4,000.

Marbles have been made of stones, clay, steel, glass, agate, or plastic. In the United States, glass marbles are made primarily in West Virginia, where the required sand, soda ash, and natural gas are abundant. American manufacturers turn out about 350 million marbles a year. Most are for use in industry: to smooth the finish on engraving plates, as filters and condensers in the chemical industry, as agitators in aerosol cans. Because marbles are impermeable, they can be sterilized and reused without spreading disease. That's why fish hatcheries fill the bottom of spawning pools with marbles, and pet owners decorate their fish tanks with them. Paper mills use glass balls in paper-feeding devices, and some funeral homes use them to roll caskets into crypts.

In the 1980s the game of marbles made a modest comeback as an organized event. The Boy Scouts, looking for a low-cost alternative to team sports, instituted a Cub Scout belt-loop award for boys who increase their proficiency in the game. Several newspapers revived local marbles competitions, and in 1991 more entrants showed up at the National Tournament in Wildwood than had participated in any of the previous twenty years. For these serious players, however, marbles is a formal spring sport like tennis or track. They've never played a pickup game with neighborhood kids on a vacant lot. □

81

Everyone's mother had a sewing basket. It contained all conceivable colors of mercerized cotton thread, several thimbles, needles of all sizes and shapes (including the one that was black at the tip because it had been sterilized over a flame and used to dig out splinters), scraps of fabric that might come in handy for a patch, and sometimes a ball of string. It sat beside her chair in the living room, and in the evening, after supper, while the children did their homework, she did her mending.

Some mothers made clothes. Several times a year, they spread out yard goods on the dining room table, got busy with the pinking shears, and whipped up the latest fashions, according to the dictates of a McCall's or Butterick's pattern designer. That was Sewing.

But mending was something as ordinary as ironing or doing the dishes. "Mending," according to a book on needle skills, "will bring much pleasure, save many a dollar, and give a certain satisfaction that nothing else quite equals." No matter if she hated it, mending torn school clothes—to say nothing of darning socks, turning the collars on dress shirts, and letting down the hems on last year's dresses—was just part of a mother's job description.

Sewing on buttons was so easy even boys could learn to do it. But the tricks of mending were handed down from mother to daughter like recipes and how to remove raspberry stains from a white summer dress. Darning socks was a basic task. Mother stretched the torn heel of a sock across the open mouth of a glass or around the contours of a darning egg. Next, she put down a series of parallel stitches across the hole. Then, turning the garment ninety degrees, she neatly and patiently wove another series of stitches through them (over and under, and over and under, and over and under. . .) till the hole was completely covered by her stitches, and the sock was ready for further wear.

Boys' corduroy school pants were patched at the knee with squares cannibalized from a pair that had deteriorated too badly to salvage. Men's shirts got a second life when their frayed collars and cuffs were carefully detached and sewn back on with the worn part turned under and the previously protected side facing the world.

The demise of the sewing basket is undocumented. It must have happened during the early 1960s when the women of America decided it was more important to expend their time and energy on jobs and self-fulfillment than on torn socks.

Your sock has a hole? Throw it out. Buy by the dozen, and put two survivors together, but never mourn and never repair when a decent burial is indicated. The collar on your shirt is tattered? Throw it out. If you are really frugal, you can experiment with iron-on patches, but they seldom last. Some people are so unfamiliar with needle and thread they have to ask the tailor to sew on buttons.

Sometime in the mid-1980s, the tattered look became a fashion statement. Young people bought new jeans and cut holes in the knees. Secondhand shops did a brisk business in distressed denim. One mother mended a pair of badly torn jeans her son brought home from college. "Mom," he cried, "you ruined them!" □

Mending

If you are a little girl just learning to handle needle and thimble, you can be a life-saver to a busy mother by learning to mend. . . .
If you are a big girl with a new husband's shirts and socks to take care of, your alertness to his material needs is sure to make a real hit with him. . . .
If you are a man? . . . If you can become expert in button sewing, patching and darning—and you can—you will have the admiration of all your girl and women friends and be as independent as you please.
— Mary Brooks Picken, *Mending Made Easy*, 1943

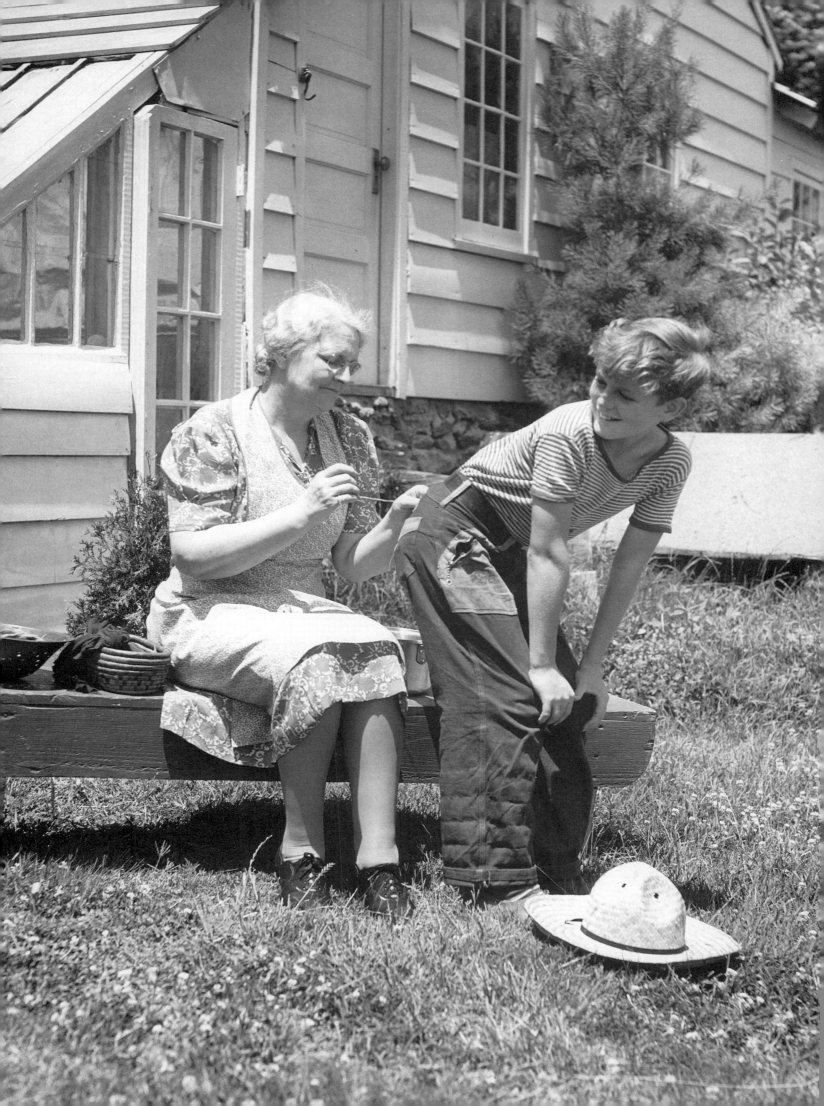

The Menopause Taboo

No one even said the word before the 1870s, when it was coined from the Greek terms for *month* and *cessation.* Until then, people spoke of "the changes" or "Indian summer." Women confided in each other about hot flashes and night sweats, and women's magazines gave tips on how to weather the "change of life," but until recently, a frank public discussion of menopause was largely taboo. Menopause has been neglected in research and theory, and even in novels, dramas, and poetry. According to one professor of English, "women of the ages from forty-five to sixty are literary missing persons."

For hundreds of years menopause has been associated with a host of negative connotations about aging and about women. The very word has evoked embarrassed laughter. Few studies have been done on middle and old age, for either men or women, in contrast to the overwhelming amount of material on infancy, childhood, and adolescence. Menopause reminds people of aging, and aging reminds people of death—subjects that our youth-oriented society would rather avoid. In popular culture, "change of life" has really meant "end of life."

It was a Victorian notion that a woman's reproductive capacity determined her value. Motherhood was revered. But as families got smaller and better health care added years to life, motherhood occupied an ever smaller portion of a woman's life span. What was she to do when faced with an empty nest? Illness was an acceptable solution; middle-class and upper-class women were excused if they took to their beds.

The Victorians perpetuated a medical explanation of menopause that was first expressed by Galen in the second century A.D. The Greek philosopher-physician described menstruation as the result of a "plethora" of blood that required periodic discharge. He believed that when a woman's aging blood vessels could no longer

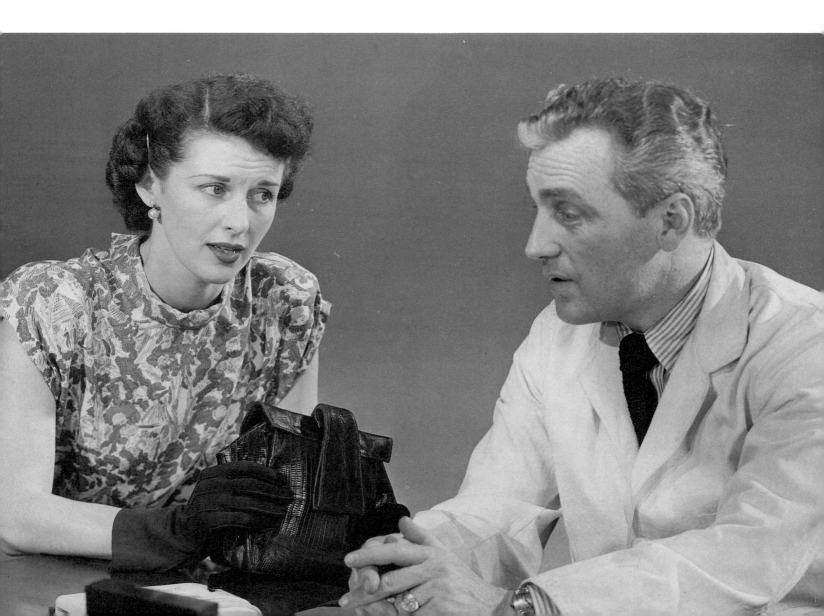

discharge the accumulated fluid, the accumulation could rise toward the brain and cause her to go mad. Galen's explanation was relied upon until the discovery of sex hormones in the 1920s.

The presumed link between menopausal women and insanity and the etiology of their strange and undiagnosable "diseases" were among the first concerns addressed by members of a new medical specialty—gynecology. In 1882 an influential GYN, Dr. Edward Tilt, wrote *The Change of Life in Health and Disease*, which lists over one hundred ailments accompanying menopause, including many kinds of insanity: delirium, melancholia, suicidal tendencies, uncontrollable peevishness, impulse to deceive, apoplexy, demonomania, and erotomania. The U.S. surgeon general's *Index Catalogue*, published in 1888, directed readers looking for information on cessation of menses to "See also: insanity in women, and uterus (cancer of)."

Popular turn-of-the-century sex and marriage manuals advised women that difficulties they experienced in menopause were caused by earlier abuses of their systems, such as immodest dress, sexual passion, lewd reading, or masturbation. Many women were afraid to mention menopause to their doctors and relied instead on patent medicines. Lydia Pinkham's Vegetable Compound, marketed in 1875, promised relief from "female complaints," such as "Leucorrhea, Painful Menstruation, Inflammation, Ulceration of the Womb, Irregularities, and Floodings." Aside from vegetable extract, the compound offered the balm of nineteen percent alcohol.

By the beginning of the twentieth century, some feminist reformers and doctors began to recognize that menopause was a normal stage of life. They said that doctors who talked of it only in terms of pathology ignored the millions of women for whom it caused little or no problem. Most radically, they argued that postmenopausal women could still lead full and satisfying lives. As one female physician wrote, "when there are no more children to be born, no more teeth to come, no more measles or whooping cough, and no more babies' deaths to break her heart. . . 'Mother' is left alone again to the renewed love of her husband."

By the 1920s researchers were developing a fuller understanding of the female reproductive system. Having established that lowered estrogen levels caused hot flashes, sweats, and crying jags, they prescribed estrogen replacement therapy to give women relief. Nonetheless, the perceived link between menopause and depression was maintained well into midcentury. Even in the 1960s and 1970s, when so many social constraints were relaxed, myths about menopause persisted. In his 1969 bestseller *Everything You Always Wanted to Know About Sex but Were Afraid to Ask*, which referred approvingly to the new sexual freedom, Dr. David Reuben had this to say: "When a woman sees her womanly attributes disappearing before her eyes, she is bound to get a little depressed and irritable. . . . Having outlived their ovaries, they may have outlived their usefulness as human beings. The remaining years may be just marking time until they follow their glands into oblivion." In an era that worshiped human potential, it was painful to think about aging and decline.

Social excesses, late hours, high living, nervous excitement, faulty dress . . . have a marked influence for evil during the menopause. —Emma F. Drake, M.D., *What a Woman of Forty-Five Ought to Know*, 1902

In the early 1990s menopause came out of the closet. Emboldened by the feminist exploration of all aspects of their lives, women began speaking out about the subject. The sheer number of aging baby boomers ensured they would be heard. During the 1990s the number of American women between forty-five and fifty-four will increase from thirteen to nineteen million. By the year 2010, over forty million will have passed through menopause. Although a fifty year old used to be considered on her last legs, today's menopausal woman can expect to live thirty more years—almost one-third of her life. In a February 5, 1991, article enticingly titled "Golden Women," the *Los Angeles Times* reported that for many women menopause was a liberation rather than a "tumultuous transition in life."

Books and surveys shattered the myth of the mature woman as over the hill physically and emotionally: Gail Sheehy's *The Silent Passage: Menopause* was on the *New York Times* best-seller list for thirty-eight weeks. Menopause was the topic of the month on talk shows, at women's forums, and in the popular press. Advertisements and television programs began to hint that aging women could have status and be glamorous. At least one woman decided that instead of referring to *hot flashes*, she was going to call them *power surges*. □

Every summer since 1878, America's power elite has gathered for a two-week outing at a remote compound in a forest sixty-five miles north of San Francisco. Campers skinny-dip in the Russian River, urinate among the redwoods, listen to lectures, and mingle at various campsites within the compound. For years, the main course at one of the parties—the Bulls' Balls Lunch—was fresh testicles supplied by a rancher-member.

These rituals have taken place at the Bohemian Grove, a retreat owned by the Bohemian Club of San Francisco. The club's motto, "Weaving spiders come not here!" (borrowed from *A Midsummer Night's Dream*), implies that no one will discuss serious matters during the encampment. But despite the motto, daily activities include informative talks and seminars led by members and guests, who happen to be the nation's leading intellectuals and political figures. Almost every American president, cabinet officer, and CEO of the country's leading industrial corporations and banks has attended.

In prestigious American clubs like the Bohemian, business and political leaders meet to discuss deals or simply to take the measure of each other, candidly and off the record. And in most, women were not admitted.

Clubs justified their exclusionary policies by claiming constitutional rights of freedom of association and privacy. The Civil Rights Act of 1964, which proscribed discrimination, specifically exempted private clubs from having to comply with its requirements. When a group of women applicants was rejected for membership in New York's Century Association, one member muttered approvingly that the club was founded "by gentlemen for gentlemen."

The ensuing Battle of the Century was covered closely by the national press. Several Centurions, among them Max Frankel, then editor of the editorial page of the *New York Times*, and Robert Bork, then a judge of the United States Court of Appeals, resigned in protest against the continued exclusion of women. On the other hand, Lewis Lapham, editor of *Harper's* magazine, characterized the advocates of female membership as the sort of people who are in favor of saving the blue whale and sympathetic to the North Vietnamese.

In 1987, responding to complaints about several men's clubs, the New York City

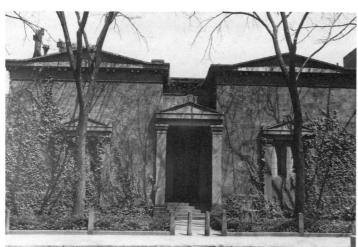

Council passed a law stipulating that an organization with more than four hundred members where meals were served and regular business was conducted could not discriminate against potential members on the basis of gender or color. In the March 16, 1987, issue of the *New Republic*, Michael Kinsley speculated that the ordinance represented a dubious victory for the female sex. "It is tempting to say that the women who engineered this legal triumph," he wrote, "should be condemned as punishment to spend every lunch hour for the rest of their natural lives eating overcooked beef in surroundings of stifling gloom while listening to some half-stewed, self-important old bore recount the exploits of the 1937 Princeton football squad."

In 1988 Justice Byron White wrote the Supreme Court's unanimous decision supporting the New York City law, although his opinion left unclear the status of golf clubs, as well as fraternal and religious organizations. The Century Association promptly accepted all twenty women whose names were recommended for membership. A male Centurion characterized the group, which included Jacqueline Kennedy Onassis, Brooke Astor, Toni Morrison, and Marietta Tree, as "superior in talent and affability to most of the members already in the club."

Other prestigious organizations like the California Club in Los Angeles, St. Botolph's in Boston, and the Cosmos Club in Washington quickly opened their doors to women. By the end of 1991, the Union League of New York had accepted all four women who applied, and forty of the fifty most prestigious golf clubs in America had female members. So did about a third of the nation's fifteen thousand chapters of the Lion's Club.

Gloria Allred, a feminist attorney who was the first woman to join the Los Angeles Friars, had trouble establishing her gym privileges at the clubhouse. The men

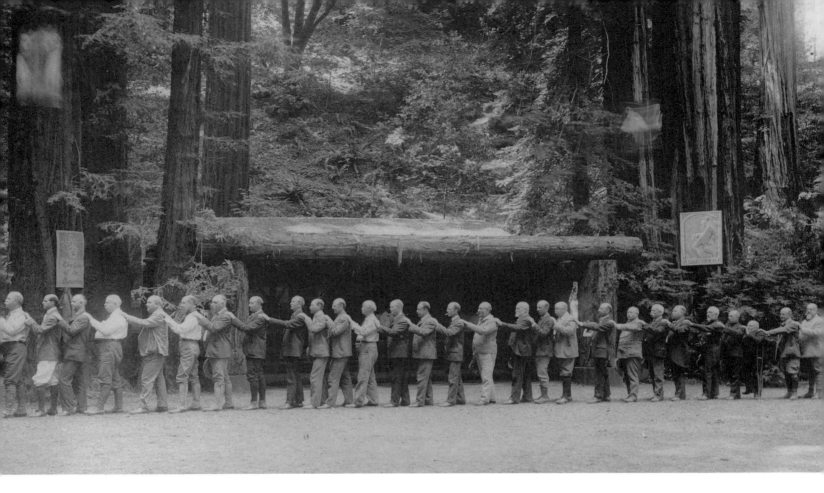

complained that because there was no separate locker room for women, she would inhibit their usual practice of walking around the locker room undressed. After Allred explained that she was interested in "naked justice, not naked men," the club set up a schedule that allowed women members some time of their own to work out.

Some male bastions tried to resist. Two eating clubs at Princeton University that were sued for alleged sexual bias in 1979 finally admitted women twelve years later. The biggest dust-up on campus came over the proposed admission of women to the Yale University senior society, Skull and Bones, which was founded in 1832 and includes ex-President George Bush, several U.S. senators, and many heads of corporate America among its famous alumni.

In 1991 the undergraduate members voted unanimously to offer membership to seven women. In recent years the organization had found itself in the unaccustomed position of being turned down by prospective members. The young men believed that the society was becoming "a source of ridicule," which was "both drastically out of step with Yale and, what's worse, flagrantly discriminatory and bigoted."

It is as if several governor's mansions, the Stock Exchange, the Supreme Court, the Pentagon, the Capitol, a flock of law offices, the boardrooms of several major corporations and of the nation's largest banks had all suddenly emptied into Fraternity Row. — Waiter at the Bohemian Grove

Irate alumni responded by changing the locks on the society's grim windowless clubhouse—called the Tomb—and suspending activities for the coming year. After several rounds of squabbling, a splinter group of alums, including William F. Buckley, Jr., sued. According to their lawyer, if Skull and Bones were to go co-ed, the club's "rituals, secrecy and confidentiality" would be lost forever, and troubling social and sexual issues between young Bonespersons might arise. "Date rape, I assure you," the lawyer said, "lies in our medium-term future."

When calmer counsel prevailed, the suit was withdrawn. The old boys voted again, and by what was reputed to be a bare majority, they agreed to accept the women.

On the whole, the transitions have been smoother than expected. A member of the California Club said some of his buddies had been afraid that "the lunch room would turn into a den of noisy cackling women, but even though there may be a dozen women at lunch that just hasn't happened." The executive director of the New York Friars Club was pleased to report that new women members "make it much prettier around here at lunch," which indicates there is some consciousness-raising still to be done. □

87

Garters were first and foremost intended to keep up socks. But they were also a sign of male vanity: for decades fashionable men would rather endure a constricting band of elastic around their calves than expose their shins.

Turn-of-the-century socks were made with ribbed tops and were held up with special elastic bands or garters of silk webbing. In the 1920s, as American men became more fashion conscious, garters in snappy striped or checked patterns were very popular. Those of the 1930s and 1940s were less jazzy. Garters were sold in haberdasheries and in department stores, where they could be found with neckwear and socks at the first counter inside the door. Like linen handkerchiefs and matching cuff links and tie tacks, they were a staple Christmas gift for father.

One-size-fits-all, ankle-length socks of crimped nylon were introduced in 1951. A sock that could stretch to fit many sizes was most appealing. For a brief time, men were even willing to wear short socks and show a bit of leg. But by the end of the decade, the garter was back. *Apparel Arts* of March 1957 noted: "the longer 'half hose' designed with elastic top or to be worn with garters are expected to stage a minor revival; we are coming to realize again that few parts of a man's anatomy are so improved by being covered as are his ankles and shins." One man remembers putting on garters with such diligence during his college years that he wore them even with his sweat socks.

In the early 1960s, men began to have a "sock wardrobe," with styles appropriate for sports, weekends, and business. They had crew, midcalf, and over-the-calf lengths to choose from. Even so, the average man wasn't paying the attention to his hosiery that the fashion industry thought he should. He tended to wear his socks until they wore out—which took longer and longer given the near indestructibility of the new synthetics from which they were made. He also regarded his socks merely as something to be worn in his shoes or under his trousers.

In 1966 Du Pont hired Dr. Ernest Dichter, president of the Institute for Motivational Research, to help position men's hosiery in the years to come. Dr. Dichter produced a seventy-three-page study titled "Soxology: a Strategy for Stimulating Sock Sales." He reported that men's feet and, by extension, their socks are charged with sexual significance that should be utilized in sensual advertising and fashion copy. He also noted that socks are an indicator of a man's status: "in successful business circles 'showing the leg' is just not done." Over-the-calf socks were associated with the executive, ankle-lengths with the "unsuccessful middle-aged man."

The hosiery industry responded by stepping up the manufacture of over-the-calf socks with elasticized tops or with stretch fibers that would stay up without garters. There was a problem, however: the synthetic fibers in a man's trousers were apt to cling to the synthetic fibers in his over-the-calf hosiery, creating what designer John Weitz called "the Du Pont stomp—that's when you see men rising from the conference table and pounding their feet on the floor." Antistatic socks soon solved that particular problem. Made of a special nylon yarn, they eliminated "trouser 'hang-ups,'" wrote a fashion commentator. "You stand up, trousers slide down."

In 1970 the *New York Times* reported on the popularity of over-the-calf hosiery: "according to the dictators of male fashion, everybody who's anybody wouldn't be seen in anything else." Argyles, Italian jacquard paisleys, beige- and black-ribbed models were available, all with what the industry called "stay-up performance."

Today dress socks are made with a new fiber called corespun Lycra, which provides even more elasticity. Men sometimes wear garters with formal clothes, and the "maturer" man might still stick with them out of habit. If he wants to buy a new set, however, he must seek out imports. Domestically, garters are a "discontinued item." □

Men's Garters

Calf gap, the patch of hairy skin between the top of the sock and the bottom of the trousers, reveals a great deal about a man's self-image. — R. Norwood Tolbert, fashion director for *Esquire*, quoted in the *New York Times*, July 4, 1970

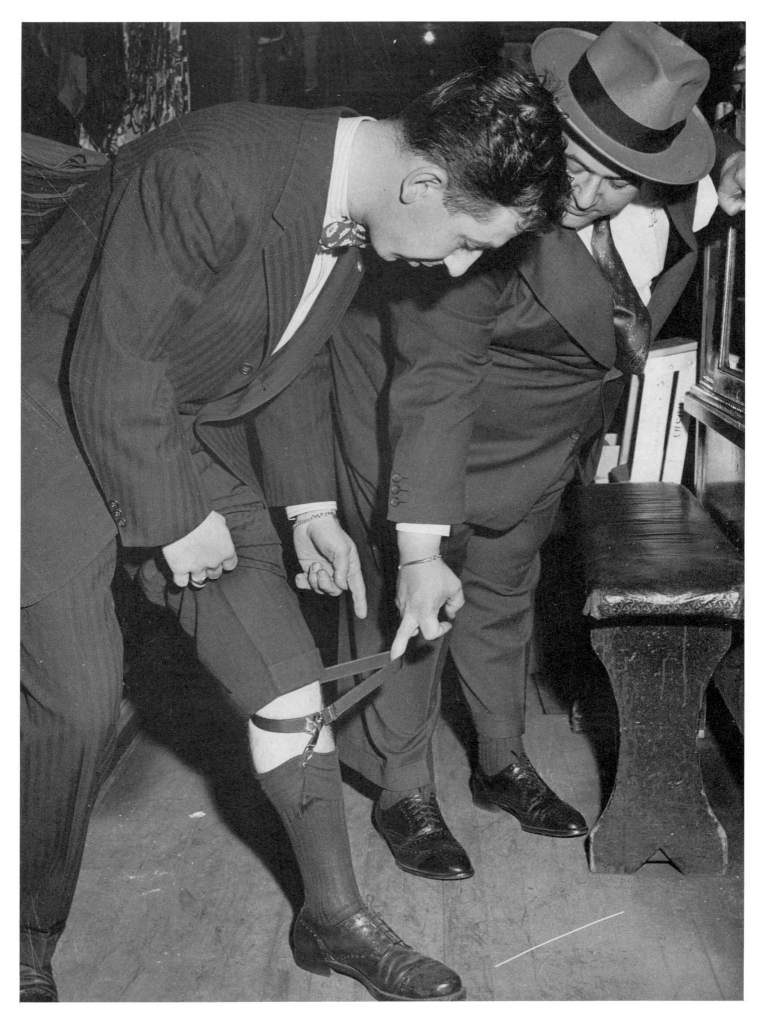

The Milkman

A milkman went to a Catholic church to make a confession. "Father," he told the priest. "I've made love to sixteen different women this past month."

The priest said, "And you consider yourself a good Catholic?" "Shucks, no," replied the milkman. "I'm a Baptist, but I had to tell someone."

The sexual prowess of the milkman, like that of the iceman and the postman, was a staple joke on the vaudeville circuit when women stayed home all day and deliverymen brought goods to their door. Every day before dawn, Sundays and holidays included, the milkman set out on his route. He filled the milk box on each doorstep with quart bottles of cold milk and pints of heavy and light cream. Then he carried the empties back to his truck. He knew each family's standing order, but sometimes he found a note inside an empty bottle asking for something special, such as buttermilk or cottage cheese. The milk he delivered had three inches of yellowish heavy cream on top. In cold weather the cream expanded and forced its way out of the bottle into little "high hats."

The milkman was a consummate salesman. He convinced the lady of the house that she really needed an extra pint of cream or should try his new roquefort cheese spread. He deciphered barely legible notes. One pro decoded the message "pliyz, milkman, Nak unoldo whyan puddy milk" as "please, milkman, knock on the door when you put [leave] milk." Sometimes a milkman performed extracurricular chores, like moving a trunk for an elderly woman or leaving a saucer of milk for the family cat. A seasoned routeman was alert: If diapers suddenly appeared on a clothesline, they indicated potential new business; if a family placed an unusually big order, they might be planning to skip town without paying.

In 1930, seventy percent of the milk sold in America was distributed door-to-door. There were twelve thousand home-delivery dairies in the United States and seventy thousand milkmen. Large companies had training programs for fledgling routemen. The trainee was taken for a day to a dairy farm where he learned about cows. He visited a processing plant where pasteurization and bottling were explained. He learned the nutritional value of each product he would sell. Company manuals instructed him in salemanship. To make sure he appeared "healthy, attractive, wide-awake, and prosperous," he was told to eat leafy vegetables, sleep with the window open, and bathe once a day. He was advised to "study the customer": was she the "Impulsive Type," the "Vacillating, Indecisive Type," or the "Suspicious Type"? Let the customers know, one manual advised, that "First in Mother Nature's Plan/Comes good Milk as food for Man."

Until the mid-1930s, milk was delivered by horse and wagon; the horse knew the route by heart and stopped automatically at each house. In the 1920s the Divco company adapted a truck specifically for milk delivery. It had a low entry step and could be driven while the operator stood and steered with a lever. The four-cylinder engine was economical for frequent stops and starts. It could run all day on a gallon of gas. The design became standard for many kinds of deliveries, though eventually a steering wheel replaced the lever and a seat was added.

During World War II, the government called on American industries to cut back on the use of gas and manpower. The dairy industry responded by trimming home delivery service. Deliveries to retailers were increased—reinforcing a trend on the part of consumers to do more of their shopping in food stores and supermarkets. Dairies stepped up their use of waxed paper containers, which weighed less than glass, took up less space, and didn't have to be recycled. Paper containers made possible big savings in gas, tires, trucks, and manpower. Dairies saved a fortune—before paper, one New York milk company had to replace ten million broken bottles a year.

Following World War II, supermarkets opened everywhere. Most families filled up their cars with supplies for the week. Milk was one of the staples they bought in bulk along with paper towels and juice. Before long, dairies couldn't afford to send a milkman out on a truck to private homes, since the dollars he brought in were well below the take from supermarkets. Individual dairies, which had advertised their brand names and fostered brand loyalty through the milkmen's routes, lost their identity. Consumers began to think of milk as a mass-produced generic product.

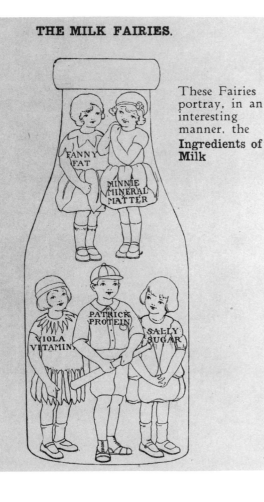

THE MILK FAIRIES.

These Fairies portray, in an interesting manner, the **Ingredients of Milk**

FANNY FAT

MINNIE MINERAL MATTER

VIOLA VITAMIN

PATRICK PROTEIN

SALLY SUGAR

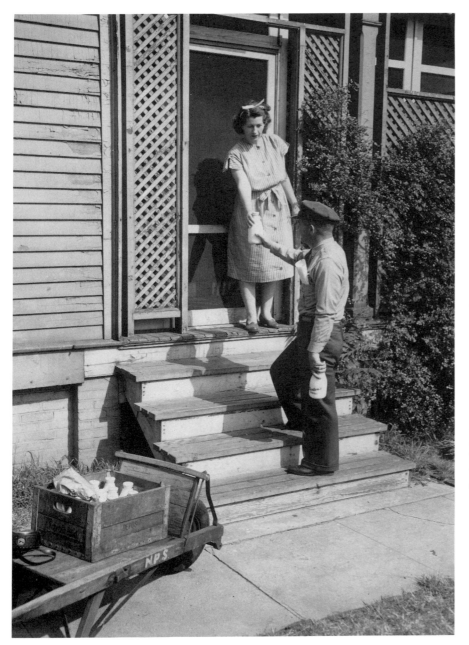

By 1990 milkmen delivered only one percent of the milk sold in America. One of the last, whose route included nearly two hundred households in suburban New York, said, "When I tell people what I do for a living, they don't believe me." His customers appreciated that his milk came straight from the dairy; milk in supermarkets may have sat around for several days. Conservation-minded clients liked his recyclable glass bottles. They also insisted that bottled milk stayed colder and retained its flavor longer.

Above all, his customers loved the *idea* of a milkman, the luxury of service in this day of voice mail, bank machines, and take-out food. One woman said, "I grew up with home deliveries in the 1950s and it's just nice having that home-on-the-farm, personalized service again." □

SELLING MILK

Things to Talk About

1. The Goodness of Milk
2. The Health Value of Milk
3. The Economy of Milk
4. Milk for Increased Efficiency
5. Milk for Beauty
6. Milk for Athletes
7. Milk for Long Life
8. Milk for Endurance

Things NOT to talk About

1. Germs
2. Your Competitor
3. Sediment Tests, slime, etc.
4. Tuberculosis, and other diseases of cattle, and such diseases as are carried in milk
5. ALL negative things, which result in the housewife questioning milk in general

— M. O. Maughan, *Milk and How to Sell It,* 1926

The Motion Picture Production Code

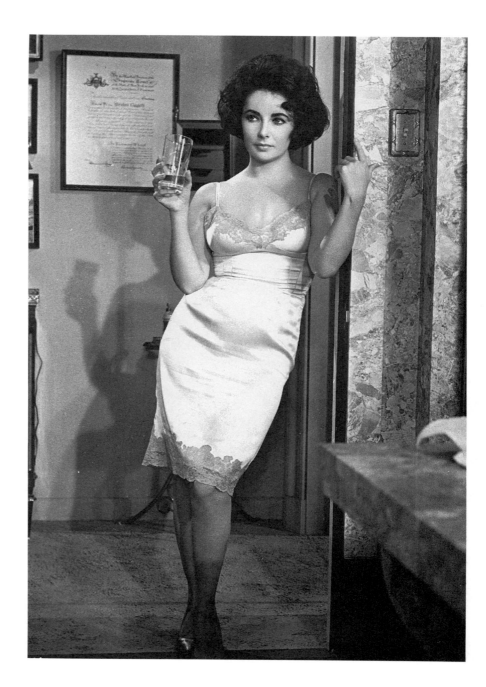

The enormous popularity of movies has always frightened people who are convinced that films encourage immorality. Hollywood and self-appointed watchdogs began tussling early. In 1907 Chicago passed an ordinance barring films that failed to meet local standards. By 1922 seven states had censors. At various times at least ninety different cities had their own boards of review.

The censors were responding not only to the content of films but also to Hollywood scandals involving drugs, murder, and—in the case of Fatty Arbuckle—an orgy involving a young girl. Movies like *A Shocking Night, Their Mutual Child, Forbidden Fruit, Two Kinds of Woman,* and *She Could Not Help It* led one United States senator to say, "Hollywood is a colony of people where debauchery, riotous living, drunkenness, ribaldry, dissipation, and free love seem to be conspicuous.... From these sources our young people gain much of their views of life, inspiration and education."

The crash of 1929 precipitated a backlash against those who typified the excesses of the jazz age that preceded it: flappers, rumrunners, gangsters, and Wall Street speculators. Reformers hurried to shore up what they saw as the collapsing moral

Take a last look at movie pretties in sweaters and shed a
gentle tear. Warning has gone out by grapevine telegraph
that the Hays Office is working up an official frown for all
pictures of actresses in these snug, curve-hugging
garments. Hand knit or machine made, fuzzy or plain, wool
or cotton, pullover or buttoned style—sweaters are out.
— Lucie Neville, *New York World-Telegram*, 1941

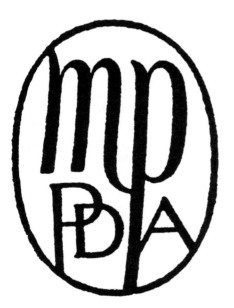

order of the nation. The Securities and Exchange Commission was created to oversee the stock market, the FBI took on organized crime, and, in a preemptive move, Hollywood promised to control itself.

In March 1930 the Motion Picture Producers and Distributors of America (MPPDA) under its president Will H. Hays announced the adoption of the Code to Govern the Making of Talking, Synchronized and Silent Motion Pictures. The Code was the direct result of Hays's effort to clean up the movie business. Hays was a puritanical Indiana Republican who had been postmaster general under President Warren G. Harding. The studios hired him to be the "Czar of Hollywood." His job was to mute criticism of the stars' private lives and the industry's product.

The Code was essentially a list of moral prohibitions, which sought to ensure that "the sympathy of the audience shall never be thrown to the side of crime, wrongdoing, evil, or sin." The problem with the Code at first was that compliance was voluntary and therefore unenforceable. In fact, as the Depression wore on, falling box office receipts intensified producers' temptation to make films with more sex and violence than ever. Mae West's popularity proved that lack of virtue had its own rewards.

In 1934, the Roman Catholic church announced the creation of a Legion of Decency to fight for better motion pictures. At Mass, millions of Catholics around the country recited an oath of obedience promising to boycott films the Legion listed as offensive. Hays and the MPPDA acted quickly. An amended code with powers of enforcement was adopted on June 13, 1934: directors of MPPDA agreed that no member company would distribute, release, or exhibit any film unless it had received a certificate of approval signed by a newly established Production Code Administration and bearing the PCA seal. Since the big studios owned most of the major movie theaters in the country and abroad, a film without the seal was doomed.

The Code affected a film long before a frame was shot. Producers and Code administrators discussed the plot in relation to the Code. They poured over drafts of the script; letters back and forth outlined cuts in language and action, suggested alternate scenes, and pointed out areas to be treated with discretion. The script, song lyrics, costumes, and sets were all subject to scrutiny. PCA personnel screened the finished picture; if they said it violated the Code, scenes or dialogue had to be cut before the seal was issued.

The Code forbade the use of terms like *damn, hell, SOB, God, Lord*, and *Jesus*, "or every other profane or vulgar expression unless used reverentially." Article IX consisted of one simple sentence: "The treatment of bedrooms must be governed by good taste and delicacy." Over time, Code censors red-penciled words like *alley cat, chippy, broad*, and *pansy*. They disapproved of *hot* when it described a woman and *tom cat* when it applied to a man. A woman had to wear a full slip—she could never appear in a half-slip and brassiere.

It's a myth that the Code forbade a married couple to be together in a double bed; a variant, equally unfounded, said it was all right if the man kept one foot on the floor. However, the PCA did advise producers that sharing a bed was anathema to English censors, who viewed any revelation of intimacies of married life as profanity. To ensure English distribution, no one was filmed in a double bed for years.

As mores changed, the censors occasionally relaxed. In 1939 they permitted the filming of naked "natives" on location if they normally went around without clothes. That same year Rhett Butler was allowed to tell Scarlett, "Frankly, my dear, I don't give a damn." In 1956 abortion could be discussed so long as the word was never mentioned.

At first, the Code represented the attitudes of the mainstream audience. During the upheavels of the 1930s, people wanted moral certainty and happy endings. Virtue was rewarded, good and evil were clear-cut, the hero got the girl, and the villain was punished. Even though the Code condemned brutality, violence was tolerated more than explicit sex. Villains got it in the end, but they had their moments of glory along the way.

Eventually, the audience became more sophisticated. They expected greater relevance and realism than the Hays office permitted. While Hollywood was still constrained by a blinkered vision, European masterpieces like *Bicycle Thief, Virgin Spring*, and *Open City* made the petty concerns of the Code seem ridiculous. finally, the studios challenged the censors head-on. In 1953 Otto Preminger made *The Moon is Blue*, which used the taboo words *virgin, seduce*, and *pregnant*, and treated "free love" with moral indifference. It became a hit even without the seal.

By the early 1960s, Hollywood producers paid lip service to the Code but did their best to get around it. The censors lost their zeal. The James Bond movies with their endless double entendres and stylized sex and violence slipped in under the Code. Billy Wilder's *Kiss Me, Stupid*, set in Climax, Nevada, dealt with the problems of a man who got headaches if he spent a night without sex. It also got a seal.

When Jack Valenti was appointed head of the Motion Picture Association of America (as the MPPDA had been renamed) in 1966, he said, "I did not take the job of President of the Motion Picture Association in order to preside over a feckless Code!" He was immediately faced with *Who's Afraid of Virginia Woolf?* The script included the expressions "screw you!" and "hump-the-hostess." After meeting with Valenti, Warner Bros. agreed to substitute "goddam you!" for "screw you." "Hump-the-hostess" was allowed to stand. Warner Bros. introduced a new descriptive rating when it advertised the film— "Suggested for Mature Audiences"—which indicated that people could presumably make up their own minds with proper guidance.

In April 1968, the U.S. Supreme Court upheld the constitutional power of states and cities to prevent children from seeing specific films. The MPAA, fearing government interference with moviemaking, was determined to allow filmmakers the artistic freedom denied them by the old Code. Valenti abolished the PCA and set up a new, voluntary Classification and Rating Association (CARA) that producers, distributors, theater owners, and film importers could all support.

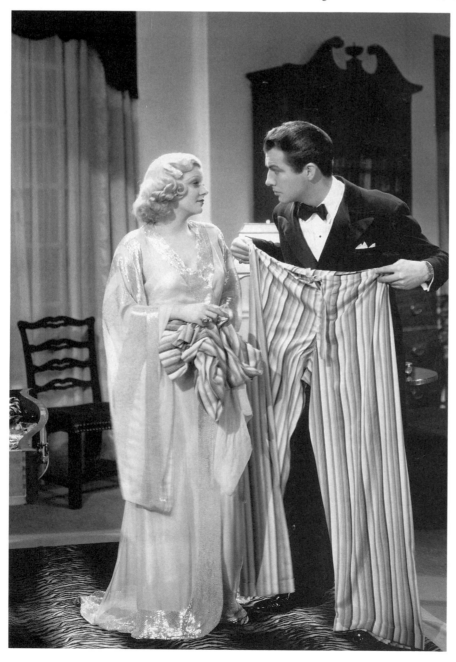

94

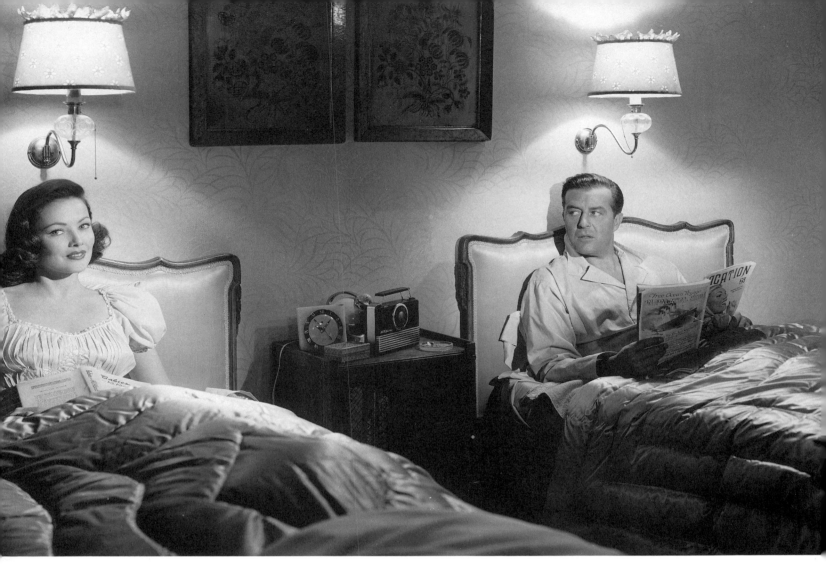

The word *code* was deliberately omitted from CARA's title. Films were to be divided into four categories: G, for General Audiences, all ages admitted; M, for Mature Audiences (later changed to PG, Parental Guidance suggested, but all ages admitted); R, for Restricted, children under sixteen (later seventeen) not admitted unless accompanied by parent or guardian; and X, for no one under seventeen admitted. In 1984 PG was split into PG and PG-13; in 1990 the X category was renamed NC-17.

The purpose of the rating system is to help parents decide what they want their children to see. Most producers and distributors submit their films to the rating board, though no one is forced to. If the producer is unhappy with the assigned rating, the decision can be appealed or the film reedited and resubmitted. Over the years the PG category has been broadened to include more nudity, violence, rough language, and controversial themes.

Some people think Hollywood should get out of the ratings business altogether because it is a form of censorship. The Motion Picture Association believes that the industry should police itself rather than give others the opportunity to decide what the public can see. Certainly, in the 1990s there is almost nothing that films do not show or say. The CARA rating board survives because it has kept up with the times; the Production Code failed because it tried to hold back the clock. □

The Navy Blue Suit

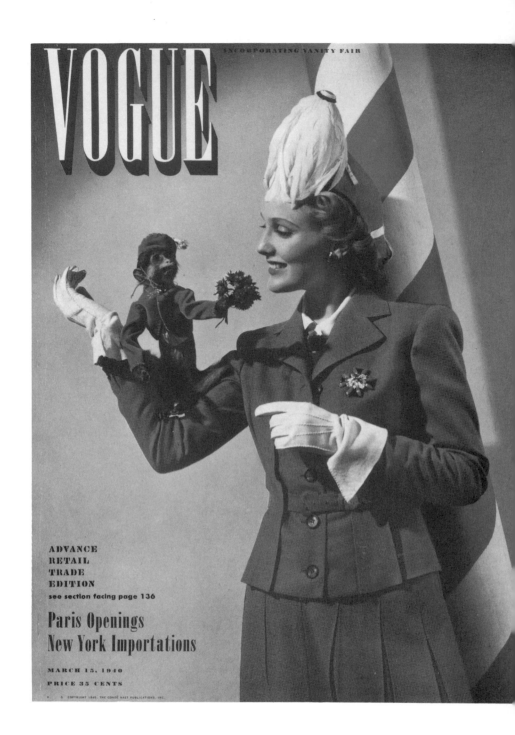

Your suit is a suit of conventional navy blue, a soft little suit and a young little suit, distinguishable from last year's because the skirt is always swirling or pleated and always very short. — *Harper's Bazaar*, April 1937

Triumphantly and happily sailing into this spring is sheer navy blue. You take it to your heart each year. For its fresh, clean look, especially with feminine white touches. For its go-everywhere quality. For its fine ability to carry on, cooly, into warm summer days and nights. — *Vogue*, April 1, 1941

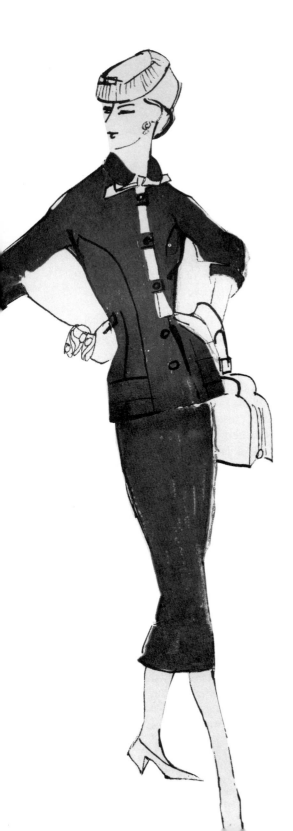

For nearly half a century, year in and year out, the spring issues of every women's fashion magazine forecast the "freshest" look of the season—the Navy Blue Suit. Not last year's suit, with its "below-the-knee heaviness" and "pointedly slim" pleats, but This Year's Suit, with the "new, more-hat silhouette" or the "frisky, almost giddy kickiness of the schoolgirl." Trimmed with a crisp white or polka-dot blouse, topped off by a straw sailor hat or a printed silk turban, it was always, always accompanied by white gloves, navy calf shoes, and navy calf bag.

Leisure clothes with military and nautical motifs were a feature of late nineteenth century resort life. At spas and the seaside, when the weather turned warm, middle-aged gents dressed up like admirals; their ladies sported middy blouses and straw boaters. Children of both sexes wore blue-and-white-striped sailor suits with blue or red knotted scarves. Even for folks who got no closer to the ocean than the shorefront promenade, the color navy became indelibly linked with spring.

Women began adapting men's clothes for themselves in the late nineteenth century. For the first time, they worked in offices, they traveled, and they wheeled across cities and countryside on the newly invented bicycle. Emancipated women needed clothes that provided freedom of movement, and they believed the new fashions reinforced their claim to be taken seriously. British tailors take credit for first applying men's fabrics and styling to women's costumes. They created *amazones*—riding habits—and daytime suits for duchesses, suffragists, and even spies. Mata Hari was executed in a suit made for her by the English House of Creed.

After World War I, couturiers like Chanel, Schiaparelli, Vionnet, and Molyneux made dogma of the notion that Madame must have a new suit to welcome spring—when, as *Harper's Bazaar* noted in 1934, "a simultaneous mutter of 'suit' occurs all over the land." Two years later, the magazine reported that whether the skirt was straight or pleated, and whether the jacket was buttoned or loose fitting, nipped at the waist or straight to the hip, "five to one the suit will be dark blue."

The reign of Fashion Correctness was overthrown by Carnaby Street and the mod movement of the l960s. Fashion developed a youth-driven, democratic spirit. It added spice to the lives of women, many of whom now worked, and all of whom were much less respectful of tradition than their mothers were. According to a trade magazine for retail merchants, the mature woman "who has bothered to keep in shape isn't ready to be returned to a plain navy suit."

Sportswear became, and remains, the style of choice. Skirts and sweaters, man-tailored jackets and slacks, and the yuppie's blue serge and floppy bow tie are perfectly acceptable versions of The Suit. Navy can be worn in winter, summer, or fall. Women no longer need a distinctive spring wardrobe, because in many parts of the country, the season itself is disappearing.

Comtemporary designers are revivifying the spirit of exuberance and appetite for change that characterized the best of the 1960s. Today's women are unwilling to submit themselves or their fashion budget to rigid formulas. The obligatory navy blue suit has passed into fashion history. □

The Nuclear Family

In the course of *Falsettos,* the 1992 hit musical about a family in transition, the father moves in with his homosexual lover. The mother remarries.

Neither parent abandons their son; in fact the lover and the new husband become caring stepparents. Two lesbian neighbors become the boy's surrogate aunts. When the boy plays Little League baseball, the extended family cheers him on. They all attend his bar mitzvah.

By the time *Falsettos* came to the stage, the traditional nuclear family with a working father, a stay-at-home mother, and two or more kids was almost a novelty. The number of households consisting of a married couple with young children had fallen from forty to twenty-six percent within two decades. Both parents often held jobs. One American child in four lived with a divorced or unwed single parent, compared with one in ten in 1960. Adults living with stepchildren, unmarried couples with children, gay and lesbian couples with and without children—all demanded to be considered families.

Despite these realities, most people's image of the ideal family is still based on a stereotype from the 1950s, when the American dream of upward mobility was represented by a three-bedroom ranch house with a two-car garage. The nuclear family took on special significance in the suburbs. Suburban life stressed togetherness—car pools, coffee klatches, Little League baseball, and the Girl Scouts. But it also separated families from their old neighborhoods and ethnic enclaves. Husbands who worked for big corporations were transfered frequently, and families lost touch with friends and relatives left behind.

The 1950s were a period of rigid sexual morality and sharply defined gender roles. Women were told that their identity came from marriage and motherhood. Coeds hoped to marry or, short of that, be pledged, pinned, or engaged by graduation. Turning their backs on the gains made by earlier generations, even serious female scholars believed that their educations were valuable primarily so they could be better wives and mothers. At least one of the Seven Sisters colleges offered workshops about grocery shopping and living on a budget to seniors who were getting married in June.

The television console was the hearth of the suburban home. The networks presented shows that young children, teens, and parents could enjoy together. "Family Time is Prime Time," one industry ad stated. *Leave It to Beaver, Father Knows Best,* and *The Adventures of Ozzie and Harriet,* the leading sitcoms of the day, portrayed cheerful, prosperous, white suburban families whose greatest dilemma was who got the car on Friday night.

Americans measured themselves against families like Ozzie and Harriet Nelson and their sons David and Ricky. Ozzie's job was never mentioned. He hung around the house a lot. In reality, though, suburban dads were frequently on the road or got home from the office too late to put the kids to bed. Ozzie's life was much more carefree. He was a pal to his kids, and a slightly foolish yet endearing husband to his wife.

The mission of *Father Knows Best* was to teach proper family conduct. Jim Anderson sold insurance. He owned the house, set the family rules, and refereed spats among the kids. His wife Margaret kept their domestic life running smoothly but left the big issues to Jim. The children, although occasionally headstrong, deferred to their parents in the end. A woman who grew up in the Midwest was given

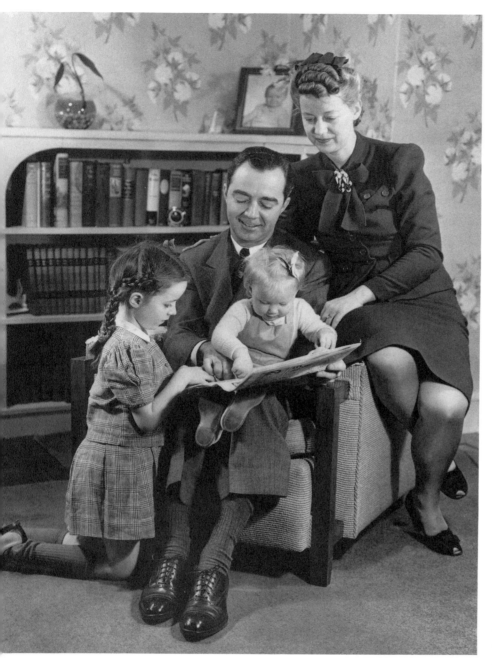

"Honey, I'm home!"

her weekly allowance only if she watched the show. At the end of the program her mother would always ask, "Susie, why can't you help make our family be more like that?"

In their long lives as afternoon reruns, sitcoms reinforced the notion that the 1950s family was a timeless institution. In fact, the decade was an anomalous interlude in the history of the American family—the last efflorescence of a Victorian ideal that had been fading for half a century. The Victorians believed that a woman's place was at home. Maintaining the household was her moral responsibility. As early as the turn of the century, however, family life was quite different: families were getting smaller, divorce was rising, sexual activity was starting at a younger age, marriages were delayed, and women were entering the professions and struggling for equality.

Families of the 1950s weren't actually all that perfect. The majority of women interviewed for a Gallup Poll in 1962 said they were "very happy," but an equally large percentage wanted their daughters' lives to be different. A woman who "had to get married" in 1957 said, "I had a shotgun wedding in order to give my child a name. I was miserable, but I stayed married for sixteen years. I didn't want to be labeled a 'divorcee.'"

In the 1960s and 1970s, the long-term trend toward looser social mores reasserted itself. Those were the days of swinging singles, open marriage, no-fault divorce, communes, alternative life-styles, and women's liberation. The birth control pill eliminated the terror of unwanted pregnancy as the price for sexual activity. Abortion was legalized; homosexuals came out of the closet; unwed mothers kept their babies. The middle class appropriated what had been considered deviant family patterns— working mothers, premarital sex, unwed couples living together, serial relationships, and divorce.

Throughout the century, the shifting role of women from passive to active partner has shaped how the family evolved. After the 1950s, the women's movement called for transformation of marriage and family life. Fewer than two percent of the women surveyed by *Redbook* in 1973 believed that "women could fulfill their potential through marriage and motherhood alone." In the mid-1970s, more than a million families broke up each year, and half of all married women worked.

By the late 1970s, a reaction set in. Many people were tired of change and frightened by the breakdown of parental authority. After Watergate, Vietnam, inflation, and economic stagnation, Americans yearned for the stability and tradition of a bygone time. Although conservatives tried to restore a social vision based on the traditional nuclear family and established moral codes, it was, however, impossible to turn back the clock. Young children of the 1990s who watch reruns of *Leave It to Beaver* or *Father Knows Best* often find the shows as fanciful as *Batman* or *The Flintstones*. The families they know have working moms, single parents, and stepbrothers who are the children of their father's second wife by her previous husband—families united by bonds of love rather than blood. ☐

Nuns

Catholics who went to parochial school have vivid memories of Sister Immaculata, who gave them a lifelong passion for social justice, and Sister Margaret, who banged their heads on the blackboard in a rage because they couldn't master long division. One former student likened parochial school to boot camp: he was being whipped into shape, and he knew it was good for him even when it hurt.

Author Mary McCarthy dreamed as a girl of becoming a "Carmelite nun, cloistered and penitential." Another woman was so awed by Sister Mary Alonzo, her second-grade teacher, that she set up an altar in her closet and prayed for the day she could join a convent. Phil Donahue and Clarence Thomas give credit to sisters for their success in life.

On the other hand, Martin Scorsese, the film director, believes that most of the nuns who taught him were hopelessly ignorant and politically conservative. One sister wouldn't permit students to use red ink because she believed it showed Communist sympathies. A number of former students say that nuns fostered a sense of "them versus us." A man who acknowledges that the sisters encouraged his ambition to be an artist nonetheless complains that he was taught to be wary of non-Catholics. "They made us believe that if we made friends with the Protestants, they would put a microscopic sliver of bacon in a cupcake and give it to us on Friday."

Nuns censored and censured even the subtlest sign of sexual interest or activity among their students. They warned young girls not to wear Mary Janes because their underwear might be reflected in the shiny patent-leather surface of their shoes. One convent-educated woman recalls being told that she should eat a banana only with a knife and fork. Although the sister couldn't bring herself to say so, she was clearly uneasy about a young girl holding the phallic-shaped fruit in her hands.

Among the first nuns in the United States were members of the Ursuline Order, who were already active in Louisiana when it was annexed in 1803. By the 1820s a few tiny communities had been established elsewhere, mostly by upper-class women who sought solitude and religious expression in cloistered communities. Mother Elizabeth Seton founded the Sisters of Charity in 1821 to serve the poor and to educate impoverished youngsters. The nuns took in some paying pupils to support their work. Catholic immigrants arriving from Germany and Ireland around midcentury wanted their children to be educated in the faith. By 1900 some forty thousand nuns taught in parochial schools. Their numbers continued to grow through the 1940s.

Novices had a "vocation." Answering a spiritual call, they committed themselves to a life of chastity and the renunciation of material comforts in order to become a bride of Christ and to serve his people. For young women whose mothers may have been worn down by the strain of bearing and raising eight or ten children, celibacy often looked attractive. For poor girls with ambition, becoming a nun was the best route to a career as a teacher or a nurse.

Taking the veil meant accepting the discipline of a highly structured community. A novice who entered an order like the Sisters of Notre Dame changed her name. Her hair was shaved, and she donned a habit that covered her whole body except her hands and face. A member of the Sisters of St. Joseph, a teaching and charitable order, rose at five, spent the next two hours at prayer and Mass, and ate a quick breakfast before going to work in a school, an orphanage, or a hospital. She returned to the convent for prayers before dinner. Her evenings were filled with several hours of devotional reading before final prayers and bed.

In 1965, parochial schools reached their highest enrollment of nearly 6 million students, and membership in American religious orders also hit a peak of 180,000 nuns. Then, almost overnight, nuns (like priests) began leaving their orders, and the number of young women who chose a vocation fell off sharply. Fewer women were attracted by religious life. A girl who wanted a career had many more opportunities, and those who wanted to remain single didn't need the protection of the veil.

Suffused with the reforming spirit of the Second Vatican Council, the religious orders tried to modernize. The Sisters of St. Joseph discarded their habit in 1967 in favor of a simple black dress. Three years later, the order let nuns wear whatever they wanted. Sisters branched out to work in many kinds of social agencies—from soup kitchens to shelters for the homeless. Some taught sociology on college campuses.

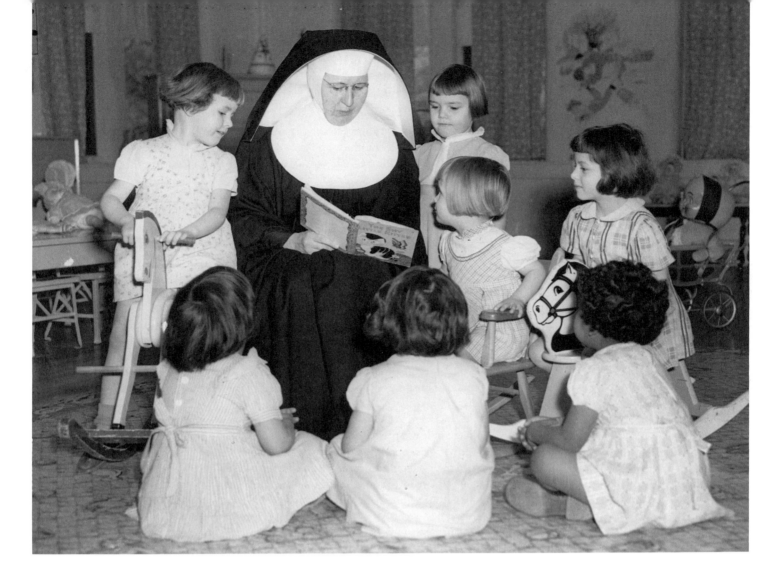

The sense of community within the convent diminished as nuns went their own way and often didn't even come home at night. Efforts to reform, rather than reinforcing a nun's vocation, often diluted her commitment to her order.

Many nuns who abandoned their vows in the 1960s and early 1970s were opposed to the Vietnam War and the hierarchy's support for it. Most felt betrayed because the promise of the Second Vatican Council was not fulfilled. The next wave of women who left were offended by the church's position on issues like birth control and abortion. They resented that nuns remained subordinate to priests in prestige and position.

Above all they were disenchanted with the ideal of celibacy. It seemed too great a sacrifice, and there were other ways to serve God. Many ex-nuns continued to be active in the church community. These "formers," as they called themselves, often taught Sunday school or took jobs as parish administrators. Some became lay teachers in parochial schools. They believed that church work was their true vocation but didn't feel compelled to be part of a religious order to do it.

By 1992, in all of America, only twenty-five hundred women were training to become nuns. The sisters of popular lore—the gentle nurse or the dedicated third-grade teacher—have virtually been replaced by lay professionals. Only ten percent of the teachers in parochial schools are nuns.

The cloistered orders, which were never large, may hold their own. They attract a few devout young women who follow a calling to serve God by withdrawing from the world and devoting themselves to prayer. But in 1992 there were fewer than one hundred thousand women in all the religious orders combined—half the number who served in 1965. There were more nuns over the age of ninety than under thirty, and their average age was sixty-five. □

No social conflict in twentieth century America has surpassed in violence or passion the decades-long struggle by working men and women to achieve job security and a living wage. The campaign to organize blue-collar employees into labor unions polarized the nation. By the 1950s, when over thirty percent of the country's industrial workforce was enrolled in unions, it seemed as if organized labor was inexorably on the rise.

It was only twenty years earlier that the federal government had first guaranteed the right of workers to organize. The Wagner Act of 1935, passed by Congress in response to armed struggles in the coalfields of Appalachia and the auto plants of the Midwest, required companies to negotiate in good faith with any union the workers chose to represent them.

In the next decade and a half, the number of unionized workers increased fivefold. Nearly fifteen million industrial workers signed up with unions that promised them protection against bosses who had previously downplayed their safety or economic needs. Unions like the International Ladies Garment Workers and the United Auto Workers (UAW) fought for a social agenda that would transform the incomes and aspirations of the American working class. Under the leadership of John L. Lewis, the United Mine Workers (UMW) spent nearly $30 million of union funds to set up a chain of hospitals that brought high-quality medical care for the first time to Appalachia.

Lewis and Walter Reuther, his counterpart at the UAW, were among the most hated or loved men in the country. When they called their members out on strike, the nation's economy came to a halt. Organized labor became a key factor in local and national politics; it forged an alliance with the Democrats that helped define the party for years to come. In the booming postwar economy, the unions delivered higher wages and better benefits that gave workers economic security, two cars, recreation vehicles, and other symbols of the American dream. Unions fought for and protected workers' safety on the job and their right not to be fired without cause. In some cases, the unions got companies to agree to underwrite the costs of higher education for members and their families. The UAW pioneered the concept of health benefits tied to employment. Individual labor leaders were among the earliest supporters of the civil rights movement.

Sometime during the late 1970s, the marketplace changed. American steel and car manufacturers made a series of bad management decisions. The rising value of the dollar froze American products out of foreign markets and made imports cheap in the States. Arrogant union leaders were slow to acknowledge new conditions. They seemed interested only in protecting their own power. They demanded that wages and benefits continue to rise while productivity remained the same or even fell.

People felt that union members did shoddy work, were lazy, and made too much money. A nation that still revered Horatio Alger heroes and the individual entrepreneur was ambivalent about work rules that interfered with the right of the boss to run his own business.

Many labor leaders were perceived as corrupt, and often the accusation was apt. The United Brotherhood of Teamsters was so crooked it was kicked out of the AFL-CIO as early as 1957 and not reinstated until 1988, when it promised extensive reforms at the national and local level. Four out of five recent teamster presidents were indicted for racketeering and related crimes; three were convicted and the fourth died before he came to trial. Jimmy Hoffa, the most notorious, was probably murdered in 1975 by associates who feared he might give evidence on labor racketeering to federal prosecutors.

During the 1980s, jobs in America's basic industries were reduced by one-third. As industry collapsed, so did union membership. Fewer people belonged to blue-collar labor unions than at any time since the 1920s. Since health insurance was tied to employment, workers who lost their jobs stood to lose their insurance. If the company went out of business, they could lose their pensions as well.

In 1988, Chrysler shut its Kenosha, Wisconsin, assembly plant, throwing five thousand members of the UAW out of work. The United Steelworkers, which had 1.6 million members in the mid-1970s, was reduced to about half a million by 1990.

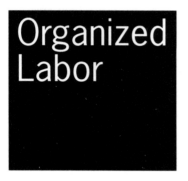

Organized Labor

The mission of trade unionism is to protect the weak against the strong. Trade unionism has fought the battle of the workman. And in fighting for the wage-earner it has fought for great liberty to man. — Clarence Darrow, *The Open Shop*, 1907

Labor union organizers are the worst thing that ever struck the earth. — Henry Ford

Seventy thousand steelworkers in Chicago alone lost their jobs. At its peak, the U.S. Steel plant in Homestead, Pennsylvania, employed thirty thousand men, but the mill was shut down in stages during the mid-1980s. In its place is a water-slide park whose few employees are mostly unskilled, low-wage part-timers. None belongs to a union.

Starting in the early 1980s, it became increasingly common for management to play hardball and win. Most industrial contracts included wage and benefits concessions by the unions. Though union members still earned more than nonunion workers in comparable jobs, their protections were precarious. Most no longer had the right to strike. A series of court decisions during the 1960s had established the rule that workers who walked off the job to highlight a grievance, even over a serious safety issue, could be forced to return to work by a court injunction.

Strikes were only legal when a contract negotiation had broken down, and they were a dubious weapon. Two widely publicized strikes were the 1985 walkout by Local P-9 of the United Food and Commercial Workers against the Geo. A. Hormel Company meat-packing plant in Austin, Minnesota, and the 1991-92 dispute between the UAW and Caterpillar Inc. in East Peoria, Illinois. In each instance, management threatened to replace strikers if they wouldn't come back to work. The prospect of permanent unemployment broke the strikes.

Given increased automation and the breakup of giant industries like steel and auto making, it's improbable that organized labor will ever regain the political and economic clout it once had. Most workers are pessimistic. One striker at the Caterpillar plant in Peoria told reporters, "If they can break the UAW, they'll have broken the back of American labor. We might as well give up everything the unions have won for workers in the last century, because bit by bit the companies will squeeze it out of us anyhow." □

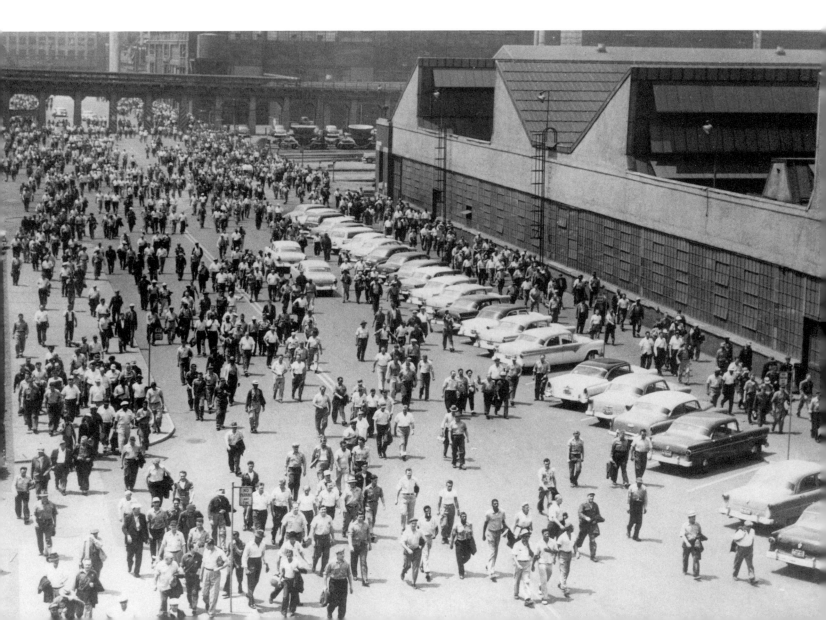

Paperboys

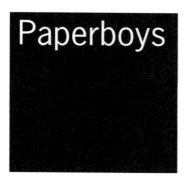

Some members of the
International Newspaper Carrier
Hall of Fame:

Isaac Asimov
Warren Buffett
Eddie Cantor
Bing Crosby
Richard Cardinal Cushing
Walt Disney
William O. Douglas
Jimmy Durante
Dwight D. Eisenhower
Julius Erving
John Glenn
Wayne Gretzky
Arthur Godfrey
Herbert Hoover
J. Edgar Hoover
Bob Hope
Rafer Johnson
Fred MacMurray
Willie Mays
Norman Vincent Peale
H. Ross Perot
Jackie Robinson
Red Skelton
Ed Sullivan
Danny Thomas
Earl Warren
John Wayne

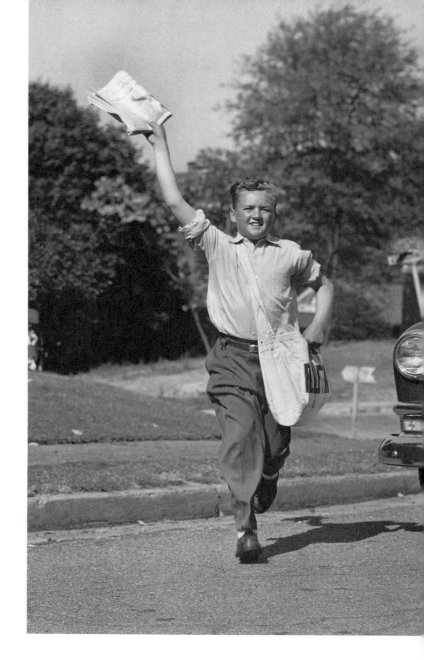

Russell Baker, writer and public television host, started delivering papers in 1937 when he was twelve. The district circulation manager came to his family's apartment in Baltimore and gave him an account book for keeping track of customers' bills, and a long brown web belt. Slung around one shoulder and across the chest, the belt enabled him to carry fifteen or twenty pounds of papers on his hip. Baker kept his paper route for almost four years. By the end of his career he had doubled the number of his customers and was earning four dollars a week. The job had drawbacks: his boss always gave him more papers than he had clients, and he had to pay for them out of his own pocket if he couldn't find new customers. The manager kept upping the ante, so that as soon as Baker signed up five new subscribers, five more papers were added to his burden.

Delivering papers gave generations of American youngsters their first taste of capitalism. When a prospective paperboy applied for a job, a circulation manager explained to him and his parents the duties of a "carrier salesman." If his parents agreed, the boy might be invited to visit the newspaper plant. He would be shown everything from the reporters' bull-pen to the mailing rooms where the papers were dispatched to pickup points across the city. He'd attend a class given by a veteran newspaperman, who would stress "courtesy, honesty, cleanliness and dependability."

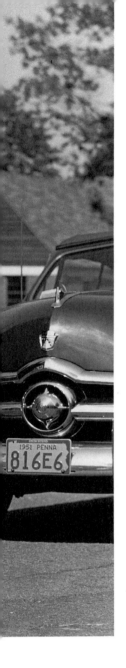

Unfortunately, paperboys were prey to unscrupulous publishers, who often took advantage of them. In 1935, the government issued a report on the employment of forty-two hundred paperboys in seventeen cities. Some started work before 4 a.m., most before 5. They worked at least fifteen hours a week. Delivery took about an hour. But under the "little merchant system" devised by the publishers, the boys were responsible for soliciting new subscribers, making collections, and keeping accounts. The boys bought their papers at wholesale rates. They had to pay their bills every week, but they collected from their customers weekly, biweekly, or monthly. Bad debt was *their* problem. Circulation managers fined them if they missed district meetings, picked up the papers late, or didn't deliver them at all. The report concluded it was "a task out of all proportions to the pay and to the maturity of a grade-school boy."

After a struggle between publishers and reformers, paperboys were exempted from the Fair Labor Standards Act of 1938 that otherwise prohibited children under the age of fourteen from working. The publishers argued successfully that the boys were not exploited like children on assembly lines and that the little merchant system taught valuable lessons about enterprise. During the Depression, in fact, some boys had been responsible for ensuring that their families had food on the table. Many states set a minimum age for newspaper work, generally ten or twelve.

Well into the early 1970s, most American papers depended on youth carriers. More than one million boys and girls delivered the daily papers before or after school. Phil Simms, the quarterback for the New York Giants, helped his three older brothers deliver the *Louisville Courier-Journal* and the *Times* until he was old enough for a route of his own. Simms got up before 5 a.m. to make his morning rounds and delivered the afternoon paper between the end of school and football practice.

As the 1970s wore on, "little merchants" were confronted with some harsh lessons in capitalism. Faced with competition from television, afternoon papers lost readers and ads. Many of them disappeared, throwing paperboys out of work. Youngsters with morning routes found their jobs threatened by retirees, homemakers, and people with full-time jobs who needed supplementary income. Adults in cars could cover more ground more quickly than teenagers on bicycles.

Many adolescents decided they didn't want to compete for the remaining delivery jobs. Teens felt they could make more money and have better hours at fast-food restaurants. Fewer young people were willing to get up before dawn to deliver the morning papers, and fears about crime make parents reluctant to send their children out. One single mother took up a paper route after her son quit his because he hated the early hours. By 6:30 a.m., she had already delivered the *Hartford Courant* and was on her way to work.

Youngsters still outnumber adult carriers, but between 1980 and 1990 the number of paperboys dropped sixty percent, while the number of adults more than doubled. When the *Asbury Park Press*, the third largest paper in New Jersey, switched from afternoon to morning publication, it replaced all its paperboys and papergirls with adult carriers. The circulation director admitted, "We had preached for years that this was the first business experience that a twelve year old or thirteen year old would get in life. We sold newspaper routes to parents and to young people that way for years, and all of a sudden we're saying that doesn't hold water anymore."

In 1992 the *Pittsburgh Press* and the *Pittsburgh Post-Gazette*, like most big-city dailies, were faced with declining readership and dwindling advertising revenues. The papers tried to cut costs by organizing a more efficient home delivery service. This included cutting the jobs of many teamsters who dropped the papers at carrier pickup sites. They also planned to replace forty-three hundred paperboys and papergirls with a much smaller number of adults who could cover longer routes in cars. The Teamsters Union went out on strike.

When the eight-month-long strike ended in January 1993, the *Press* had folded. The surviving *Post-Gazette* settled with the teamsters and rehired some three thousand carriers, of whom only fifteen hundred were paperboys and papergirls. A newspaper official said, "We can't stay in business trying to stick with a tradition that has outlived its usefulness." □

Paper Dolls

Paper dolls—the very words summon up preadolescent girlhood. They evoke long Saturday afternoons sitting on the floor, cutting carefully around the tabs with blunt-tipped scissors, and arguing with your best friend over who got the bridal gown and who was stuck with the pedal-pusher outfit. Once your doll was dressed, you could spin your own fantasy—you could take her to Hollywood, make her fall in love, pretend she was the most popular girl in school.

Paper dolls date from the mid-eighteenth century—the first era when Western societies acknowledged that childhood was a distinct stage and that children needed to play. Because printing was inexpensive and good-quality paper was available, paper dolls, which had been a whimsical item for adults, were among the early playthings adapted for children. By 1760, they were sold at the new toy shops that were beginning to appear in London.

By the mid-nineteenth century, the format and conventions of paper dolls were fixed. The most popular figures were babies or celebrities of the day, like Victorian royalty or Mr. and Mrs. Tom Thumb. Entire families of parents and children often came in a set. Dolls and their clothing were printed on flat sheets and boxed or bound into books; less expensive versions were folded loose in envelopes. The dolls, which were sometimes printed on heavier paper, came dressed in undergarments. Little girls cut out the doll's attire—a fashionable swimsuit, an opera cloak, or a wedding gown—placed it on the figure, and let their imaginations fly. Other dolls came with a stand. Often their garments had a front and a back attached at the shoulders, leaving an opening at the neck. A child cut out the costume and slipped it over the doll's head like a poncho. Tabs that hooked the costume to the doll at the shoulders and legs appeared around 1850. They were the definitive solution to the problem of transforming a doll from bride to ballerina in the shortest amount of time.

Newspapers and women's magazines printed pages of paper dolls from midcentury on. A kind of ad hoc baby-sitter, they kept the children occupied while mother caught up on her reading. Little girls, who spent hours at embroidery and darning, were very adept with scissors. In an era when most clothes were made at home, girls were familiar with pattern making and were eager to try their hands at

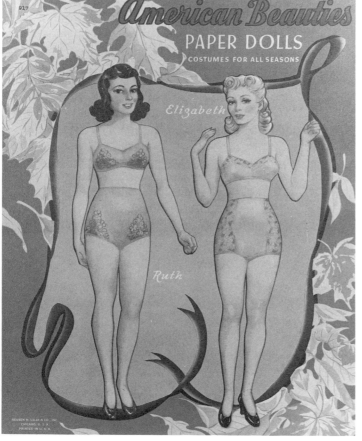

creating additional designs. Their brothers played with paper dolls of military heroes or lads who went to sea, and no one called them sissies.

By the early years of the twentieth century, five-and-dime stores attracted young buyers with books of dolls published by firms like Merrill, Saalfield, or Whitman. At first the books sold for five cents; by the late 1920s the price had doubled. So-called Dolls from Many Lands were popular, with their exotic costumes and vaguely educational value. History, literature, and Hollywood movies supplied an endless variety of characters: George Washington, Pocahontas, Robinson Crusoe, Little Women, the Five Little Peppers, Tillie the Toiler, Fatty Arbuckle, Jackie Coogan, Sonia Henie, and Princess Margaret Rose. Shirley Temple's maturation from tap-dancing toddler to wholesome teenager was chronicled in nearly twenty "authorized editions" of paper dolls issued in the late 1930s and early 1940s. *Gone with the Wind* paper dolls copied authentic costumes from the movie, such as Scarlett's famous dress made from green velvet curtains. GWTW dolls, manufactured by several publishers, were among the most popular sets of all time.

Paper dolls went to war. A large set in 1943 was titled "Ten Beautiful Girls in Uniform." Other books featured "WACS and WAVES" and "Girl Pilots of the Ferry Command." After the war, Rosie the Riveter retired. Books called "Paper Doll Wedding" and "Bride and Groom" featured starry-eyed all-American girls standing at the altar with their beribboned war heroes.

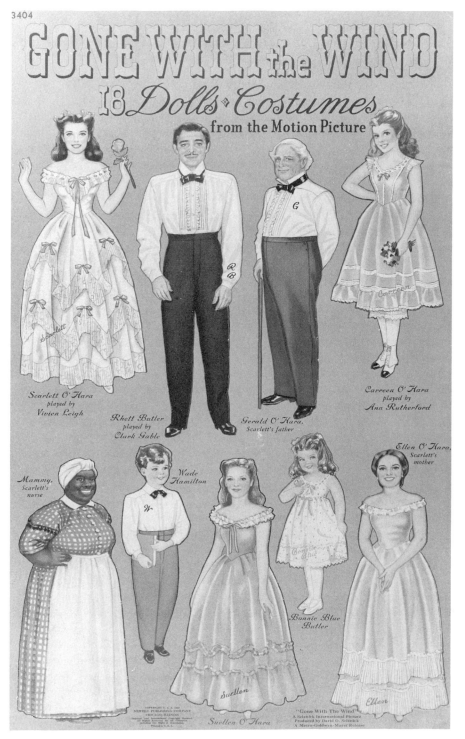

Gone With the Wind. 18 Dolls · Costumes from the Motion Picture.

Scarlett O'Hara played by Vivien Leigh

Rhett Butler played by Clark Gable

Gerald O'Hara, Scarlett's father

Carreen O'Hara played by Ann Rutherford

Mammy, Scarlett's nurse

Wade Hamilton

Bonnie Blue Butler

Ellen O'Hara, Scarlett's mother

Suellen O'Hara

The 1950s was the last great age of the paper doll. The dolls were made of heavier cardboard and often had little platforms so they could be freestanding. Movie stars like June Allyson, Natalie Wood, Diana Lynn, Grace Kelly, and Rock Hudson were equaled in popularity by TV personalities Ozzie and Harriet, Lucille Ball and Desi Arnaz, Faye Emerson, and the Mouseketeers. Strapless evening dresses and revealing swimsuits were popular. Female dolls were more curvaceous, more "sexy" than in the past.

When Barbie—three-dimensional, plastic, cheap—appeared in 1959, paper doll manufacturers tried to fight back. Reasoning that little girls no longer liked to do all the work of cutting out, they furnished perforated punch-out dolls. They experimented with plasticized paper dolls with plasticized clothes. They even marketed a Barbie paper doll.

Paper dolls limped on into the 1960s. Jackie and Caroline Kennedy were dolls—as was Tricia Nixon. Betsy McCall, launched by *McCall's* magazine in 1951 as a cute little girl of about eight, was the only paper-doll character in a major magazine who out-lasted the 1960s, and she disappeared for good in 1974.

The convention of character dolls with changeable apparel lives on in so-called adult paper dolls. There are books of Carmen Miranda and Marilyn Monroe, Pope John Paul II and Santa Claus, "Great Black Entertainers" and the "Families of American Presidents." Grown-ups collect adult paper dolls for their humor, history, and kitsch. Although the dolls come with stands and the clothing with tabs, the books are usually kept intact. Adults may be sentimental, but they rarely play with scissors. ☐

Parietal Rules

Men's colleges in America traditionally tolerated bad conduct. A real man was expected to drink till he dropped. Flirting with barmaids or having a fling with a townie was part of the education of a postadolescent privileged male. But in 1865, when the founders of Vassar College established America's first women's college, they instituted the office of lady principal to control the students' social life.

A report issued by Vassar on its fiftieth anniversary said that the principals instilled "regard for law, religious interest, hatred of the coarse, ungentle and bizarre, and respect for the characteristics in speech and acts of the true, refined lady." The first incumbent also decided that the young ladies should take at least two baths per week.

Vassar set the tone for the other women's colleges founded in the late nineteenth century. And as the big state universities across the country went coed, they too wrote parietal rules—policies that governed behavior between the sexes. The underlying goal was to keep women chaste and above reproach.

In practice this meant that, well into the twentieth century, if female students went to the movies or motoring with men, they had to go during the day. At most schools, women had to sign out when they left the campus, indicating where they were going, with whom, and at what time they would return. Usually they had to have their parents' permission in writing in order to visit a men's college or a neighboring city for a weekend.

In 1913, a restaurant owner in Berea, Kentucky, challenged the right of college administrators to declare his establishment off-limits to its students. The state Court of Appeals rejected his claim, ruling that "college administrators stand in loco parentis concerning the physical and moral welfare and mental training of the pupils."

Because colleges interpreted this guardianship very broadly, parietal rules defined a wide range of acceptable behavior. Until the 1940s, Wellesley women were not allowed to wear slacks. Sweet Briar women who went to dances at the University of Virginia had to be accompanied by college chaperones. At many universities, coeds who married had to leave school.

After World War II, campus life was transformed by older students back from the war and by large numbers of married undergraduates, but vigilance wasn't altogether relaxed. College housing continued to be single-sex. No man except a father was permitted upstairs in the women's dorms, and no woman except a mother in the men's.

In the 1950s, at the Seven Sisters colleges, men were allowed in the women's rooms on Sunday afternoon from two to five as long as the door was open. At Swarthmore, students caught breaking a similar rule could be expelled. A young man got in trouble for falling asleep in a female friend's room, during the proper hours, but with his shirt off.

One Swarthmore coed spent the night on the couch in her boyfriend's off-campus apartment because she was afraid to walk back to her dorm during a thunderstorm. Caught, and facing expulsion, she challenged the system. She denied that she had had sex with the man and demanded a gynecological exam to prove her virginity. The deans were so abashed by her audacity that they let her stay in school—without the examination.

In 1962, responding to student requests for an explicit code of behavior, Vassar president Sarah Gibbons Blanding said that a Vassar girl should not get drunk or have premarital sexual relations. Any student who was unable to live up to this expectation, said Miss Blanding, should resign from the college or be asked to leave. Fifty-two percent of the students polled agreed with her, but one cynic said that if the practice were enforced, two-thirds of Vassar's students would be gone.

In the late 1960s, the old order collapsed. The impact of the civil rights movement and protests against the Vietnam War led to student rights demonstrations. Undergraduates demanded the autonomy to run their own lives. Claiming rights of due process and freedom of speech, they challenged college rules or penalties in the courts. Most colleges gave in completely.

Single-sex schools went coed. Dorms—sometimes individual floors—were integrated. People came and went at will. "The dorms turned into Ramada Inns," said one Wellesley student. "Boyfriends, girlfriends, old friends from high school, some people no one had ever seen before used the room down the hall as a crash pad for several weeks." By the early 1970s, the only rules still in force at most colleges were

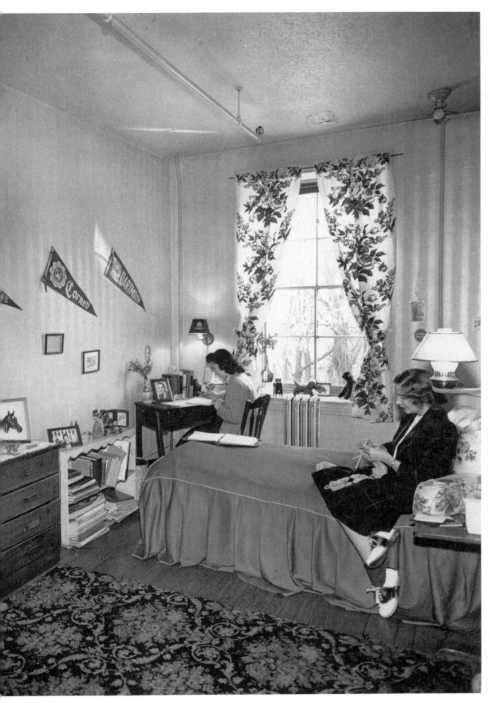

local laws governing alcohol use, and drinking was essentially a nonissue in the face of the widespread use of drugs.

Laissez-faire created problems: Where could a student go when her roommate's boyfriend slept over? What if he stayed for a semester? What would you do if your roommate were gay and her lover moved in? What if raucous parties across the hall interfered with your ability to study? Or your roommate's best friend threw up all over your bed? What ever happened to privacy?

In 1988, responding to what he called "roommate abuse," John Silber, the president of Boston University, announced that his institution would reintroduce some rules limiting guest privileges and alcohol use in the dorms. Students reacted calmly to the new strictures about alcohol but hit the roof about the guest rules. After a task force looked into the matter, new rules were adopted in 1989: No overnight visitors of the opposite sex would be tolerated at BU dorms unless they were members of a student's immediate family, and roommates would have the right to object to any overnight or late-evening guests.

Many other universities now ban opposite-sex guests from sleeping in the dorms. Many have reinstated single-sex dorms or floors justified not by in loco parentis but because many students prefer them. In addition, schools need to protect themselves against lawsuits. Crimes of violence are on the rise. Urban campuses—even rural ones—cannot protect everybody, yet students who have been raped or assaulted on campus have sued their colleges. The potential liabilities from unsupervised parties and unrestricted access to campus facilities are worse than the occasional pregnancy that used to haunt college administrators' dreams. ☐

*Permissions for absence from dormitory after 10:00 PM
—Freshmen*

A total of fifteen 1:00's and overnights used interchangeably may be taken in the first semester and a total of eighteen in the second semester.

During the first six weeks of the academic year only one 1:00 a week may be taken and only two a week thereafter.

One 11:30 may be taken each week throughout the year.

Free permissions may be granted for off-campus Placement Office work, which should be indicated by a notation such as "baby-sitting" in the Permission Remarks Column.

— Wellesley College Government Handbook, 1958–59

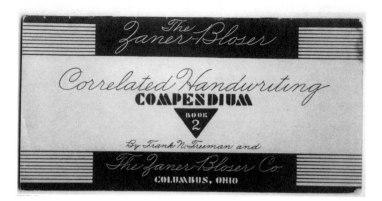

Penmanship

Elementary education used to be dominated by the Three Rs—Reading, 'Riting, and 'Rithmatic. Even today, adults of a certain age remember their grade school teacher's daily announcement of "Round, round, ready, write!" and other slogans designed to encourage the proper formation of cursive letters. The teacher encouraged her charges to believe that ornate yet precise penmanship indicated not just literacy, but refinement and social grace. First graders started with fat pencils and progressed to pen and ink, always working on fresh sheets of preruled paper. They spent hours smoothing out circles and loops, slanting the letters just so, and always Keeping Between the Lines. Capital F and G were very hard. After years of indoctrination in the methods of Palmer, Peterson, Stillman, or any of several other formal systems—each of which had its share of idiosyncratic flourishes and odd capital letters—graduates could produce "a lovely hand." Girls were better at this sort of thing than boys.

Since midcentury, however, the business world has been dominated by first by typewriters and then computers, diminishing the need for clerks and other office personnel to write neatly. Executives dictate. Society women, who formerly carried on a copious correspondence of invitations and thank-you notes, use the phone. Friends correspond via E-mail. Students and teachers alike write longhand poorly. The mark of good handwriting is no longer beauty but simple legibility. Sometimes people can't read their own writing: shoppers in a supermarket puzzle over their lists, and callers from an airport telephone wonder if that hastily scrawled digit is a 4 or a 9.

The whole world suffers from what a German scholar calls "analphabetism," the inability to write legibly. Handwriting drill is no longer stressed in most American schools. Young children are still taught to make joined letters in the second, third, and fourth grades, but the prevailing theory of learning called "whole language" preaches that what they write is more important than how they do it. For the teacher to interrupt the flow of a child's ideas with technical advice is considered a mistake.

Some children never master script, or cursive writing. Many fourth through eighth graders hand in their work in what used to be called printing and is now called manuscript handwriting—that is, single detached letters. Some schools are satisfied if students can produce legible printing; after all, most forms you have to fill out in life say "type or print clearly." By the time students reach junior high, they are expected to type term papers rather than submit them in labored and incomprehensible longhand.

Nonetheless there are times when people have to take pen in hand to sign bank checks, fill out health insurance claims, and address invitations. Even if the handwriting measures up to the best of bygone standards, organizations that sift through reams of handwritten forms spend too much time processing them.

The United States Postal Service, which must cope with over one hundred million pieces of hand-addressed mail each day, longs for electronic help in speeding them on their way. The postal service, which already sorts typed or printed envelopes automatically, wants computers to read the address and zip codes on handwritten

Handwriting can provide an outlet for skill and aesthetic feeling, particularly when the ability to draw is lacking. How worthwhile when handwriting interests the writer and pleases the reader. How satisfying when something ordinary and commonplace is raised towards the beautiful. Just as speech can be a delightful vehicle of words and thoughts, so too can handwriting; and language is served.
— Alfred Fairbank, *A Handwriting Manual*, 1975

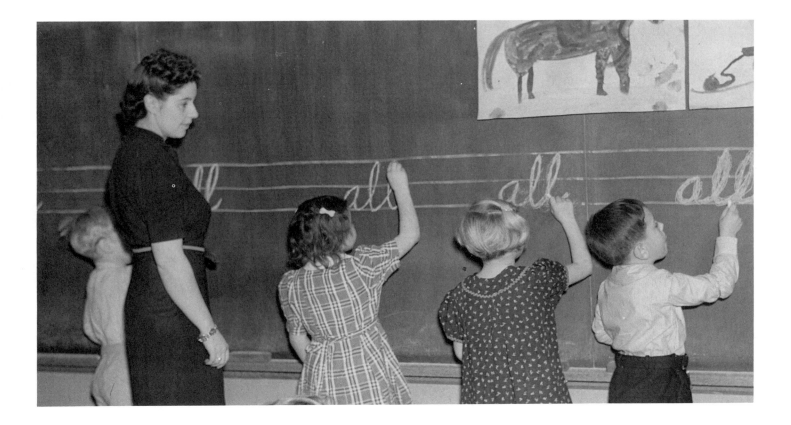

envelopes as well. Banks and credit card companies want computers to verify signatures in order to cut down on fraud and forgeries. All kinds of businesses expect white-collar productivity to increase when sales personnel can write up sales directly into a laptop computer, rather than fill out a paper form for someone back at the office to transcribe into the system at a later time.

Software designers trying to develop programs that will decipher any scrawl have been frustrated by the fact that handwriting styles are as unique as fingerprints, and most of them are terrible. They've come up with various systems that permit the user to print individual letters by hand on a specially prepared surface that looks something like ordinary notepaper. The software program instantaneously reproduces on the screen what it thinks has been written. The user proofreads the information, makes corrections if necessary, then saves the data as if it had been typed in a conventional system. Most programs can interpret upper- and lowercase detached letters that are hastily, even sloppily, inscribed.

Programs to read cursive writing are just beginning to deal with the problem of wretched penmanship. One prototypical version has seven hundred thousand samples of handwriting stored in its memory so it can recognize almost anybody's style. In extreme cases, a user can teach the machine to remember personal tics—if someone shapes the letter a in a way that the computer interprets as an *r*, the program can be customized to recognize the variant form. With the day dawning when machines will easily read a doctor's prescription and print out a legible version for the pharmacist, there's little incentive to practice good penmanship again. ☐

Polio Scares

Anyone who grew up in America before the late 1950s recalls the fear that struck as summer approached. Movie houses and swimming pools were closed all over town. Children were taken home from camp in the middle of the night. A school chum who had played softball on Friday died over the weekend.

The annual summer polio epidemic was always accompanied by panic. At the first sign of a sore throat and a stiff neck, people envisioned spending a lifetime flat on their backs encased in an iron lung—as very large respirators were called—or paralyzed from the waist down. Or ending up dead from an appalling disease for which there was no cure.

Poliomyelitis—also known as infantile paralysis—is a combination of two Greek words: *polios*, meaning "gray," for the gray matter of the nervous system, and *myelos*, "marrow," for the myelin sheath that surrounds certain nerve fibers. The potentially fatal viral infection attacks those nerve cells in the spinal cord that control muscle movement. Children were the primary victims.

Polio invades the body through the mouth and passes from the gastrointestinal tract into the blood stream, causing a fever and aching muscles for several days. If the virus then reaches the central nervous system, it attacks the nerves that send messages to the limbs and other muscles. A victim may become partly or completely paralyzed. If the virus enters the brain, it paralyzes the muscles needed for breathing and swallowing, and the patient can die.

Actually, paralytic polio is a fairly infrequent complication. Even during the worst epidemics, most infected children suffered nothing more serious than a fever. When they recovered, most were immunized for life.

Major epidemics ravaged the United States in the first decades of the twentieth century. When the future president, Franklin Delano Roosevelt, was stricken in the summer of 1921, the history of polio was changed forever. Roosevelt was thirty-nine years old, tall, and athletic. One of the nation's most promising young politicians, he had been the candidate for vice president on the losing Democratic ticket in the 1920 election.

The 1921 epidemic was one of the worst outbreaks in history. In New York City alone, nearly ten thousand people were infected; two thousand of them died. Hysterical families trying to flee the city were turned back on roads or at train stations by the state police. Many hospitals refused to admit polio cases. Policemen had to break into apartments to take dead children from their mothers.

Roosevelt got sick at his summer home on Campobello Island just off Maine. He later recalled what happened to him on the morning of Thursday, August 11: "When I swung out of bed my left leg lagged, but I managed to move about to shave. I tried to persuade myself that the trouble with my leg was muscular. . . . But presently it refused to work, and then the other."

Roosevelt went back to bed with a fever of 102. The next day he could not move his legs, his whole body ached, and his hand was too weak to direct a pen to paper. Finally a specialist confirmed what the family had begun to fear: Roosevelt was suffering from an attack of infantile paralysis.

He was hospitalized for six weeks in New York City. His legs were completely paralyzed, his arms were weak, and his back muscles so debilitated that doctors feared he might never be able to sit up. But by sheer willpower, he learned to stand

112

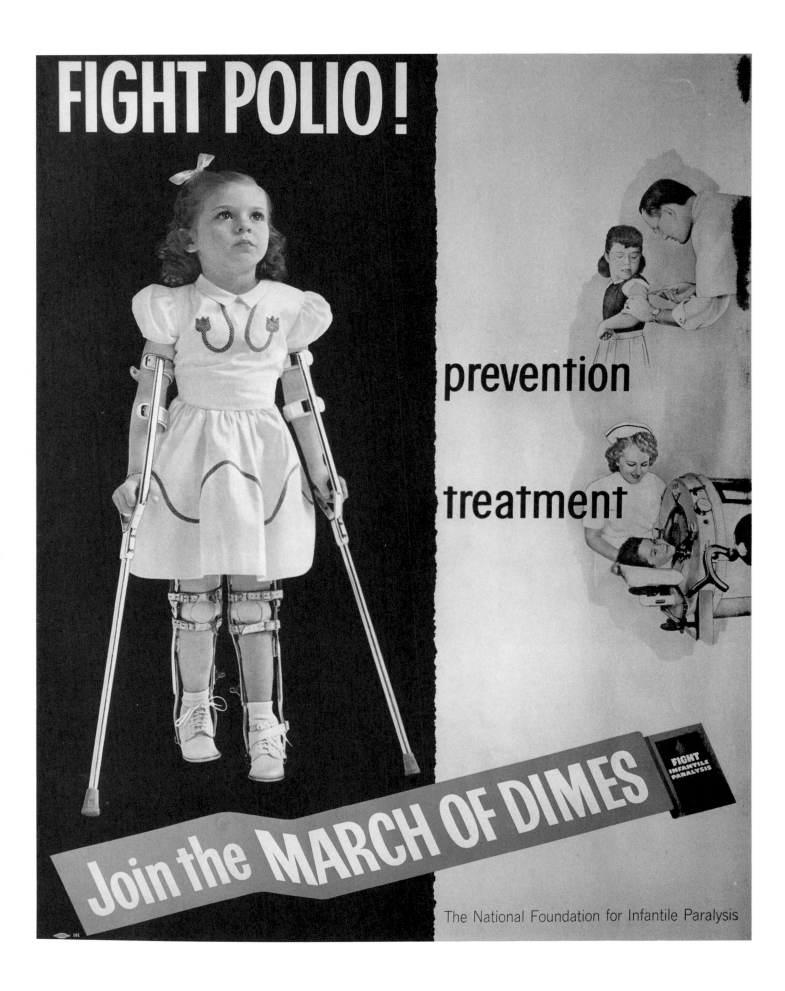

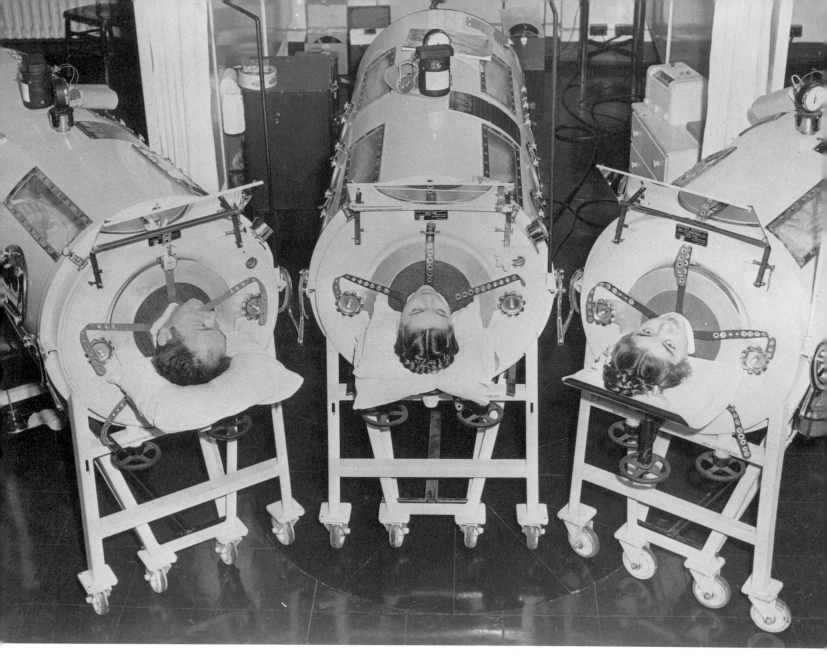

and walk with the aid of hip-to-shoe steel braces and crutches. He spent hours dragging himself up the stairs. Over the next few years he practiced getting out of a chair without help. He learned to lean unsupported against a wall. Eventually he could substitute two canes for his bulky crutches, but he could never abandon his despised leg braces.

FDR was elected governor of New York in 1928. Five years later he was president of the United States. In late 1937 he announced the formation of the National Foundation for Infantile Paralysis, mobilizing scientific and lay resources to conquer the disease. To kick off support for the foundation, singer-comedian Eddie Cantor broadcast a radio appeal in January 1938 for Americans to send in dimes to fight polio. Within days the White House received 2,680,000 dimes—thrown loosely into envelopes, baked into cakes, embedded in wax, or glued onto the eyes of paper portraits of the president. The March of Dimes—a phrase coined by Cantor—was born.

On the eve of World War II, the nation was obsessed with polio. On one front, matters improved. The traditional treatment for polio patients had been to straighten their weakened muscles by immobilizing them in splints or plaster casts. In 1940, an Australian nurse, Sister Elizabeth Kenny, revolutionized treatment by insisting on hot packs to relieve pain and tightness, followed by a regimen of physical therapy. The national foundation endorsed her new treatment and, over the next six years, sold thousands of unused splints for scrap. Kenny's treatment made patients more comfortable and helped some regain mobility, but it was certainly no cure.

On April 12, 1945, Franklin Roosevelt died. Though people feared that the campaign against polio would now falter, scientists pressed on in their search for a vaccine. Newspaper headlines in 1946 reported "the worst polio epidemic in thirty years," then proclaimed the outbreak in 1949 "the most devastating in medical annals."

In 1949 John Enders of Harvard managed to grow polio viruses outside the body in tissue that could be injected into human beings without risk. It was now possible to produce a large, safe source of the virus for vaccine experiments. By 1951 Jonas Salk, a young, audacious researcher at the University of Pittsburgh Medical School, had shown that all the known strains of poliovirus fell into three main types. He also determined that people could be immunized against the many forms of the disease by a vaccine containing one strong strain of virus from each of the three types. This simplified the design of a potential vaccine. Within a year Salk was convinced that he had developed a killed-virus vaccine powerful enough to produce antibodies against polio in human beings.

In the summer and fall of 1952, Salk inoculated 160 people in the Pittsburgh area with vaccine from little vials of pink solution. At a January 1953 meeting of leading immunologists he reported his results: blood samples from the people vaccinated revealed the presence of antibodies capable of neutralizing the virus, and none of the subjects had suffered serious reactions or side effects.

In a hurry-up campaign to protect potential victims before the expected summer outbreak of the disease, the March of Dimes organized a nationwide field trial of the Salk vaccine. In the spring of 1954, 650,000 children in forty-four states received a series of three shots each, 440,000 received the actual vaccine, and the rest, who acted as the control group, got a neutral substance. (When the vaccine proved successful, these 210,000 youngsters were the first to be inoculated.)

In the largest peacetime mobilization effort in America's history, twenty thousand doctors and public health officials, forty thousand nurses, sixty-four thousand school teachers and principals, and over two hundred thousand volunteers cooperated in running the trials and analyzing the results—no mean feat in the days before the computer. The trials proved so successful that Salk's vaccine joined those against diphtheria, whooping cough, and tetanus in the standard protection every American child received by the age of five.

The Salk vaccine was supplanted in the United States in 1962 by the attenuated

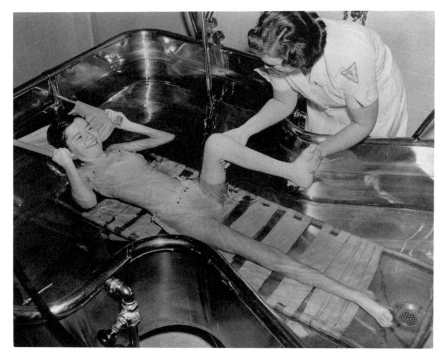

virus vaccine developed by Dr. Albert Sabin. Wherever there have been systematic inoculation programs—North America, Europe, Australia, and parts of Asia—there has been a dramatic decrease in polio. In the United States twenty-eight thousand cases were reported in 1955. One year after the vaccine went on the market, the number of cases dropped nearly fifty percent. Every year thereafter the incidence of polio declined. Between 1973 and 1981 an average of fewer than fifteen cases per year was reported in the entire country.

Poliomyelitis is now a rare disease in the United States. Most young doctors have never seen a case. The last outbreak due to natural infection occured in 1979. In 1991 only nine cases of polio were reported in the western hemisphere. Although about two hundred thousand children a year still get polio worldwide, the World Health Organization is determined to wipe out the disease by the year 2000. □

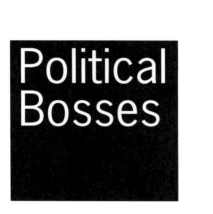

Political Bosses

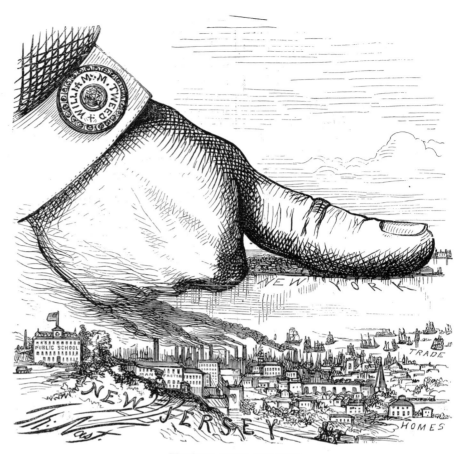

UNDER THE THUMB.

THE BOSS. "Well, what are you going to do about it?"

Chicagoans know that a drunk lawyer who is an alderman can often perform greater legal miracles than a smart lawyer who isn't. — Mike Royko, *Boss: Richard J. Daley of Chicago*, 1971

The Pendergast organization ran Kansas City from the late nineteenth century until the early 1940s. Tom and Jim Pendergast, the sons of Irish immigrants, started out as saloon keepers in the West Bottoms, a tough neighborhood where poor families crowded into dilapidated tenements and the unpaved streets were open sewers. The Pendergasts recognized that slum dwellers would receive public services only when they could get the attention of local elected officials. Gradually the brothers organized enough voters to control the city council and the police. Soon they extended their power and their connections with the established politicians who ran the city and the state of Missouri.

The Pendergasts discovered that political power had economic consequences. They put together a network of construction companies that built most of the roads in western Missouri. Their companies charged fair prices and did solid work, and the brothers had a reputation for personal honesty. But they lived in a world of quid pro quo. Officials they helped to elect were expected to approve big construction projects and assign them to Pendergast-controlled companies. "Politics is a business," Tom Pendergast said. "Nobody gets a job or an appointment because he's a nice fellow. He must deserve it politically. It's the same as any other business."

The Pendergast organization had its counterpart in most major cities in the country, where powerful cliques organized by political bosses dominated the activities of a political party for their private good. These organizations worked so smoothly that by the 1870s they were commonly referred to as machines. Everything depended on personal contact. Machine bosses appointed a leader for every block in a district they controlled. These block leaders reported to precinct captains, who in turn reported to the ward leader. The precinct captain visited every new family in the neighborhood and made sure they had water, gas, and electricity. At Christmas, the Kansas City machine handed out three thousand free turkeys. During the flu epidemic of 1918, Tom Pendergast visited every house in his wards to see who was sick and needed help.

Constituents were expected to return the favor by voting for the machine candidate on election day. One young woman voted four or five times; she and several friends were driven from precinct to precinct in a fancy car, changing costumes and sometimes donning a wig en route. "I knew it was illegal," she recalled, "but I certainly never thought it was wrong."

But it was wrong. Although the Pendergasts and their most famous protégé, Harry Truman, didn't take any public money illegally, some of the machine's other pols did. The city manager of Kansas City during the 1930s misappropriated some $20 million in public funds, and that's only what the prosecutors were able to document. Reformers estimated that the machine arranged for approximately sixty thousand spurious votes to be cast in the 1936 elections. Tom Pendergast, who had squandered his family fortune in gambling debts, was convicted of tax evasion in 1939 and sent to Leavenworth. The machine floundered for several more years under his nephew, but its power was broken.

The best-known machine in the country was probably New York's Tammany Hall, which was incorporated in 1789 by anti-Federalist allies of Thomas Jefferson. Under Boss William Tweed, Tammany had agents in every precinct in the city and stole an estimated $20 to $40 million from the public till between 1868 and 1871.

A subsequent Tammany leader, George Washington Plunkitt, distinguished between what he called "honest graft"—influence peddling, patronage, selling judgeships, awarding city contracts to firms that would kick back a piece of the action—and "dishonest graft"—extortion and the direct theft of public funds. On a typical day, Plunkitt noted in his diary, he went to court to bail out four constituents who had been arrested for vagrancy, paid a widow's rent, found jobs in city offices for four men, and attended an Italian funeral, a bar mitzvah, and a church fair.

Not all political bosses based their strength on the urban poor. Mark Hanna of Ohio, who represented the interests of midwestern businessmen, dominated the Republican party during the golden age of the robber barons. Hanna was generous with his own fortune and solicited big contributions from his peers. In exchange he ensured that governors, senators, and presidents were attentive to big business and opposed to organized labor.

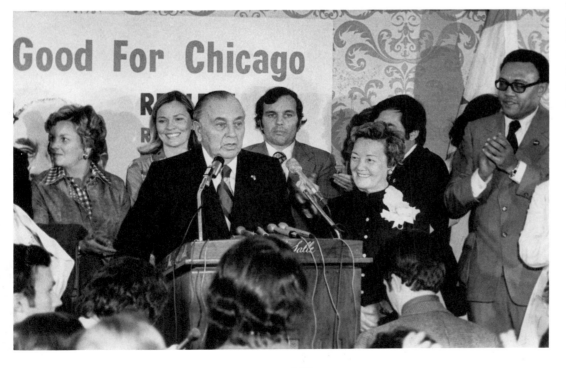

Few political bosses took so much and gave back so little as Frank Hague, who ran Hudson County, New Jersey, in the 1930s and 1940s. Hague, who once said "I am the law in Jersey City," rose from ward healer to mayor. The boss and his cronies made lucrative real estate deals with city agencies and took over banks with which the city did business. To pay for the elaborate public works projects that lined Hague's pockets, taxes in Jersey City by 1939 were the highest in the country. Yet after twenty years of Hague rule, the schools, roads, and garbage collection in the city were a disgrace.

People were afraid to vote against the machine. In the rare cases when they did, their ballots often disappeared. When voters moved, they stayed on the rolls at their old addresses and registered as well in their new districts. When they died, the election board was never notified. Hague said that anyone who complained about the way things worked in Hudson County was anti-American and should be thrown into a concentration camp in Alaska.

The last two nationally known bosses were Richard Daley of Chicago and Carmine De Sapio of New York. Both came to power as reformers, pledged to throw other bums out. De Sapio was the little-known precinct leader of an Italian neighborhood in Greenwich Village when he took over the New York Democratic Party in 1949. He purged the machine of petty hoodlums, and he helped elect good-government candidates like Robert Wagner, Jr., as mayor and Averell Harriman as governor. Although De Sapio continued the old Tammany practice of selling judgeships, he sold them only to reasonably competent people and sometimes waved the fee for an especially deserving candidate.

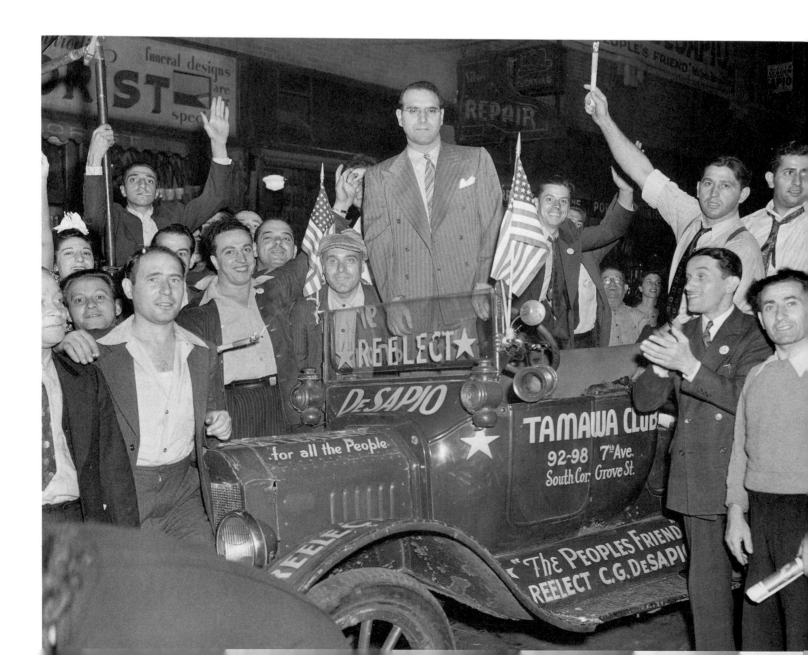

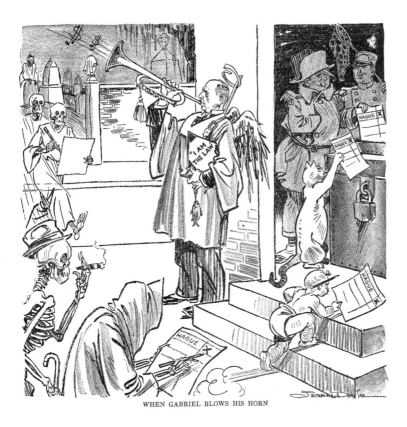

WHEN GABRIEL BLOWS HIS HORN

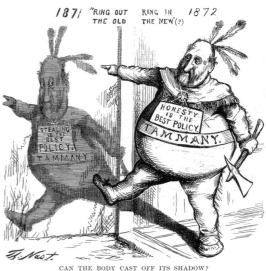

1871 "RING OUT RING IN 1872
THE OLD THE NEW(?)

CAN THE BODY CAST OFF ITS SHADOW?
The Tammany Society has expelled TWEED as Sachem. — *Daily Papers.*

Richard Daley's Chicago had been controlled by the Democratic machine for decades. Daley rose through the ranks in classic fashion: After working for a neighborhood club in his teens, he became a precinct captain and got a city patronage job in his early twenties. Elevated to the chairmanship of the Cook County Democrats in 1951, he was elected mayor in 1955.

The Chicago machine in Daley's heyday probably controlled twenty to twenty-five thousand jobs on the city payroll, and the mayor kept tabs on every one. Despite civil service reform, it was possible to postpone exams and make "temporary" appointments that sometimes lasted for years.

Daley's great day in national politics came when he delivered Illinois to John Kennedy in the 1960 presidential election. But the alleged fraud in that year's vote count, which was startling even by Chicago standards, became a national scandal. Daley's image was hopelessly tarnished after the brutal attacks by his police force against demonstrators at the 1968 Democratic National Convention in Chicago.

Daley and De Sapio were the last of their breed. Most would-be urban political bosses no longer had the connections to get out the vote. Their core constituents moved to the suburbs, weakening loyalties to old neighborhoods or parishes. Reformers could put together a coalition of agitated citizens galvanized by a single issue a few weeks before an election. Civil service covered more and more former patronage jobs. Lawyers took over government. The bosses were often undone by their racist attitudes; the machines that had accommodated successive waves of Irish, Italian, Jewish, and Slavic immigrants were less willing to work with blacks and Hispanics.

Some people think the collapse of the machines did more harm than good. When residents needed to get a streetlight fixed, the garbage picked up, or an extra cop assigned to a tough block, their precinct captain knew whom to call to get it done. Machines may have been corrupt, but they had a rough kind of accountability. The people who held city jobs at the pleasure of a political boss have been replaced by bureaucrats who are protected by civil service and union rules. Serving the public often seems like the last thing on their minds. □

119

Sigmund Freud's couch is enshrined at the Freud Museum in London. It is the archetype for thousands of others—some equally ornate, some in tufted leather, some tattered, some replaced every year—that dominate the offices of orthodox Freudian psychoanalysts across America. Patients lie down on the couch four or five times a week, except in August, for four or five years, to reveal their dreams, fantasies, childhood memories, daily trivia, and innermost thoughts to a doctor, seated out of sight, who rarely says anything but "ummm" or "ahhh" or "what do you think?" By the end of the process they hope to understand why they behaved the way they did in order to act differently the next time.

Psychoanalysis was invented around the turn of the century by Freud, who was then a little-known Austrian neurologist. Psychoanalysis provided a theoretical structure that promised to explore and explain the hidden workings of the mind. It described a psyche composed of the self, the ego; untamed biological urges, the id; and a moralistic censor, the superego. It argued that forces of which the conscious mind was unaware could dominate one's waking and sleeping moments.

Freud constantly modified his own theories and practice. He once analyzed his disciple, Sandor Ferenczi, during a series of horseback rides they took together in Vienna. Freud's followers were much more strict. By the time psychoanalysis received the imprimatur of the American Medical Association in 1939, the formal patterns of the "talking cure," as it was called, were set in stone.

After the upheavel of two world wars, which revealed much about the dark side of human nature, many intellectuals looked to psychoanalysis rather than religion for a coherent explanation of the human psyche. Popular novels and plays featured characters who were undergoing Freudian analysis or whose behavior was explained in terms of psychoalanytic theory. Nearly one in ten medical school graduates chose to specialize in psychiatry; a number committed themselves to the years of rigorous postgraduate study and treatment required to become anaylsts. The general mood of the country was optimistic; business was booming. With a characteristic American zest for self-improvement, many people went into treatment. Even those who didn't picked up psychoanalytic jargon: "He's sublimating." "She's orally fixated." "You're such an anal compulsive." It was fashionable to talk about your analyst at cocktail parties. There were more would-be analysands than doctors available to see them.

Classical psychoanalysis always had critics; some of the most vociferous were from within the psychiatric profession. Detractors labeled the process an "intellectual charade" or "little more than a collective contagious delusional system."

By the third year, I was spending more on cabs to my analyst than on food. — Dan Wakefield, "Six Years on the Couch," ***The New York Times Magazine,*** **December 20, 1987**

In disparaging articles and books, analysis was taken to task for its clinical rigidity and paucity of scientific validation. Analysts were attacked for their lack of warmth and their unwillingness to give guidance to perplexed or despairing patients. Some critics questioned Freudian causal reasoning, which blamed past conflicts for present neuroses. Others challenged Freud directly. One adversary, while acknowledging that Freud helped the modern world break free of sexual hypocrisy and supernatural belief, concluded that "so far as we can tell, the only mind he laid bare for us was his own." As time went on, many opponents charged that analysis lasted too long and its goals were too vague.

Nevertheless, in the 1950s, if you thought you needed psychological treatment, chances are you found yourself on the couch. During the next two decades, however, many other therapies became available. In the 1960s you could be treated with electric shock, psychochemotherapy, existential psychotherapy, group therapy, psychodrama, crisis intervention, hypnosis, and the new behavior therapies, as well as one of several psychoanalytically oriented psychotherapies. By the 1970s you could turn to the human potential movement or to self-help measures like biofeedback, autohypnosis, and meditation. You could get into Zen or yoga or a "feel" group or a weekend marathon group.

By the mid-1970s patients in analysis were hard to find. One doctor said, "It is incontestible that classical psychoanalysis (five times a week, on the couch, etc.) has become a *rara avis*." The central role that psychoanalytic concepts formerly enjoyed in the training of psychiatrists had diminished, and the number of medical school

Psychoanalysis

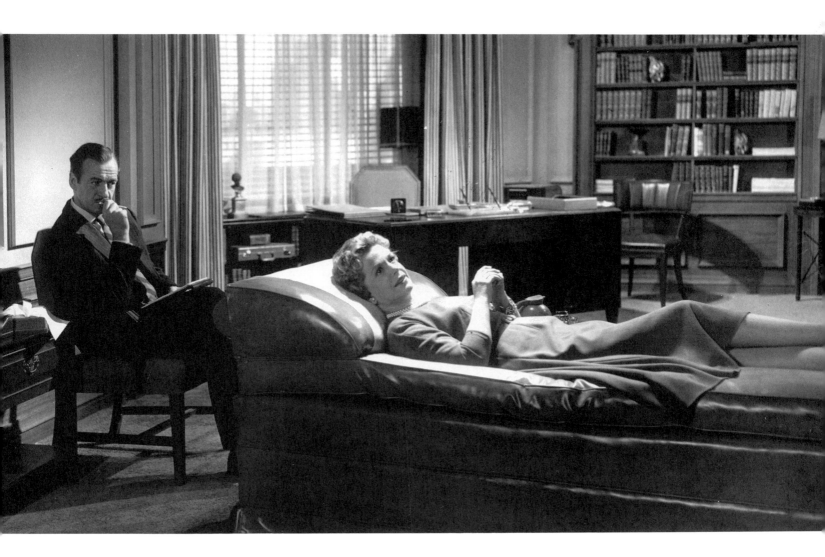

graduates applying to psychoanalytic institutes declined. Therapies based on psycho-active drugs were considered the new cure-all.

In 1988 *Newsweek* quoted a practitioner as saying psychoanalysis was "starved" for patients. Many communities had not a single analysand. Few doctors could afford to practice analysis exclusively. Most patients demanded brief goal-oriented treatment instead of a hypothetical restructuring of their personalities. They wanted psychotherapy with a doctor who would look them in the face and talk about the here and now, rather than sit silently and focus on the past. Medical insurance reinforced the trend; benefits didn't come close to covering the total costs of four or five sessions a week for years on end.

In hopes of revitalizing the profession, the American Psychoanalytic Association admitted nonmedical analysts—many of them women—for the first time in 1989. It's unlikely, however, that fresh blood can restore psychoanalysis to a central place in the constellation of available treatments. If psychoanalysis does not survive as a treatment, it will have left an extraordinary legacy. Freud's assessment of his theories in the 1926 *Encyclopedia Brittannica* may have been prophetic: "The future will probably attribute far greater importance to psychoanalysis as the science of the unconscious than as a therapeutic procedure." □

Analysis was like being wrapped in a protective cocoon of gentleness, permitted to find a safety I never knew. It was an experience through which I lived, comparable to growing up again. It was like receiving painless injections of love and trust which gave me the strength to accept myself.
— Lucy Freeman, *Fight Against Fears*, 1951

The Red Menace

Russian Communist party chief Joseph Stalin was on the cover of *Time* magazine twelve times, more often than either of his contemporaries, Franklin Roosevelt or Winston Churchill. Such continued fascination with the leader of a country halfway around the world was only one indication of Americans' obsession with the man and his cause. From the time of the Bolshevik Revolution, many Americans feared that Communism would eventually reach these shores. They were convinced that the U.S. was the target of spies, secret agents, and traitors aiming to subvert "the American way of life."

After World War I, a coalition of American isolationists and anti-Communists forced the deportation of some 550 suspected anarchists and Communists, including some poor souls who simply didn't speak English. During the 1930s, people who sympathized with the Republicans in the Spanish Civil War and those who defended victims of social and racial persecution at home were often accused of being Communists because the Party also supported those causes.

The anti-Communist crusade was put on hold during World War II while the Soviet Union and the United States joined to defeat the Third Reich. Hollywood did its part to support the wartime alliance with films like *The North Star* (1944) based on an original story by Lillian Hellman. Walter Huston, Farley Granger, and Dana Andrews starred as a group of heroic Russian villagers fighting against Nazi invaders led by the villainous Erich von Stroheim.

When the war ended, rivalry between the two great powers resumed, and the worst fears of anti-Communists seemed to be coming true. The West "lost" China. The Iron Curtain clanged down across the middle of Europe. The Russians exploded their own atomic bomb in 1949, and the U.S. was shocked to discover that spies and traitors inside the American scientific community helped to make it happen.

There were never many "card-carrying Communists" in the United States. Party membership had hit its all-time high of about eighty thousand in 1944. Nevertheless, superpatriots were convinced that there were Reds everywhere. Publicity-seeking congressmen looked into alleged Communist influence in Hollywood. Throughout the 1940s, the House Un-American Activities Committee dominated the headlines and newsreels. The committee subpoenaed many famous actors, producers, and writers of films like *The Red Star*, which they said were too sympathetic to the Soviet Union.

Ten writers went to jail rather than cooperate with the committee. The heads of the entertainment industry protected themselves by blacklisting scores of other writers, actors, and directors, often without a shred of evidence. The movie studios rushed to release *I Was a Communist for the F.B.I.*, the story of a heroic double agent; *The Whip Hand*, about an enemy germ-warfare plant in the Midwest; and *Invasion, U.S.A.*, which, Hedda Hopper warned, "will scare the pants off you."

Such hysteria may have contributed to the convictions of Alger Hiss for perjury and Julius and Ethel Rosenberg for treason. After three years of legal maneuvering, President Eisenhower refused a final plea for clemency for the Rosenbergs, who were the only Americans ever executed for treason in peacetime.

East-West confrontations dominated the headlines. Following the Berlin blockade and the Communist invasion of South Korea, many Americans feared that a war between two superpowers armed with atomic weapons could lead to annihilation. They marched, signed petitions for nuclear test-ban treaties, and proclaimed that they'd rather be Red Than Dead. People on the right were sure these "Comm-symps" or "fellow travelers" underestimated Russia's designs on the "free world" or, worse, supported them.

By the 1950s, over ten million American were under investigation of some kind by Congress, the FBI, antisubversive units of various municipal police forces, or the loyalty committees of many public institutions, including schools and universities. The U. S. attorney general ordered the preparation of six detention camps in which to lock up reputed spies and saboteurs. Yet when pollsters asked a number of Americans in 1954 if they knew any Communists, only three percent said they did. Another ten percent had suspicions about some of their neighbors. Asked for evidence, they cited people who never attended church, dressed poorly although they were known to have money, or showed no interest in major league baseball.

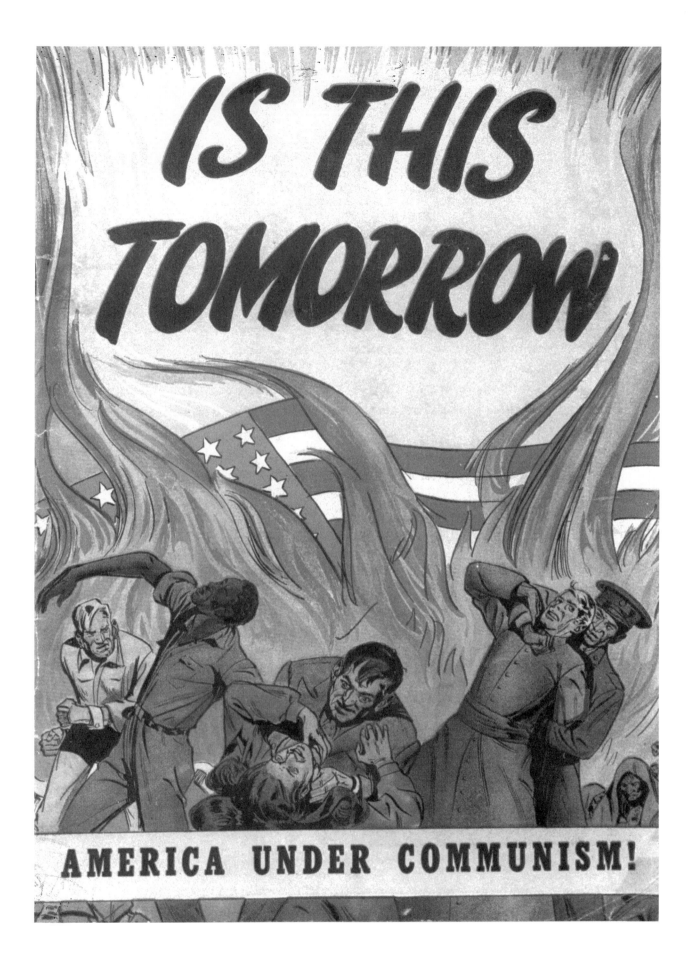

Traitors in the high councils of our own government have made sure that the deck is stacked on the Soviet side of the diplomatic tables. — Richard Nixon, 1950

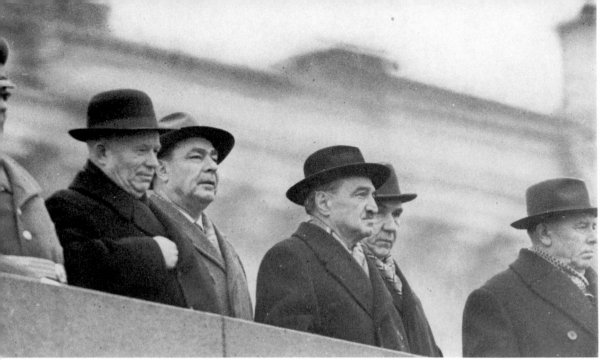

Virulent anti-Communism was responsible for the meteoric career of Sen. Joseph McCarthy of Wisconsin. In 1950 McCarthy was a freshman senator looking for a cause to ensure his reelection. He hit the headlines for the first time after a speech in Wheeling, West Virginia, in which he announced that he had a list of 205 security risks employed at the Department of State. Two days later in Salt Lake City, he declared his list contained the names of "fifty-seven card-carrying Communists." Two weeks after that, he charged that there were "eighty-one cases" of subversion. He never substantiated a single claim.

McCarthy's Permanent Subcommittee on Investigation looked into alleged Communist penetration of the U.S. Army. Among other charges, the senator maintained that higher-ups had permitted a dentist named Irving Peress, a self-identified Communist sympathizer, to serve in the army for nearly a year before giving him an honorable discharge. There was no evidence that the dentist was a traitor or had improperly prepared a filling.

Nonetheless, in the spring of 1954 McCarthy called the secretary of the army and other witnesses to testify about Major Peress and other so-called security leaks. For a time the senator, and his assistant, Roy Cohn, had the army on the ropes. Then the army's counsel, a Boston attorney named Joseph Welch, challenged the senator's wild allegations before a television audience of twenty million people. "Until this moment Senator, I think I never really gauged your cruelty or your recklessness. . . . Have you no decency, sir, at long last? Have you left no sense of decency?" After McCarthy was shown up as a bully and a fraud, his reign of terror ended. His conduct was condemned by the Senate in August 1954, and he soon drank himself to death.

Joseph Stalin died in 1953 during the height of McCarthy's power. But the goals of his successors remained essentially the same. Photographs of the Politburo on review at the annual May Day parade featured a dozen men in lumpy gray suits and shapeless overcoats, wearing funeral fedoras and grim expressions. Kremlinologists argued about who stood closer or farther from the center each year, but to the average American the men all looked frighteningly alike.

International Communism will never rest until the whole world, including the United States, is under the hammer and sickle. — J. Edgar Hoover, *Masters of Deceit: The Story of Communism in American and How to Fight It*, 1958

Soviet success seemed relentless: the Russians put down a Hungarian revolt in 1956 and launched Sputnik in 1957; Third World leaders like Fidel Castro and Ho Chi Minh goaded the U.S. into calamitous military adventures; Soviet tanks crushed the Czechoslovakian rebellion in 1968. Although the Chinese Communists drove the Dalai Lama from Tibet in 1959 and intermittently threatened to attack the nationalists on Taiwan, Americans never worried as much about Mao and his minions. The USSR remained the embodiment of the world revolution. When Khrushchev boasted to Nixon, "We will bury you," Americans visualized Russian soldiers taking over city hall.

During the late 1960s, J. Edgar Hoover and the John Birch Society were convinced that students protesting the Vietnam War and black activists in the civil rights movement were in cahoots with Communist agents. The New York Police Department kept files on 250,000 people who might be "subversive," and the Los Angeles police accumulated six tons of files on fifty thousand people. Ronald Reagan traveled the

HELP!
DEMOCRACY IS IN DANGER!
MOSCOW WITHIN OUR GATES!
FIGHT COMMUNISM
at the **MASS RALLY HIPPODROME·**
FRIDAY · FEB. 12th 8 P.M.

lecture circuit asserting that the antiwar and antinuclear movements were run by people who were "being manipulated by forces sympathetic to the Soviet Union."

After the fighting stopped in Vietnam, international tensions in the Middle East, Africa, and Southeast Asia kept the Cold War alive. But by 1985, when Mikhail Gorbachev took power, the Soviet system was collapsing from within. On December 25, 1991, Gorbachev resigned as president, ending seventy-four years of Communist rule in Russia. The USSR disbanded into old and new republics.

The death of Russian Communism also finished off the convention of Soviet agents as standard-issue villains in the popular mind. Scruffy Middle Eastern terrorists and sinister Asian and Latin American drug dealers replaced them as the major threats to international peace. But even paranoids had trouble making a case that they posed a clear and present danger to the American way of life. ☐

NOW YOU CAN DIAL!—a public service film made by the Bell Telephone Company—was shown throughout America in the 1950s. A pretty actress stood next to a five-foot-tall model of a telephone dial. She explained cheerily how the letters and numbers worked and how to use the directory. "Pick up the receiver and listen for the tone. Instead of the operator's familiar 'number please' you'll hear a steady hum. While the receiver is still off the hook, pull the dial around to the finger-stop for each number. Be sure to let it return to its normal position before you go on to the next digit. An interrupted *brrring* sound lets you know the number is ringing. A busy signal—a *buzz-buzz* sound—means you should hang up and try your call a little later."

The dial telephone was invented in 1891 by Almon B. Strowger, a Kansas City undertaker, supposedly because he was convinced that operators were being bribed to switch his customers' calls to competitors. Strowger was determined to find a way to skirt the central exchange. When the Bell System eventually converted to dial phones, it used some of his ideas.

The conversion went slowly. For decades operators in many towns continued to place local calls. One New Jersey Bell operator who ran a switchboard for twenty-five years was warned not to get friendly on the phone. "Have a nice day" had not yet been invented; her patter consisted of "number please?" and "I can connect you now." Small-town operators sometimes disregarded their employers' instructions. They took messages or told callers, "I don't think your party is home now. I just saw her walk by the office on her way to church."

Although the phone company began installing dial systems, exchange by exchange, as early as 1919, twenty years later only half the country had dial service. Meanwhile, Bell engineers were trying to accommodate different styles and speeds of dialing. An engineer's report explained: "An individual's accuracy and speed in operating a dial, apart from his ability to remember the telephone number, depends on proper coordination between his eye in picking the right letter or digit, and his fingers in finding the corresponding hole in the finger wheel. To dial in the least possible time, he must locate the next digit while the finger wheel is in motion, and have his finger poised ready to wind up the dial as soon as the wheel comes to rest."

For both company and customer, the dial system was too slow and inaccurate. In 1963 AT&T introduced a "completely different concept in telephone calling and signaling"—a ten-button keyboard. The shape, size, and spacing of the keypad buttons were determined after tests using people whose hands presented a range of variations—men with blunt finger pads, women with long nails, children with stubby fingers. Bell researchers asked them to "touch" circles, rectangles, and triangles, in various number sequences. The winner was three rows of three buttons each, with the numbers 1, 2, and 3 across the top and the operator button set by itself at the bottom.

The touch-tone system was a technological revolution. A rotary phone, as the dial phone came to be called, generates pulses of direct current—like the action of turning on and off an electric light switch. Each digit dialed opens the circuit momentarily and then closes it from one to ten times. This produces a small pulse which is transmitted to the central office where the pulses for each digit are tabulated. These pulses are then released at the proper rate to complete the call.

Touch-tone signals, on the other hand, are alternating current tones, similar to some of those produced by the human voice. When a button is pressed, a signal generator within the phone produces two discrete musical tones that identify the digit and transmit it to automated switches in the central office. The designers selected frequencies sufficiently distinct from those of speech, music, and noise to avoid the possibility that a caller's voice could replicate the sound of a digit and result in a wrong number.

Soon the Bell Lab design team figured out that a touch-tone pad could produce twelve signals almost as easily as the ten that were in common use. Two extra spaces could be added on either side of the operator button and used in data messages. Choosing the symbols and names for the two new keys was a challenge. The asterisk

Rotary Phones

As far as I am concerned, the entire New England Telephone & Telegraph Co. deserves to be shut up in a closet for having saddled us with dials and deprived us of our beloved operators, who used to know where everybody was and just what to do about everything.
— E. B. White, *The New Yorker*, December 24, 1955

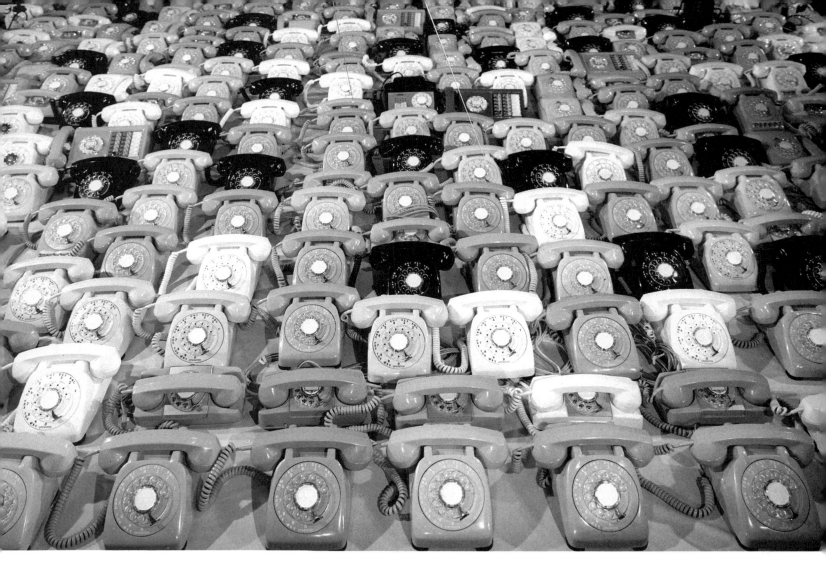

(*), commonly used in handwriting and typing, was selected for the button on the lower left. The design team wanted the other symbol to be a dot, but since it might be mistaken for an asterisk, the team settled on the pound sign (#).

Like the transition from operator to dial, the change from rotary to touch-tone was done one exchange at a time. Individual subscribers had the option of sticking with their old equipment or paying a small premium for the new. Most customers loved the speed and convenience of the touch-tone keypad. Numbers that used to take eight to ten seconds to dial could be sequenced in half that time. Subscribers wrote the company that touch-tone was like "magic" and made dialing "a game instead of a chore."

Although speed was the initial stimulus for touch-tone, the engineers quickly realized that the keypad could be linked with other emerging technologies. As early as 1963 a Bell Telephone article prophesied that a housewife might use touch-tone to turn on a household appliance when she was out shopping or a merchant might query a computer to check a customer's credit. It was even conceivable that someday the telephone could get a "voice answer from a computer simulator"—voice mail as we know it today.

In the mid-1980s, AT&T stopped making rotary phones, although it continues to lease and refurbish old ones. Millions of them are still used by people because of habit or because they are wary of new technology. The dial may be familiar, and therefore comforting to some, but many more people are outraged if the only phone available won't allow them to punch in their credit card numbers or check their messages. ☐

Sanitary Napkin Belts

No woman ever had anything nice to say about sanitary napkin belts. They dug into the skin, stretched out of shape, and turned gray. Worst of all, they didn't keep a sanitary napkin in place. The napkin started out centered, but after an hour the belt pulled it up toward the spine or the belly button. Young girls were terrified that a boy could see the outline of the belt under their skirts and know it was "that time of the month."

In the first decades of the twentieth century, menstruating women wore washable cotton cloths, which they secured with safety pins to long tabs that hung from the front and back of an elasticized belt. Belt manufacturers referred discreetly to their product as "a personal necessity." One of the most popular brands, Hickory Belts, came in several styles: slip-on elastic, fabric with elastic, or soft mesh and elastic that fastened in front with a pearl button. In 1925, Hickory advertised, "Even our least expensive model is cut to fit easily and gently. The elastic portions are skillfully placed to relieve all strain and the belts themselves are so light and soft you can wear one night and day scarcely knowing it!"

In those days the belt was less of a problem than the napkin. To meet the needs of young women who were beginning to participate in active sports and take jobs outside the home, various manufacturers experimented with combinations of cotton and synthetic materials in a napkin that was absorbent yet cheap enough to throw away after one use. One company made a serendipitous discovery. Kimberly-Clark, a producer of paper products, was stuck with a surplus of highly absorbent cellulose wadding that had been used as surgical dressings to treat the wounded in World War I. The company learned that during the war army nurses had packed the wadding in gauze and used it for sanitary napkins. The material was much softer and more effective than the felt or cotton rags they had used till then. It was also easily discarded.

In 1920 Kimberly-Clark marketed its first disposable sanitary napkin. Kotex brand napkins had several layers of cellulose wadding cut into a rectangular shape and wrapped with gauze. They were five times as absorbent as cotton. The potential demand for the product was enormous, but a hush-hush attitude surrounded the subject of menstruation. Stores were reluctant to display or stock feminine napkins, and most magazines refused advertisements for them.

Kimberly-Clark, like its leading competitor, Johnson and Johnson—the manufacturer of Modess—needed a tasteful way to inform women about its product and had to find dealers who would sell it. The companies awarded prizes to merchants who were willing to display the controversial items in their windows. Since women were embarrassed to ask a clerk for help, dealers were persuaded to place the product—wrapped in plain paper—on top of the counter so women could simply pick it up, pay, and walk out. Customers could also order free samples—in unmarked parcels—through the mail.

In 1939 one in five women still used homemade napkins, despite the number of brands on the market. World War II changed all that. Women who went to work every day in factories and shipyards needed the ease and comfort of disposable pads. By 1945, nearly all American women had switched to store-bought napkins and belts.

For a long time, makers of pads and belts had recognized that many of their customers knew very little about their bodies and less about the menstrual cycle. Millions of young girls experienced their first period without any idea of what was happening to them. Manufacturers tried to educate the public through pamphlets that explained the process and how to use their products. Kimberly-Clark's first publication, "Marjorie May's Twelfth Birthday," described feminine hygiene in terms a baffled teenager could understand. Some states banned shipments of "Marjorie May" through the mail, but the demands of parents and educators overcame the opposition.

A later pamphlet illustrated the female reproductive organs, explained ovulation, dispelled superstitions about menstruation, and defined terms like *vagina, uterus,* and *cervix.* The reassuring message was that menstruation is a healthy bodily function.

The booklets mentioned tampons as well as napkins. Although tampons were first introduced in the 1930s, for decades they were considered taboo for young women who were not yet sexually active. Pads and belt were the beginner's only choice, and many women remained loyal to them all their reproductive lives.

I locked the bathroom door and attached a *Teenage Softie* to the little hooks on my pink belt. Then I got dressed and looked at myself in the mirror. Would anyone know my secret? Would it show? — Judy Blume, *Are You There God? It's Me, Margaret*, 1970

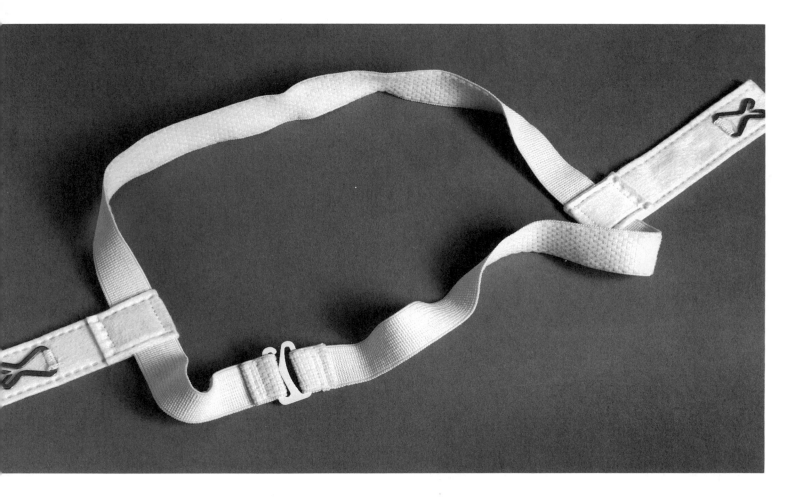

In the early 1970s, a new product claimed to make women forget they even had their periods. Sanitary pads that adhered to the inside of underwear revolutionized the market. A woman simply peeled the protective cover off the adhesive strip and pressed the pad against her panties or girdle. "Goodbye, belts and pins and fuss! Goodbye discomfort!" trumpeted one manufacturer. "Your new feminine napkin locks on automatically without any heavy hardware."

By 1978, the new adhesive napkins outsold the old-fashioned tabbed ones. In the years that followed, they swept the field. No more worries about sliding napkins or telltale outlines. With a choice of tampons or adhesive pads, women were finally freed from the tyranny of the belt. ☐

There was once a time when air travel was considered glamorous. In the years after World War II, families went to the airport to visit the shops and restaurants and look at the sleek, modern DC-3s or twin-tailed Constellations or Stratocruisers. Departing passengers visited with friends and relatives in the departure lounge or strolled on the observation deck overlooking the field. Passengers and bystanders mingled at will. Baggage was checked without fuss. Ticketed passengers with carry-on suitcases and shopping bags showed up at the gate when their flight was announced and got on the plane.

All that changed after May 1, 1961, when a National Airlines Convair en route from Miami to Key West was forced to fly to Cuba by a man who said he wanted to warn Fidel Castro of an assassination attempt. Two months later an American citizen of Cuban birth diverted an Eastern Airlines flight bound for Tampa to Havana. In August a Pan Am jet flying from Mexico to Guatemala was commandeered by a man opposed to American policy on Algerian independence. The skyjacker pointed a .38 at the pilot and demanded to be taken to Havana.

Americans were outraged and frightened. President John F. Kennedy asked for special antihijack legislation. Some airlines put security guards aboard their flights. The Federal Aviation Administration required that cockpit doors be locked except during takeoffs and landings. Congress made it a federal crime to carry a weapon on board or to assault or intimidate crew members in any way that interfered with passenger safety. The mandated punishment for sky piracy was a prison term of up to twenty years.

Throughout the 1960s, the skyjack epidemic spread throughout the world. But in 1969 the FAA developed two antihijacking measures to identify and isolate potential troublemakers while they were still on the ground—the behavioral profile and a weapons-screening system. Airline employees were on the lookout for anyone with personality traits believed to be characteristic of a hijacker and scanned all passengers with a metal detector as they moved through the boarding gate. Anyone who aroused suspicion was interviewed by airline officials and sometimes arrested. Uncooperative passengers were forcibly searched. People with something to hide either changed their plans or ditched the forbidden item before being screened. Knives, guns, pornographic pictures, packets of marijuana, and even silverware filched from airport restaurants were found behind potted palms in the lounge areas.

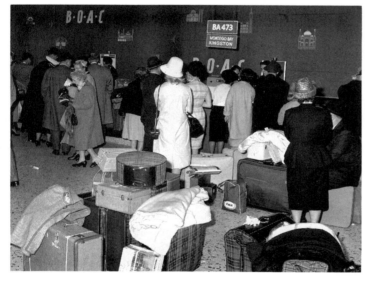

During 1970 hijacking became more violent. On February 10 three Arab terrorists in the Munich terminal lobbed grenades at passengers in the transit lounge waiting to board an El Al flight to London, wounding eleven people and killing one. Within weeks, saboteurs exploded a bomb on one plane—which the pilot managed to land—and blew up another in midair, killing all forty-seven passengers. In September members of the Popular Front for the Liberation of Palestine diverted four airliners to the Middle East, then evacuated and destroyed them. This was a new breed of hijackers—professionals who knew airplanes and weapons and whose objective was to publicize their cause. They were engaged in international blackmail with innocent civilians as their pawns.

On December 5, 1972, airlines were given one month to install electronic equipment that would search all passengers and screen carry-on baggage. Airlines warned passengers that their Christmas presents would be opened for inspection to prevent someone from smuggling a weapon on board. Travelers were advised not to gift-wrap packages since gate attendants would not rewrap them. Some people complained about their right to privacy, but most were delighted to cooperate. Ticketed passengers walked through a magnetic gate and presented their hand luggage for inspection before they were allowed into guarded boarding areas. If they failed to pass the magnetometer test, they had to produce the item that caused the high reading before they were cleared. The detectors were ultrasensitive. One was activated by shrapnel in the body of a World War II veteran. A woman traveling from New York to Miami removed her bracelets, necklace, and metal-rimmed glasses, but the sensor still went off. It was finally discovered that the metal stays in her corset had triggered the detector.

Security-Free Airports

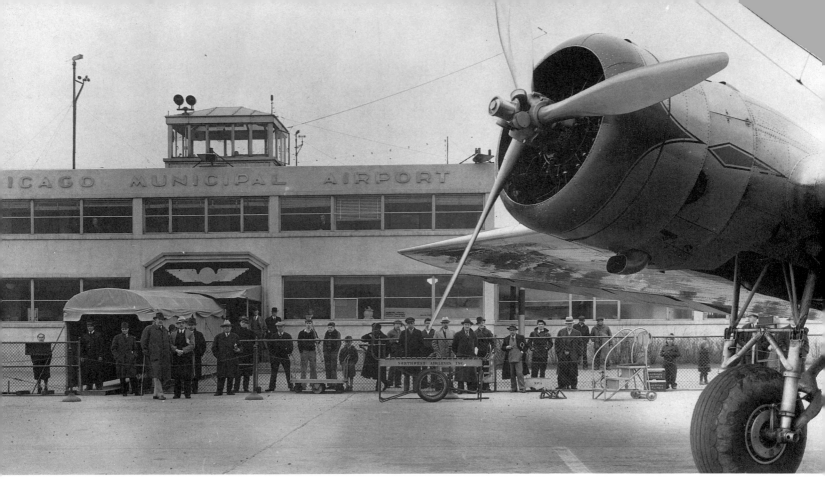

Security measures gave airports a new look. Many adopted the "sterile corridor," a concourse used only by passengers who were cleared at security barriers. Friends no longer saw travelers off at the gate or met them as they stepped from the plane. Security officers used X-ray equipment to scan every carry-on bag and searched those that were suspicious. During the first six months of 1973, 894 guns were confiscated, 1,337 people were arrested for various crimes including illegal possession of weapons or drugs, and 1,505 were refused permission to board. No airline was hijacked after blanket screening went into effect at the beginning of the year.

Terrorists didn't give up. Between 1983 and 1989 they planted explosives on sixteen planes worldwide. Although the FAA had required American carriers to intensify security practices, the destruction of Pan Am's flight 103 over Lockerbie, Scotland, in 1988, proved that tightened procedures were fatally flawed. Investigators eventually established that a plastic explosive was concealed in a cassette recorder inside a suitcase stowed in the cargo hold. The airline had violated security regulations that prohibited a carrier from transporting baggage not accompanied by a passenger, unless the baggage was opened and physically searched.

At Heathrow, terminal roofs are laid out like seaside promenades, and airport visitors can relax in gay, candy-striped deckchairs, stroll through spacious roof gardens, or shop and eat, making a day of aircraft-spotting an outing for the entire family. — Ken Conoley, *Airlines, Airports and You*, 1968

Extraordinary procedures were put into place at high-risk airports. They remain in effect today. Passengers on international flights are advised to arrive at the airport at least two hours in advance. They are asked questions designed to determine if they might intentionally or unwittingly be carrying a bomb or weapon. Some are physically searched along with their carry-on items, even though the magnetometer has already cleared them. Each passenger must identify a bag as his or her own before it can be loaded, and some checked baggage is further searched and X-rayed. At the most vulnerable airports, all carry-on items are searched by hand. Passengers traveling within the U.S. are routinely screened by metal detectors. The only domestic airports that do not have some form of security are those in small or remote cities or those served by noncommercial planes.

So far, terrorists have changed their tactics to stay one step ahead of every protective measure. One consultant thinks he could foil them. In his scheme, naked passengers will be X-rayed and sealed in tubes before boarding the aircraft. Their baggage will be loaded on a separate, pilotless plane. With nothing to gain by blowing up luggage on the pilotless plane, terrorists will no longer threaten the friendly skies. □

Shoe-Fitting Fluoroscopes

For Americans growing up in the years just after World War II, a trip to the shoe store was as much of a treat as a ride in the family car.

You got to choose a pair of new brown oxfords for school and a pair of party shoes—shiny black Mary Janes if you were a girl and tasseled loafers if you were a boy. Occasionally you were allowed to consider saddle shoes, either in black and white or in brown and white. You might plead for moccasins, but they were Bad For Your Feet.

Best of all, when you had put on your new shoes, you stepped up on a boxlike machine, inserted your feet into an opening at the base, and saw your very bones light up within the outline of the shoe. As you wriggled your toes, your parents and the salesman took turns looking through the viewer to determine—scientifically, of course—whether or not the shoe fit.

The miraculous instrument was called a fluoroscope. Invented by Thomas Edison in 1896, it allowed a doctor to see a silhouette of the bone structure and some of the internal organs of the human body. The most common type of medical fluoroscope consisted of a large X-ray machine and a fluorescent screen that emitted light when it was struck by the rays. The patient stood in front of the machine, which generated an X-ray beam that passed through the body and projected a continuous image of the bones and organs onto the screen. If the doctor wanted a permanent record of the patient's condition, a technician took a conventional X-ray picture that preserved the image. For the first time doctors could see where a bone was broken or locate a bullet or shard of metal deep inside the body. They could study the digestive tract as barium passed through the system, or inject an iodine compound into the blood to see the arteries.

Even though the hazards of radiation were known shortly after the discovery of X-rays in 1895, enterprising companies kept dreaming up new applications of the fluoroscope in daily life—especially after World War I, when quantities of surplus X-ray apparatus became available. The shoe-fitting fluoroscope—the Foot-O-Scope—was "invented" and marketed in 1920 by the United Shoe Machinery Corporation. The device may have had its antecedents in the X-ray slot machines that could be found in some Chicago and New York restaurants around 1905. For a nickel, you could see the moving bones of your hand or your wrist and learn about the wonders of science.

By the 1940s and 1950s, shoe-fitting fluoroscopes from a variety of manufacturers were commonly found in most shoe stores in America. "The machine is particularly useful in the fitting of children's shoes because young children are not usually able to give the shoe man accurate advice as to how a shoe feels on the foot," explained a United Shoe Machinery Corporation brochure in 1951.

Many shoe-store fluoroscopes were equipped with an automatic switch to turn off the X-ray exposure after a predetermined length of time up to thirty seconds. Some models had a selector switch with three positions marked "men," "women," and "children," presumably permitting different rates of exposure. Typically, a thin plate of aluminum was interposed between the X-ray tube and the foot to lessen the X-ray dosage. In most stores, the fluoroscope was operated by a person with no knowledge of X-rays or their hazards. Often the machines had no indicator marking the amount of radiation hitting the feet; some emitted about fifty times the radiation rate of a modern hospital fluoroscopic unit. Moreover, there was no way of monitoring customers who went from store to store trying on shoes or school kids who sneaked in for a surreptitious look at the bones in their feet.

In the case of older children style is becoming increasingly important. They will often forget about comfort if the shoe is attractive enough, and the X-ray machine must be used to make sure that the shoe is right for the foot. — Store owner, cited in United Shoe Machinery Corporation records, 1951

Though shoe-fitting fluoroscopes may have had some possible value in the fitting of shoes—and even this was disputed—their widespread use worried radiologists and public health departments. For the customer, radiation exposure was momentary, but relatively intense. Direct radiation was limited to the feet, with scattered X-rays sometimes hitting the legs and the lower body. Salespeople were exposed to the scattered radiation if they stood behind the customer.

After World War II, in response to worries about the abuse and overuse of shoe-fitting fluoroscopes, state and local governments around the country began to take measures to reduce the radiation hazards from the apparatus. The New York City

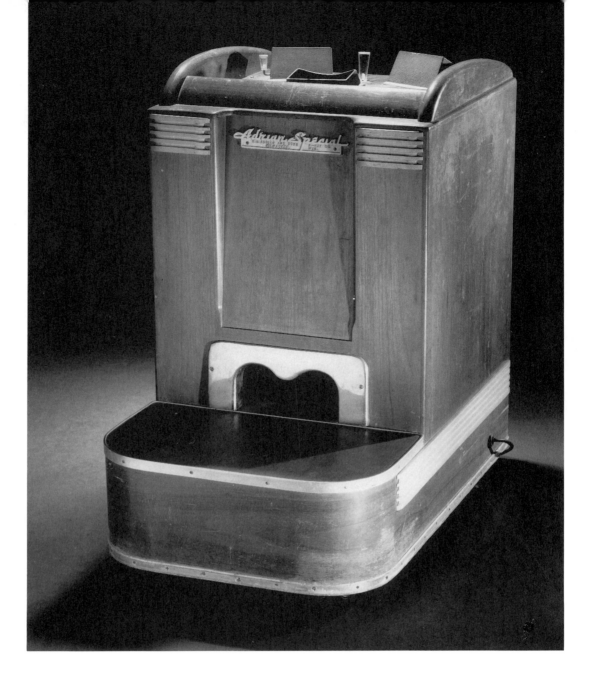

Sanitary Code of 1948, for example, required that "the maximum permissible dose per exposure ('exposure' being defined as a single viewing of one pair of shoes on the feet) shall not exceed 2 roentgens." Each machine had to be equipped with an automatic timer set to terminate the exposure after five seconds. The code required that a sign warning the customer of radiation hazards be posted in a conspicuous place with the message (in capital letters): "REPEATED EXPOSURE TO X-RAY MAY BE HARMFUL, INCLUDING THE EXPOSURE OF HUMAN FEET IN SHOES. FLUOROSCOPIC EXAMINATIONS FOR SHOE FITTING SHALL BE LIMITED TO THREE EXPOSURES IN ANY ONE DAY, AND SHALL BE LIMITED TO NOT MORE THAN A TOTAL OF 12 EXPOSURES IN ONE YEAR."

During the following decade, thirty-three states and the District of Columbia moved from regulating to prohibiting shoe-fitting fluoroscopes. The remaining states eventually fell into line. Most radiologists believe that fluoroscopes should have been banned because they could be, and probably were, used carelessly. Yet they likely did little overall damage since the feet can tolerate more radiation than sensitive areas such as the eyes and the gonads. It is doubtful that any genetic mutations resulted from their misuse. Nonetheless, they are gone, and almost totally forgotten. Salespeople of today must rely on the tried and true—unscientific, of course—thumb method to determine if the shoe fits. □

Slide
Rules

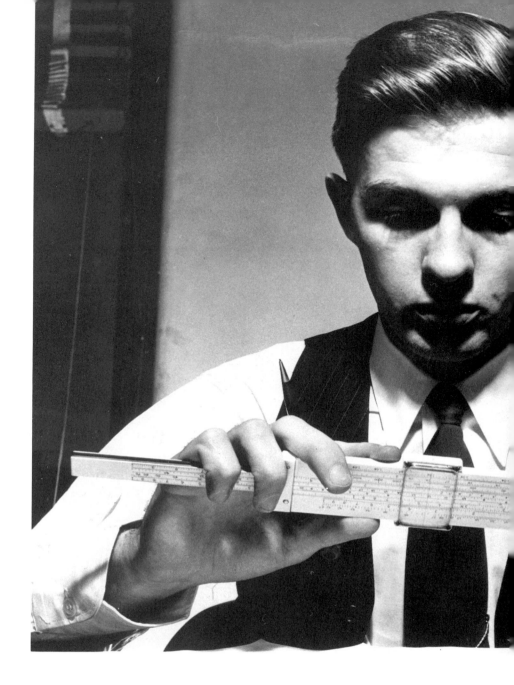

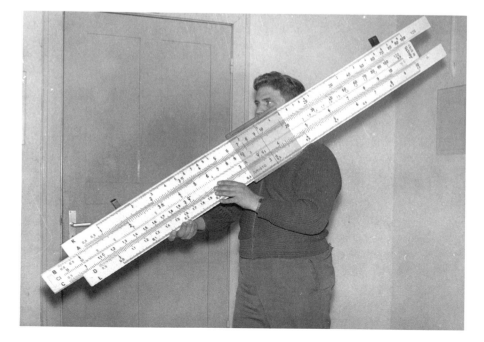

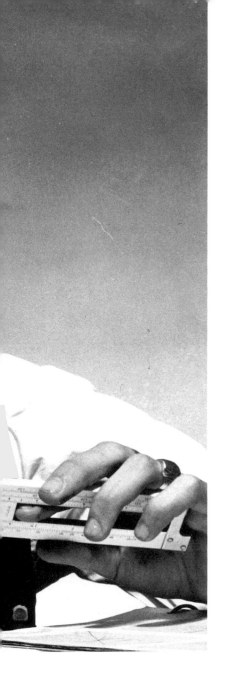

Buying a slide rule was a rite of passage for math and engineering students in the 1950s and 1960s. A boxwood and plastic model in a cardboard or Leatherette case cost $1.79. A newly graduated engineer or architect might spring for a mahogany inlaid version that cost as much as $40.00.

Despite the mystique that slide rules were only for the seriously brainy, they were actually not that difficult to use. The basic slide rule was composed of two parallel rulers that were printed or incised with numerical scales, and a third ruler, also marked with gradients, that slid between them. By lining up numbers on various scales, you could solve complicated problems of multiplication or division with simple addition and subtraction. You could also get a good estimate of the solutions to complex square root and trigonometric problems. The key word is *estimate* because the slide rule was an inexact device. If you had a good eye, you could make an acceptable approximation, and in most situations, a slight inaccuracy didn't matter.

Slide rules became common in Europe during the second half of the nineteenth century. They were indispensable to the bridge designers, railway builders, and civil engineers who built America. One engineer recalls that "nerd sticks," as they were frequently called, were "the very symbol" of his profession.

Keuffel and Esser, a manufacturer of scientific instruments, was the largest producer of slide rules in the U.S., selling as many as twenty thousand a month. In addition to basic student models, various manufacturers produced slide rules which computed the horsepower of engines and others that calculated the molecular weights of compounds. One slide rule was designed for surveyors, and another helped artillery officers calculate the trajectories of their weapons.

In 1967, Keuffel & Esser commissioned a report on the future of technology called *Life in the Year 2067*. The report predicted that people would live in domed cities and watch three-dimensional television. What it did not foresee, however, was that within less than a decade, K & E's best-known consumer product would be obsolete.

Dr. Robert Otnes, an engineer who collects scientific instruments, is the cofounder of an organization for people interested in the history of slide rules. Otnes and fellow members of the Oughtred Society (named for the seventeenth century English clergyman who invented the first slide rule) may be sentimental, but they are practical as well. "One of the happiest days of my life," Otnes says, "was when I got my first calculator."

The *Journal of the Oughtred Society* notes that "the slide rule switched from being a working tool to being a piece of junk somewhere between 1970 and 1975," when pocket-sized electronic calculators put slide rules out of business. These chip-based devices were more accurate than slides and almost as inexpensive. Parents may have deplored the introduction of calculators into the classroom, but they took the guesswork out of math and reduced the chance of computational error. In 1984, when an engineering professor asked his class of first-year students what a slide rule was, nobody could answer.

Keuffel & Esser stopped making slide rules in 1975, and their competitors soon followed. The transition came so fast that manufacturers were left with sizable inventories on the shelf. K & E now sells about a hundred slide rules a year, usually to scientific-instrument collectors and other buffs.

Once in a while, someone discovers a specialized use for the old-fashioned slide rule. Photographers, for example, who want to change the size of a print to fit into a display need to know what will happen to the height if one, or two, or three inches are added to the width. When they ask at an art store for a "proportional calculator," what they get is an old circular slide rule—one of the dwindling supply left behind by the microchip revolution. Working out the problem with an electronic calculator would require running a separate set of numbers for each inch they might add. The slide rule, on the other hand, displays at a glance the complete range of possible solutions.

While the superiority of the slide rule for such specific purposes is undeniable, it is not necessarily appealing. When one engineer showed off the versatility of a "proportional calculator" to his computer-age son, the boy said, "Frankly, Dad, I'd rather press buttons." □

As easy to set as a clock and as plain to read as a yard stick.
— Slogan for the Otis King slide rule, manufactured by Carbic Ltd., 1920s

During our Westward travels with the season, I asked many people what scent first came to mind at the mention of autumn. To some it was the fragrance of ripe grapes, to others the kitchen smells of canning and jelly-making, to others the aroma of the apple harvest; to most, I think, it was the scent of burning leaves.
— E. W. Teale, *Autumn Across America*, 1956

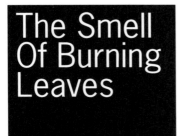

The Smell Of Burning Leaves

Across America, in the late October twilight, families gathered for an autumn ritual. Dad raked the dead oak, beech, and maple leaves from the lawn and gathered them in a big pile at the front curb. The kids jumped and rolled in the wet, sticky leaves, then helped their father reshape the pile for its real purpose: the bonfire.

Dad gave his lecture about using matches carefully. As the flames leaped high in the fall sky, kids threw chestnuts into the fire and heard them pop. Mom brought mugs of hot chocolate from the kitchen. Neighbors gathered to tend the blaze and share local gossip. An Iowa newspaperman remembers that a bonfire, like that other autumn ritual, the high school football game, needed to be watched, but not very carefully, for the chances were that nothing exciting was going to happen.

After the younger children were in bed, teenagers might linger, roasting marshmallows over the fading embers, but the night air was chilly, and there was homework to do. The sweet, pungent scent of a hundred smoking piles of burning leaves hung in the air for days.

Then, in the early 1970s, environmentalists warned that burning leaves and sap released chemicals and particles of ash that contributed to air pollution. Most communities banned bonfires; homeowners were required to use their leaves for compost or bag them and deposit the bundles at the town dump or incinerator.

Making your own compost heap is not without its problems. "To compost the leaves," instructs columnist Russell Baker, "all you do is rake them together in a pile approximately the same size as your house and then lie spread-eagled on them whenever a rising wind threatens to blow them back to where you raked them from."

Many suburbanites began to attack fallen leaves with a motorized arsenal. Having thrown out their old wire or bamboo rakes that were said to damage the lawn, they spent weekends deploying leaf blowers, choppers, and shredders that filled the autumn air with an unpleasant whine and a greasy exhaust. Huge mechanical sweepers pushed leaves that had fallen on roads and sidewalks into neat piles to be picked up by sanitation trucks and transported to at the village dump.

Within a decade, however, old dumps were overcrowded, proposed new landfill sites were rejected by local residents, and incinerators were closed down. In the late 1980s, the sanitation facilities of many towns and cities began rejecting bulky bags of leaves. Massachusetts now requires its citizens to deposit their fallen leaves in community compost heaps. Residents of Burlington, Vermont, who take their leaves to a community compost site can return in the spring to get mulch for their gardens.

Composting is expected to cost less than half the amount communities had been paying to dump or burn leaves, and it produces a rich natural soil additive that could be a low-cost benefit to nearby farmers. But kids can't jump in a compost heap, and no one would ever confuse its smell with the evocative aroma of burning leaves. ☐

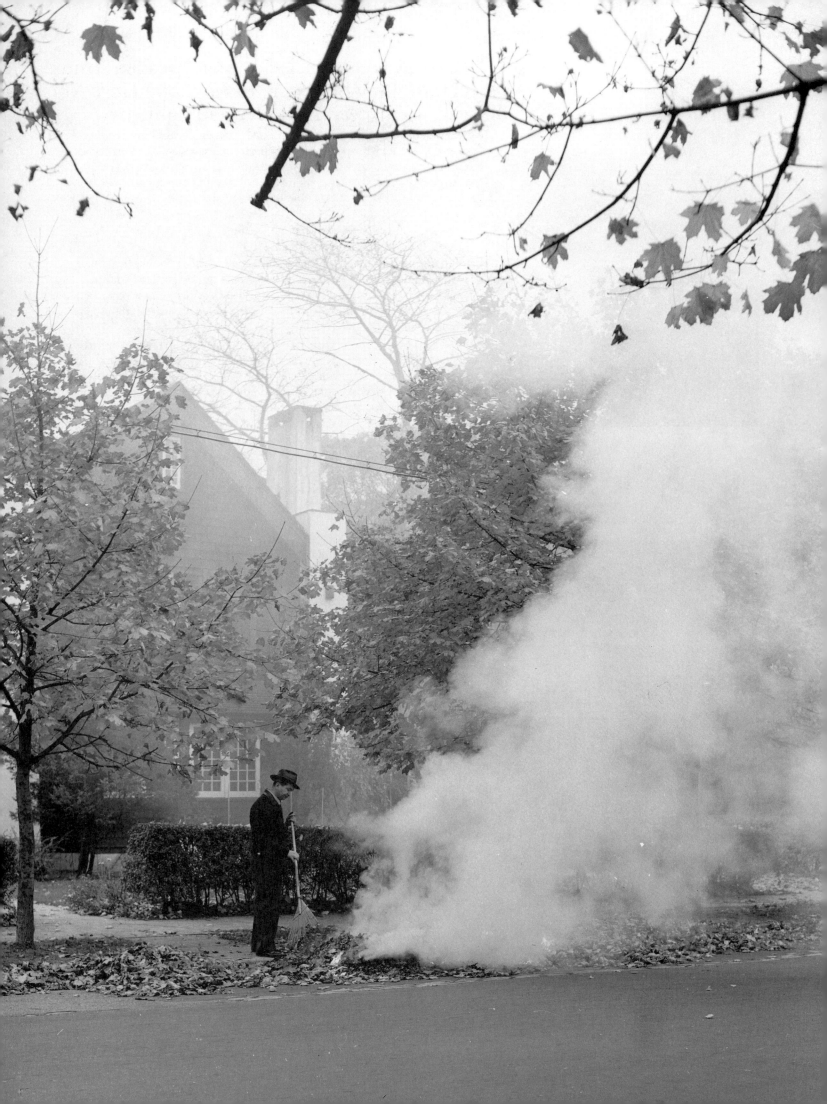

Smoking

"Anybody got a match?" Lauren Bacall murmurs to Humphrey Bogart in *To Have and Have Not.* In *Now, Yoyager,* Paul Henreid lights two cigarettes at once—his own and one for Bette Davis. In *Grease,* John Travolta makes his first appearance with a cigarette dangling from his lips, and the Pink Ladies initiate Olivia Newton-John in the ways of American high school students by teaching her to smoke. Call for Philip Morris! I'd Walk a Mile for a Camel. L.S.M.F.T.—Lucky Strikes Mean Fine Tobacco. Kent with the Micronite Filter. Us Tareyton Smokers would rather fight than switch. Winstons taste good like a cigarette should. The Marlboro Man. You've come a long way, baby.

Lauren Bacall started smoking because she idolized Bette Davis. "She was my heroine. She used cigarettes so dramatically, and I wanted to be like her." Smoking stood for sophistication and sex appeal. Becoming a smoker led to adulthood, glamorous careers, an air of worldliness. It also led to cancer, emphysema, and heart disease. Bogart, a heavy smoker on-screen and off, died of cancer of the esophagus— a smoking-related malignancy—in 1957.

Since the late 1920s, studies have connected smoking with high rates of heart and lung disease. But those unpleasant realities were ignored by the public until 1964 when Luther Terry, the surgeon general of the United States, alerted the nation to the link between tobacco and heightened risk of disease and death. Only with the surgeon general's report summarizing decades of scientific evidence did the antismoking crusade finally take off.

Since then an estimated fifty million Americans have kicked the habit. In 1964, sixty-four percent of all adults smoked; in 1990 twenty-five percent did. Antismoking campaigns spawned an industry of hypnotists, behavior modification programmers, acupuncturists, addiction counselors, and manufacturers of devices from nicotine-free cigarettes, to worry beads, to what are basically adult pacifiers. For a time, dinner parties came to resemble impromptu twelve-step confessional

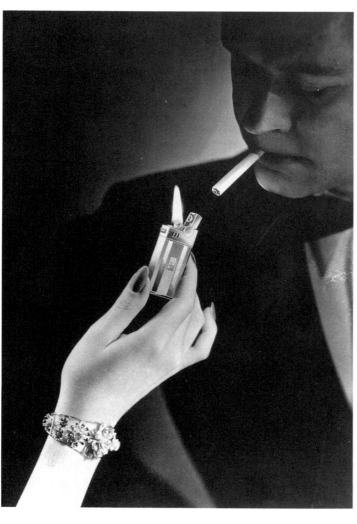

sessions, as guests competed with ever more harrowing stories about the anguish of breaking their addiction. Humorist Art Buchwald wrote that during withdrawal, he could think of little else. "I would want to write about the MX missile system and the only thing that came out was 'Puff the Magic Dragon.' The song 'Smoke Gets in Your Eyes' droned in my head."

Scorn for smokers became institutionalized in smoking/ nonsmoking divisions in restaurants and airplanes, and outright bans on cigarettes in many public places. Reprobate employees were forced to hit the streets for a furtive smoke.

On the theory that young, potential smokers are influenced by role models, antitobacco activists encouraged movie and television producers to eliminate smoking from their productions whenever possible. Major league baseball players were forbidden to smoke in uniform. In 1971 Congress banned cigarette ads on television. To get around what an industry spokesman called "health and safety fascism," the cigarette companies sponsored popular televised sports events and placed their billboards within camera range in stadiums and arenas. They widely publicized their lavish contributions to museums, opera productions, ballet companies, and traveling displays of Americana.

Public health officials originally hoped for a smoke-free America by the year 2000. A more realistic projection is that only fifteen percent of the population will be smoking at century's end. Despite repeated reminders from the surgeon general's office that smoking remains the "chief avoidable cause of death in our society," people still puff away. One government official has said, "We've been successful convincing people to stop smoking, but we can't keep them from starting." The Federal Centers for Disease Control estimates that every day three thousand smokers take up the habit. Annual polls of college freshmen have showed that the number who smoked declined between 1966 and 1987 but has

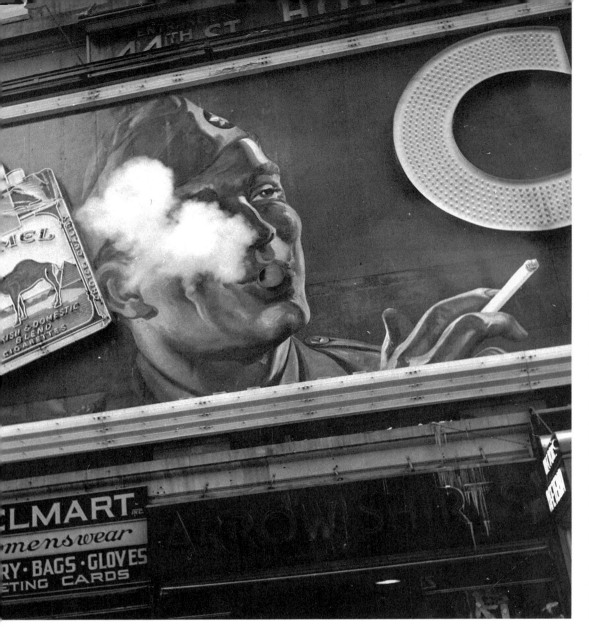

risen slightly each year thereafter. In general, the more education people have, the less likely they are to smoke. As many as seventy-five percent of high school dropouts are nicotine addicts.

Walk past any American high school at break time and see the number of students who light up as soon as they leave the building. Teenagers get hooked for the same reasons their parents and grandparents did— it seems chic, grown-up, rebellious, and besides they're going to live forever.

On March 9, 1992, Surgeon General Antonia Novello and an official of the American Medical Association announced the first-ever campaign against a single brand of cigarettes alleged to appeal especially to young people. The AMA has released studies showing that Joe Camel, a cartoon character who figures prominently in R. J. Reynolds ads and promotions, is as familiar to six-year-olds as Mickey Mouse, and Camel is the preferred brand of young smokers ages twelve to seventeen. Other brands have attracted teenaged customers with campaigns that show carefree smokers in their twenties playing tennis, skiing, sailing, and sharing intimate moments with friends. Cigarette makers deny that they're trying to woo adolescents; they claim they're pushing smoking as an "adult choice." But an AMA executive believes the tobacco companies are being less than candid. "This is an industry that kills four hundred thousand Americans per year; they have to pick up new customers." ☐

I'm sending Chesterfields to all my friends. That's the merriest Christmas any smoker can have—Chesterfield mildness plus no unpleasant after-taste.— Ronald Reagan, Liggett & Myers Tobacco Company ad, 1951

Soda Fountains

The year: 1952. The scene: Mallory's Drug Store on Allegheny Street in Bellefonte, Pennsylvania, where teenagers met every day after school.

They leafed through the latest comic books and true romance magazines, then giggled at the display of trusses and orthopedic aids. Girls swung by the cosmetics counter to try on samples of "Fire and Ice," Revlon's latest lipstick sensation. The tables in the back were reserved for couples. Everyone else jostled for the swivel stools that lined the marble counter along one side of the store.

Behind the counter, the soda jerk—who earned the name from the practice of jerking the fountain handles forward to draw soda water into a glass—served up strawberry floats, cherry Cokes, double chocolate malteds, and black-and-white sodas. It took talent to flip a scoop of vanilla ice cream into a glass, add a dollop of chocolate syrup, and shoot a thin stream of carbonated water to raise a delicious foam of chocolate bubbles.

Soda fountains were immortalized in films like *Love Finds Andy Hardy*, in which Mickey Rooney and Judy Garland flirted over straws and sodas. Offscreen, the counter at Schwab's Drugstore on Sunset Boulevard was the fabled hangout for would-be actors and starlets hoping for their first break. Legend has it that Lana Turner was "discovered" while sipping a soda at Schwab's.

From the 1860s until nearly a century later, almost every corner drugstore had a soda fountain of marble, gleaming metal, and glass. Inside an early model, ice was packed around syrup containers and tubes that carried carbonated water up from the cellar where it was stored in large vats. Silver-plated spigots—sometimes two or three, sometimes as many as one hundred—were each inscribed with the flavor of the syrup they dispensed: strawberry, lemon, and sarsaparilla, or, less frequently, claret and wintergreen. Above the spigots, larger taps pumped carbonated water and artificial mineral waters—soda water mixed with mineral salts to imitate the "curative" waters of famous European and American spas.

Soda water brought drugstores and soda fountains together. For centuries, the sick and dyspeptic drank naturally carbonated mineral waters at fashionable spas for relief from constipation, indigestion, and bad livers. People tried, and failed, to add carbon dioxide bubbles to plain water, until 1767, when Rev. Joseph Priestley of Leeds, England (who also discovered oxygen), produced a carbonated liquid by pouring water back and forth between two glasses held above fermenting mash which gave off carbon dioxide.

A New York manufacturer of carbonating machinery named John Matthews is credited with the invention of the soda fountain. Matthews was constantly on the lookout for new sources of carbon dioxide. After the completion of St. Patrick's Cathedral in New York, he bought all the leftover marble—a source of calcium carbonate from which CO_2 can be released. From it he generated twenty-five million gallons of soda water. When he died, Matthews was buried in Brooklyn in a thirty-six-foot-high mausoleum shaped like a soda fountain.

Doctors endorsed soda water as a cure for obesity, and pharmacists soon realized its money-making potential. In 1825 an apothecary named Elias Durand opened the first "modern" drugstore on the corner of Sixth and Chestnut streets in Philadelphia. Doctors, scientists, and members of the literary establishment gathered at his store to talk and gossip while drinking carbonated water drawn from the small urn-shaped apparatus that sat on the counter. Other entrepreneurs added flavored soda waters to their fountains as well as syrup pumps. The fountains were decorated in all the popular styles of the day—Roman, Gothic, Byzantine, Egyptian, Japanese—and had names like the Icefloe, the Peoria, and the Naxos.

Robert M. Green, inventor of the ice-cream soda, had the soft-drink concession at the Franklin Institute Exposition in Philadelphia in 1874. His best-seller was a concoction of sweet cream, syrup, and carbonated water—until he ran out of cream. In desperation he bought some vanilla ice cream which he intended to melt, but his customers wouldn't wait. So he used the ice cream as it was. The innovation was a hit.

By the 1900s soda fountains across the land were selling a variety of tasty drinks as fast as they appeared on the market: Hires Root Beer, Dr. Pepper's, and Moxie were supposed to be healthy, and during Prohibition, they were touted as nonalcoholic thirst quenchers. But "The Great National Temperance Drink," as early ads proclaimed, was Coca-Cola, which sold for five cents and was guaranteed to make the people who drank it "healthy and happy."

In the 1920s, refrigeration allowed fountain operators to expand their business. They prepared and served entire meals, not just a snacks. Fountains appeared in department stores, groceries, five-and-dimes, and luncheonettes. Americans got used to eating on the run.

During World War II, soda jerks were drafted, sugar was rationed, and fountain equipment was not manufactured. Afterward, soda fountains never fully revived.

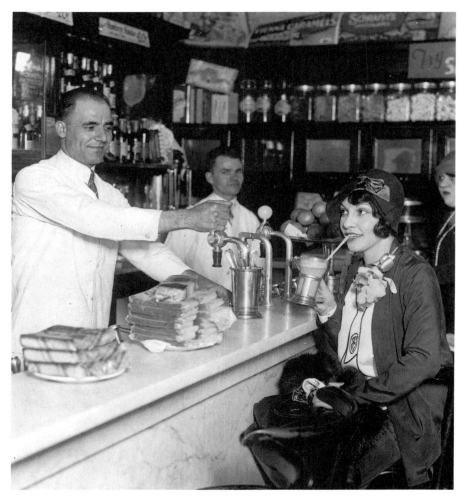

Drugstore owners earned a better return on cosmetics, nylon stockings, and packaged snacks than on handmade fountain treats. Downtown luncheonettes lost business to the restaurant chains along the interstates and in suburban shopping malls. Fast-food franchises took up the slack, and the soft-drink companies wooed them instead of fountain owners. People became impatient with the time it took to make sodas and shakes; they quickly got used to the mass-produced and prepackaged "shakes" available at the local burger joint.

In recent years, a hundred or so old-fashioned soda fountains have popped up in self-consciously restored downtown malls and urban museums. Soda jerks, dressed in immaculate white jackets and wearing caps at a rakish angle, pump drinks from vintage equipment. Fancy ice-cream "shoppes" serve expensive, ultrarich sundaes, topped with sprinkles, nuts, and whipped cream. A woman in Omaha, Nebraska, has founded a national association of former soda jerks, dedicated to the preservation of this small slice of American nostalgia. The group has a tough road ahead, because most people under twenty-five have no idea what a black-and-white soda is. □

Walgreens' Double-Rich Malted Milk Recipe (1922)

1 1/2 oz. chocolate syrup
Three #16 dips of vanilla ice cream
5 1/2 oz. cold milk
Add one heaping tablespoon malt powder.
Place on mixer only until mixed.
Use a generous portion of whipped topping in a #1808-10 oz. glass.
Pour malted milk in glass approximately 2/3 full.

Stockings

Half a century ago Du Pont announced the invention of a fiber spun out of coal tar, air, and water that was reputed to be "as strong as steel yet as fine as a spider's web." Nylon was the first textile fiber made entirely from chemicals, and it changed the hosiery business forever.

The new synthetic arrived just in time. By the late 1930s, America was the world's largest producer of silk stockings, but the possibility of war with Japan imperiled the source of silk fiber. Nylon was the culmination of work begun in the Wilmington, Delaware, lab of Du Pont chemist Wallace Carothers. In 1935 he and his research team discovered a molten polymer that could be drawn into filaments, cooled, and stretched to form very strong but sheer fibers. The new discovery combined the transparency of silk with the strength of cotton or wool.

After a two-year search for practical applications, a Du Pont researcher carried a top-secret package of the miracle fiber hidden in his coat to Frederick, Maryland, for an experiment on an industrial knitting machine. Although the first nylon stockings emerged from the dye bath yellow and wrinkled, the commercial possibilities of the fiber were striking. But what to call it? Du Pont tried to come up with a catchy name for the product. A committee considered *Wacara*, after inventor Wallace Carothers, and *Duparooh* (Du Pont Pulls a Rabbit Out of its Hat). They settled on *no run*, because the fabric was far less fragile than silk. *Norun* wasn't quite right, so they tried variants: *nuron* sounded too brainlike; *nulon* was too much like an existing patent name; finally *nylon* won the day.

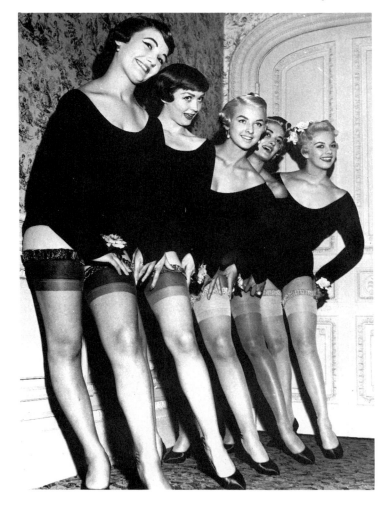

Du Pont unveiled its new product during the New York World's Fair of 1939. At the company's exhibit, four young women each nicknamed "Miss Chemistry" sat in beautiful dresses with their legs crossed to show off their glamorous sheer stockings. When the new hosiery went on sale in May 1940, crowds in many cities gathered behind rope barricades waiting for stores to open. Customers in New York City bought seventy-two thousand pairs the first day. The bottom fell out of the Japanese silk market. Even though silk stockings cost about sixty-five cents, everyone wanted nylons, as they were called for short, which sold at the then hefty price of $1.15 a pair.

After the attack on Pearl Harbor, nylon was commandeered for America's war effort. All available production went into parachutes, belts, tents, and other military uses. Women were asked to donate their old stockings to the scrap drive for recycling into aircraft tires. Reluctantly, they turned back to cotton and rayon hose, which bagged and sagged. Some women covered their legs with brown makeup and drew eyebrow-pencil "seams" up the back. A popular ditty of the day lamented that "cotton is monotonous to men, / only way to keep affection fresh, / get some mesh fo' yo' flesh.../ I'll be happy when the nylons bloom again."

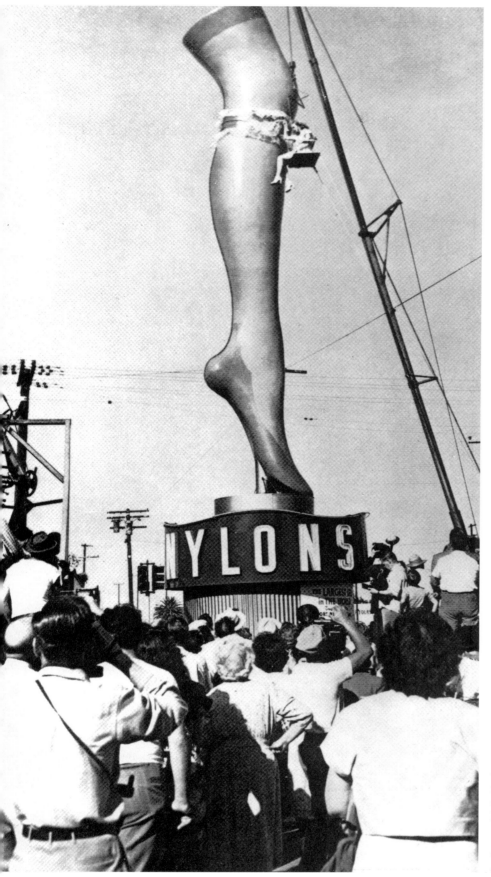

When the war ended, consumers assumed nylon stockings would be available right away. Instead, only a limited supply trickled into stores, causing near riots as thousands of women fought to get their hands on a single pair. "Nylons gobbled up by Throngs" read one Indianapolis headline. "Women Risk Life and Limb in Bitter Battle for Nylons" declared the Augusta, Georgia, *Chronicle*. Fortunately, nationwide sales resumed in mid-May of 1946; in the first few hours four million pairs of nylons were sold.

In the postwar years, innovative knitting machines produced a seamless tube of fabric, eliminating one of life's nagging little problems: "Are my seams straight?" The new yarns stretched to fit the contours of the body. Three or four flexible size ranges replaced the old increments of 6, 6 1/2, 7, 7 1/2, 8, etc., that had complicated the manufacturing process and store inventories. Runs were still a problem, but women devised a low-tech solution—a dab of clear nail polish.

In the mid-1960s, when the miniskirt placed fashion's focus on the legs, women were desperate for hosiery that went all the way to their thighs. Waiting in the wings was a garment that had only recently been introduced as a specialty item—a waist-high product targeted primarily for dancers and theater folk. Pantyhose and miniskirts were a perfect fit.

Industry analysts predicted that the craze for toe-to-waist hosiery would end as soon as hemlines dropped. But women had no intention of going back to stockings, with their uncomfortable and inconvenient garters belts and garters. By the early 1970s, pantyhose of nylon or nylon blend had captured seventy percent of the hosiery market. They maintained their dominance for the next twenty years.

Only three percent of the women in America continue to wear stockings. Most of them are elderly, though another segment of the market consists of young women who think stockings are sexy. There's something provocative about a bare bit of flesh at the top of the thigh and all that alluring paraphernalia to put on and take off: lacy garter belts, merry widows, rubber-tipped garters with satin ribbons. Since they grew up with pantyhose, they look upon stockings as a novelty—definitely something their mothers would never wear. □

Suntans

In the nineteenth century, fair, indeed pallid, skin was fashionable. It meant you were "sensitive"—possibly even tubercular—or a member of the upper classes, who stayed indoors while servants and laborers were forced to work for hours in the hot sun. After World War I, as more people participated in active sports, suntans conveyed higher status. A tan in January meant you were affluent enough to afford a winter vacation. A year-round glow indicated you were free to spend hours at the beach or on the tennis court.

By the 1950s a bronzed complexion was a summer necessity. You baked for hours, lathered with tanning creams, or cocoa butter and baby oil, which actually fried your skin. Sometimes you fashioned a foil-covered reflector to gather in every bit of the sun's rays. A lobster-colored nose and shoulders, which developed painful blisters and then peeling splotches, were explained away as "putting down a base coat."

Golden skin went with a perfect body. Starlets posed on the beaches of Cannes and Malibu, exposing as much sun-baked flesh as the censors would allow. Bodybuilders bronzed themselves so their muscles would be better defined. Actor George Hamilton built an entire career on maintaining the perfect tan. Even intellectuals liked to glow. In 1950, when she was seventeen, poet Sylvia Plath bragged to a boyfriend about a tan so admirable that women stopped on the beach to ask what suntan lotion she used. Fellow poet Anne Sexton wrote that lying on the beach and letting the sun wash over her was "like having intercourse with God."

During the 1980s, dermatologists noted an alarming increase in skin cancers. The incidence of melanoma, which can be fatal if not promptly treated, began rising faster than that of any other malignancy. By the early 1990s, melanoma was the most common form of cancer for women in their twenties and second only to breast cancer for women in their thirties.

The sun reverberated off the buildings with the brilliance of a handful of diamonds cast against an iceberg, the shimmering white was blinding, as Sabrina lay naked on a deck chair in the heat of the Los Angeles sun. She lay sparkling and oiled, warmed to a honey brown by the relentless sun.
— Danielle Steel, *Secrets*, 1985

Dermatologists have argued for years that there's no such thing as a safe tan. Basically, any tanning is a sign of injury to the skin. The American Medical Association says a tan conveys no healthy benefits except an "enhanced image of personal worth." Children are particularly at risk; their skin is very sensitive, and they're more likely than adults to spend long hours out-of-doors. Redheads know they must be careful, but dark-complexioned people forget they can get a burn from reflecting surfaces like glass, sand, or snow.

Ninety percent of the estimated six hundred thousand cases of skin cancer diagnosed each year in the U.S. are caused by exposure to ultraviolet rays emitted by the sun. During the 1970s and 1980s, scientists observed that these cancer-causing rays were becoming a greater threat than ever before. Normally the direct passage of ultraviolet rays from the sun is blocked by the ozone layer—a protective layer of gases in the earth's upper atmosphere. However, the ozone layer itself has been under assault. Ozone depletion is occurring at least three times faster than anticipated.

Ozone depletion is caused by increased levels of chlorine in the upper atmosphere. The chlorine comes from the breakdown of chlorofluorocarbon (CFC) molecules as they rise through the air. For decades, chlorofluorocarbons were used in an ever-expanding number of industrial applications: as cleansing aids, as blowing agents for plastic foam, in air conditioners for buildings and cars, in refrigerators, as fuel for space shuttles and airplanes, and as propellants in aerosol sprays.

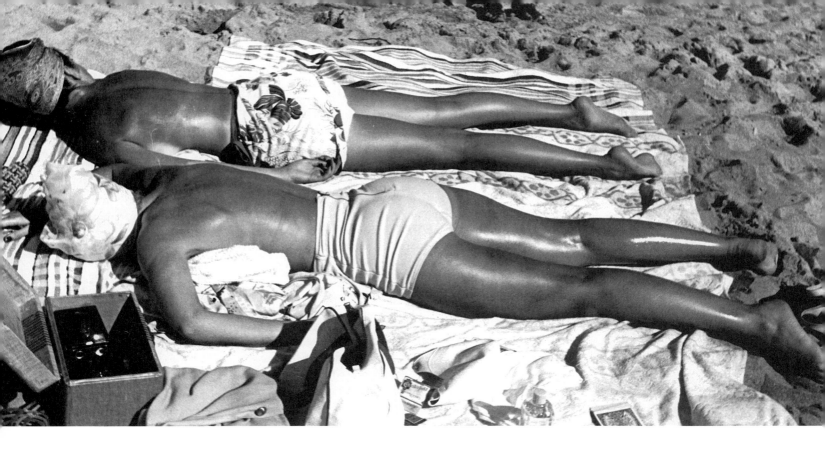

Ninety-three industrialized nations have agreed to eliminate the production of CFCs by the year 2000. CFC propellants in aerosol cans are already banned, and CFCs used in refrigerators and air conditioners will soon be recycled rather than expelled into the air. But even if CFCs are phased out completely by the year 2000, it may take fifty years for the amount of chlorine to retreat to 1990 levels, and until the end of the twenty-first century for the ozone layer to restore itself.

In the meantime people have begun to take special measures to escape the pernicious effects of ozone depletion. Skin cancers are preventable. The most dangerous ultraviolet rays can be avoided by wearing a hat and protective clothing. One dermatologist recommends adopting a "Spanish lifestyle—stay indoors from late morning till late afternoon."

Another solution is to lather on protection. Sunblocks protect the wearer by absorbing the ultraviolet rays or deflecting them away from the surface of the skin. Coppertone, which marketed the first successful tanning cream to American consumers in 1944, devised the acronym SPF (sun protection factor) in 1977. Cosmetic companies are pushing creams, lotions, and powders in a confusing array of SPFs from SPF 2 (for die-hard seekers of an old-fashioned dark, brown, leathery look) to SPF 50 (which should protect a fair-skinned Norwegian in the Sahara at high noon).

After a decade of warnings, people are certainly aware of the risks. The volleyball game on the beach begins with a debate about the merits of SPF 15 for the first twenty minutes vs. SPF 8 for the whole day. In 1991 many women reported using more sunscreen lotions and spending less time in the sun than they had five years earlier. Mothers said they were especially vigilant about protecting their young children.

But it's hard to give up the healthy feeling that comes with "a little bit of color" on your cheeks. Cosmetic companies and the fashion press still treat tans with respect. In the swimsuit issue of *Sports Illustrated*, in the annual spring fashion spreads of the glossy magazines, on billboards, and in commercials, tan gods and goddesses run through the surf, ride horseback, and hoist sails under a tropical sun without a care. Melanoma seems far away. When all else fails, dermatologists try to frighten the young and glamorous with the specter of wrinkles and premature aging.

Unlike the self-righteous citizens who publicly castigate smokers or drinkers, the sun police have not yet hit their stride. But one woman who has achieved the skin tone of a good French handbag after years of lolling on the beach says she is more defensive than she used to be. "I hear a critical note now when people comment on my tan. I don't admit to lying out in the sun. I tell them I've just been gardening too much." □

Teenage Dating

High school kids today still go bowling, they still hang out at the mall, they go to movies the minute they open, they throw parties as soon as their parents leave the house, and they hog the family car. They fall in love, and out of love, with tragic intensity. What they don't do anymore is date.

"Dating just doesn't exist," says a high school senior in New Hampshire. "What? Have a guy pick you up at your house, shake hands with your parents, and promise to bring you home by eleven? He pays for dinner and a movie. You kiss him goodnight. Then go through the whole thing all over again with some other guy the next night? Gross!"

A twenty-year-old college student from San Francisco claims, "I've never been on a date in my life. You go out with friends, and you just meet someone somewhere. You spend a few hours with her, and then you decide if you want to see her again. If you do, you're certainly not going to see anybody else. That seems to eliminate the dating process. It isn't a formal institution anymore."

Before the 1920s courtship was a precursor to marriage. A proper young man "called on" a young woman whom he or his parents had decided was a suitable potential spouse. Her parents joined them in the parlor, and everyone made small talk. Eventually the young couple were allowed to be alone in the house or the garden. If they got serious, they exchanged a chaste kiss. In theory, that's all they did until they were married.

By the end of World War II, courtship had changed. There was Dating. A nervous teenager telephoned the girl he sat next to in algebra class. They hemmed and hawed about homework. Finally he asked her for a date. If he called after Wednesday for the upcoming weekend, she was in a quandary: Should she accept, or did that make her seem too eager? She preferred to be booked two weeks in advance. Finally, they agreed on the time and place. She spent the afternoon of the big day giggling with girlfriends about what to wear. She had several pairs of "party" shoes: flats for short boys, Cuban heels for someone just her height, and spikes for a member of the basketball team. All he worried about was having a clean shirt; he owned only one good jacket and tie.

She often saw the same movie twice in one weekend because she didn't want to tell Saturday's date what she'd done the night before. All through the evening there was

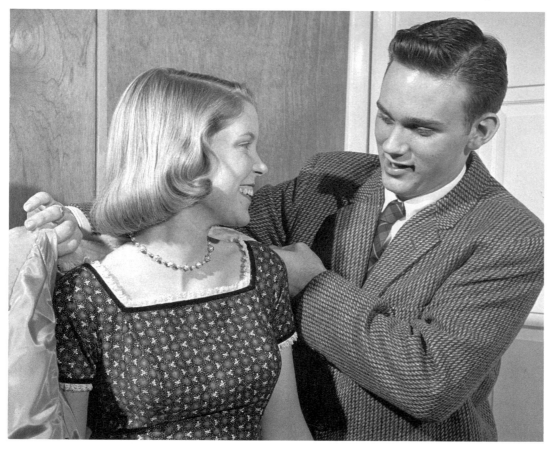

unspoken tension about how it would end. Should they kiss on a first date? When was it permissible to French kiss, neck, or pet above the waist? It was never officially acceptable to do more. Nice girls didn't go all the way, but they had more trouble saying no if they were Going Steady. Dating was not so much about collecting suitors as it was about avoiding sex.

Today kids often start going out with each other as early as fifth grade. By the time they're in high school, they have the routine down pat. They start calling each other in midafternoon to find out where the action is. It takes hours to coordinate the plans of a dozen teenagers. Sometimes they don't leave home till ten at night. They come and go in packs. Then suddenly two of them pair off and spend the next six weeks or six years together.

146

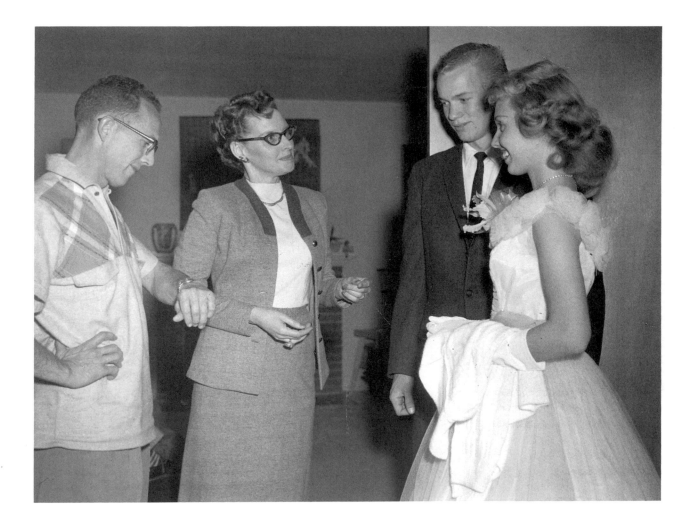

Dating is a casualty of the sexual revolution. Most teenagers who pair off are sexually active, and even in these liberal times, it is difficult to maintain two or more sexual relationships simultaneously. Anybody who tries is often condemned. An eighteen-year-old girl from San Francisco explains. "If you go out with more than one guy at a time, you're a slut. Maybe years ago, when you went out with someone several times and didn't sleep with him, you could get away with it. But now—of course you're sleeping with someone if you're dating him. So everyone would know you were sleeping with more than one person at a time. That's always been a slut." □

Marcy stood back from the full-length mirror on her closet door for a last reassuring look at herself. Her hair had turned out well too. Certainly Steve should be impressed with her tonight.

Steve stood with Marcy's father in the lower hall and, just as she had hoped, at the sound of her footsteps he turned up and looked at her. . . . Her mother came downstairs and they all stood and talked for a few minutes before Marcy and Steve said good night and started to leave.

"Take it easy Steve," Marcy's father warned. "There are so many crazy drivers on the road New Year's Eve."

— Rosamond du Jardin, *Senior Prom*, 1957

Telegrams

For many generations of Americans, news of life's milestones—birth and marriage, death and divorce, war and peace—arrived first by a yellow Western Union telegram: "IT'S A BOY." "NEED $100 STOP SEND SOONEST." "WE REGRET TO INFORM YOU . . ."

Even before the light bulb and the telephone were invented, Samuel F. B. Morse had demonstrated the first practical use for electricity: sending messages along the length of a wire. On September 2, 1835, while teaching at New York University, Morse stretched seventeen hundred feet of wire from one classroom to another. He then transmitted signals from a sending instrument at one end of the wire to a receiver at the other end by interrupting the electrical current in patterns that could be translated into text.

On January 6, 1838, Morse invited an investor, Judge Stephen Vail, to witness the machine in operation. On a slip of paper the judge wrote, "A patient waiter is no loser." The message was encoded in a series of dots and dashes forever associated with Morse's name, transmitted across three miles of wire stretched around the room, and deciphered in front of the judge's eyes.

Morse demonstrated the miracle to Congress on May 24, 1844. With Dolley Madison, Henry Clay, and other dignitaries looking on, he tapped out a now-famous message, "What hath God wrought!" The words were flashed via an experimental telegraph line along the railroad tracks linking Washington to Baltimore, forty miles away. The first telegram, which arrived at the railroad depot in Baltimore in an instant, opened the age of telecommunications.

The Western Union Telegraph Company was established in 1856, with lines crisscrossing the country as far west as St. Joseph, Missouri. Telegraph lines followed railway lines. At first the company strung wire from town to town on high telegraph poles. Later, cables—which could carry more messages—were suspended from poles in open country or buried underground in populous areas.

With the outbreak of the Civil War, communication with the Far West became essential. It was estimated that ten years would be needed to string a two-thousand-mile line across the plains from Missouri to the Pacific. President Abraham Lincoln

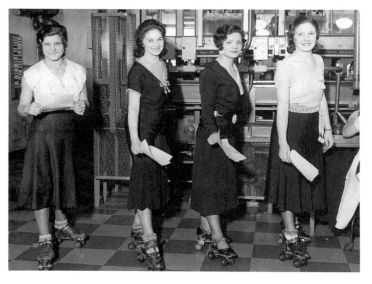

told the head of Western Union, "I think it is a wild scheme. It will be next to impossible to get your poles and materials distributed on the plains, and as fast as you complete the line, the Indians will cut it down."

In fact, the project took only 112 days. Lines uniting the East and the West were joined at Salt Lake City on October 24, 1861. In the first transcontinental telegram ever sent, Chief Justice Stephen Field of California assured President Lincoln that California would "stand by the Union . . . on this, its day of trial."

The generals of the Civil War made ample use of the telegraph on the battlefield. Telegraphese had not yet been invented, so messages were delivered in full sentences, with full punctuation. After the first engagement of the war, Gen. Pierre G.T. Beauregard, newly appointed commander of the forces of the South, acknowledged the flag of truce hoisted by Maj. Robert Anderson, the Union commander of Fort Sumter. Beauregard wired Anderson: "I SEE YOUR CONDITION THROUGH MY TELESCOPE. WE HAVE INTERCEPTED YOUR SUPPLIES. GIVE IN LIKE A GOOD FELLOW, AND BRING YOUR GARRISON TO DINNER, AND BEDS AFTERWARDS. NOBODY INJURED, I HOPE?"

After the war, Western Union expanded its network to keep pace with the westward expansion of settlers, industry, and railroads. The tap-tap of Morse key and sounder became familiar throughout the country. Because the company charged by the word, telegraphese became a noticeable style. Western Union introduced other new services for a growing America: stock tickers, money transfers, and time signals. Until time was standardized in 1883, the company was known as "The Nation's Timekeeper."

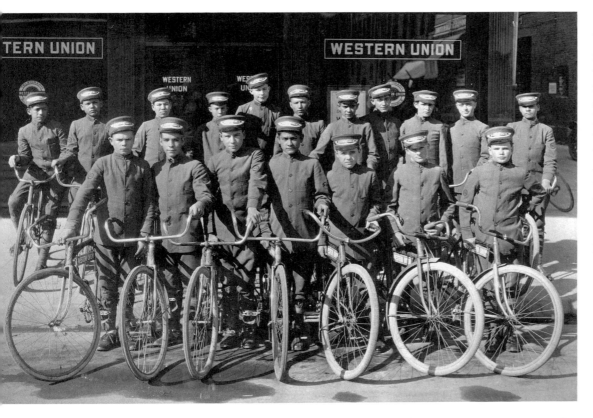

From the start, Western Union's employees were part of its public image. Rigorously trained and snappily dressed, its messengers were expected to serve the public no matter what hardship might be involved, whether sailing twelve thousand miles to hand-deliver a telegram to the president of the Boer Republic during his war with England or climbing a flagpole to deliver a message to "Shipwreck" Kelly. Company linemen braved the Johnstown flood of 1888 to relay early reports to the newspapers and raced to reestablish links with San Francisco after the 1906 earthquake. In the 1930s and 1940s, at Western Union switching centers in major cities, women on roller skates rushed reperforated tape from receivers to printers to transmit messages across the nation. So important was the company's devotion to decorum that, during the 1930s, its fourteen thousand messengers were outfitted by a department whose sole function was wardrobe.

The Singing Telegram was inaugurated in 1933 when an operator sang "Happy Birthday" to crooner Rudy Vallee. After Walter Winchell mentioned the unusual greeting in his column, the novelty became one of Western Union's most popular services. In 1935 the company offered the first of its standardized-text holiday messages, a Christmas greeting illustrated by Norman Rockwell that could be sent anywhere in the United States for twenty-five cents. Soon the company added Bunnygrams, Storkgrams, Kiddiegrams, Melodygrams, and Cigargrams.

The punch, brevity, and immediacy of telegrams made them the perfect medium for most people's messages. The impresario Florenz Ziegfeld, a prodigious telegram sender, preferred Western Union to face-to-face communication with his chorus line: "ANY GIRL WHO CHANGES OR TWISTS HER HAT WILL BE FIRED." Some telegrams have become famous. George S. Kaufman sent the following message to actor Billy Gaxton, who was performing in Kaufman's *Of Thee I Sing*: "WATCHING YOUR PERFORMANCE FROM LAST ROW. WISH YOU WERE HERE."

World War II began and ended in a hail of telegrams. From the British Admiralty, September 3, 1939: "IMMEDIATE. SPECIAL TELEGRAM. *TOTAL* GERMANY." Adm. Chester Nimitz, commander in chief, U.S. Fifth Fleet, to the forces under his command: "THE WAR WITH JAPAN WILL END AT 1200 ON 15TH AUGUST. IT IS LIKELY THAT KAMIKAZES WILL ATTACK THE FLEET AFTER THIS TIME AS A FINAL FLING. ANY EX-ENEMY AIRCRAFT ATTACKING THE FLEET IS TO BE SHOT DOWN IN A FRIENDLY MANNER."

After the war, the use of telegrams diminished. Perhaps the decline was inevitable once the telephone was invented, though it took a century before the advantages of the one technology completely swept the other away. As telephone systems improved and the cost of calls dropped, communicating by telegram became inefficient and expensive. The once-heralded messengers were a liability in time and money. Improved long-distance phone service and, eventually, computers and faxes provided faster, cheaper, and easier options.

These days, telegrams are ceremonial, since real news comes in other forms. But something has been lost. No other communication has such a sense of urgency. No other compels you to stop what you are doing and pay attention—your heart pounding until you learn the best or the worst from the terse message spelled out on the yellow sheet inside. ☐

Tonsillectomies

"You won't feel a thing" was the lure, and "all the ice cream you can eat" was the reward. In between was the tonsillectomy—a chapter in the history of American childhoods that used to be as predictable as the first day of school and the loss of baby teeth.

Tonsils are small spongy lymphoid glands designed by nature to protect the respiratory tract from infectious bacteria and viruses. There are three pairs of tonsils: the linguals, at the base of the tongue; the palatines, farther back in the throat; and the pharyngeals, also known as adenoids, which flank the back of the nose. When tonsils are swollen, it usually means that they are hard at work bringing disease-fighting white blood cells to the area to help protect a person from getting sick or sicker. Since young children suffer from so many colds and ear infections, it is sometimes hard to say the tonsils do much good. Until a few decades ago, the conventional wisdom was that, after a few infections, they might as well come out.

For the average schoolchild, a tonsillectomy—which usually involved the removal of the palatines and the adenoids—was his or her first brush with any medical remedy more complicated than Vicks VapoRub and bed rest. The frightened child was hospitalized, anesthetized, and then deposited in a strange room after a procedure that lasted about an hour. The patient woke up with a slightly sore throat,

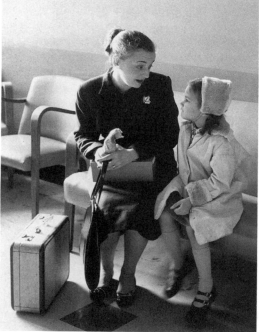

which was soothed with soft foods like egg custard and vanilla ice cream. The child went home a day or two later, although the sore throat got worse after several days. By the end of the second week, the whole experience was reduced to a vaguely unpleasant memory, with a jar containing the excised tonsils in formaldehyde as the only souvenir of the ordeal.

For much of the twentieth century, tonsillectomies were the most commonly performed surgery in America. In the mid-1960s they accounted for nearly half of all the operations each year. (Hernia repairs were a distant second, and appendectomies third.) Yet there was mounting evidence that the operation was virtually useless in an overwhelming number of cases.

Most preschoolers suffer from eight to ten upper respiratory infections a year—a figure that drops to about two or three by the time they are seven or eight years old, whether or not they have had their tonsils out. A large-scale study done in England in 1963 and widely reported in the U.S. showed that the average school-age child whose tonsils were removed was no better off than one whose tonsils remained in place. The British doctors strongly recommended that tonsillectomies be prescribed only in cases of persistent viral infection of the glands themselves and in cases where they obstructed the nasal passages.

At first the impact of the report was negligible. In 1971 American doctors still performed a million tonsillectomies a year, eighty percent of them on children under fifteen. Finally the message began to sink in. Abruptly the numbers fell to three hundred thousand tonsillectomies in 1980 and to just over one hundred thousand in 1989.

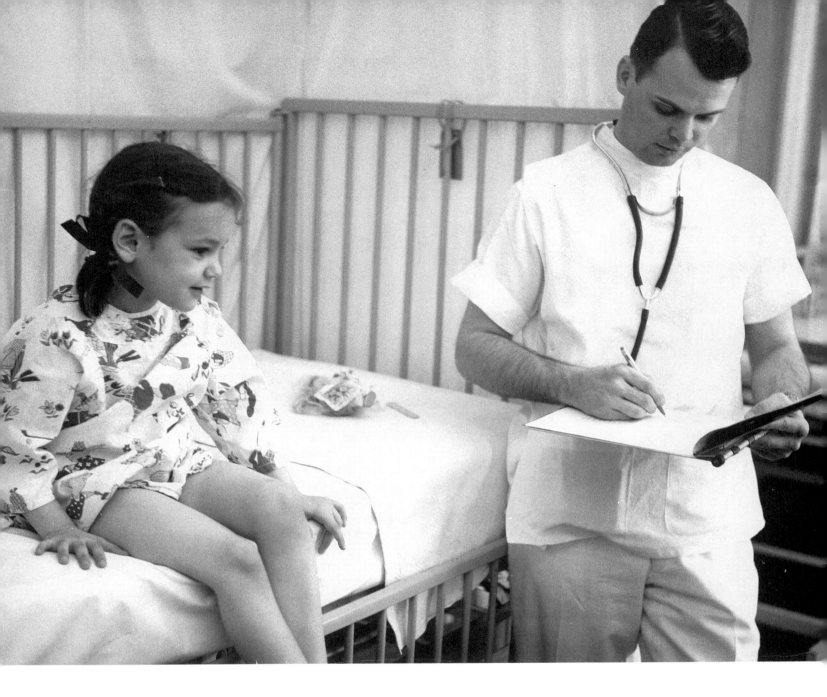

When other efforts to cure chronic ear infections fail, a doctor may still recommend removing the adenoids. Sometimes they're taken out if a child has a particularly "nasal" speaking voice or snores loudly enough to wake up the family. The palatine tonsils may be excised if they're so big they interfere with swallowing or if a teenager or adult continues to suffer from recurrent infections of the glands themselves.

Otherwise, antibiotics, which have been available since the late 1940s, are the first line of defense against bacterial infections in the ears, nose, and throat. Tonsillectomies are no longer routinely performed. Doctors are less quick to resort to invasive surgery than they used to be. General anesthesia imposes risks, and sometimes postoperative complications are worse than the conditions surgery was meant to cure. Parents' attitudes have also changed. They no longer believe that having their child's tonsils out is as important a sign of good nurturing as piano lessons and orthodontia. ☐

In spite of the prevalence of tonsils, nobody ever has a good word to say for them. . . . They have no value—except to doctors. — Kenneth Roberts, *It Must Be Your Tonsils*, 1935

TV Antennas

In the early 1950s, television entered the American home. The networks televised the 1952 political conventions live. People stayed home from school and work to watch senatorial hearings chaired by Estes Kefauver on organized crime and Joseph McCarthy on alleged Communist infiltration of the army. Families and friends made dates to watch the Friday night fights, "The Ed Sullivan Show," "Your Show of Shows," "Playhouse 90," and "Kukla, Fran, and Ollie."

The weakest link in this Golden Age of Television was its broadcast signal. Stations transmitted their signals from a tower or any high spot in town to people's homes where they were picked up by a receiver inside each set. If anything blocked their passage through the air—mountains, high buildings, even a storm front—the interference caused spots, wavy lines, or a double image, popularly called a ghost. At a tense moment in "The $64,000 Question" or "Dragnet," a passing airplane could scramble the picture.

The solution was an antenna mounted on the roof that captured the transmitted image and transferred it via a lead-in wire to the set. Manufacturers offered a confusing range of antennas: dipole, tripole, slotted pipe assembly, conical shapes, G-lines, rotating and stationery, each with features they claimed made a particular model the best at gathering in signals from stations that broadcast at various wavelengths on various frequencies.

After buying the antenna of his choice, the man of the family struggled to assemble the thing on the ground and then mount it on his roof without incident. After it was in place, he had to tune it by aiming the arms properly, while yelling to his wife below: "How's Channel Two?" "Any snow?" "How's it now?" And so on, until he had brought in the best reception for each of the two or three available channels. After a thunderstorm, the antenna had to be tuned all over again.

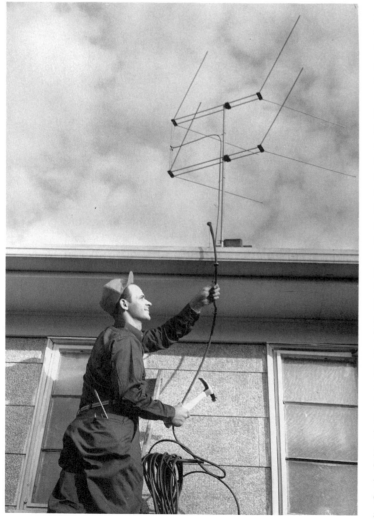

Do-it-yourself magazines explained how to make a super antenna. But the best you could hope for was two channels that worked pretty well and another one that came in only when the weather was right. The problems were worse with newly popular color sets, which had less tolerance for distortion than black and white.

Some people who lived within twenty-five or thirty uninterrupted miles of the transmitting towers—which is to say most city dwellers—tried indoor antennas. They came in various configurations of wire loops, twists, and spirals and sat in the place of honor on top of the TV set. "Rabbit ears," as they were called, could be repeatedly fine-tuned. Viewers were constantly jumping out of their chairs to rotate or bend the arms of the antenna. But snow or ghosts never really went away. Lousy reception was a staple of TV jokes. One comic said it was bad enough seeing Milton Berle once, but twice at the same time was more than a person could bear.

Imaginative businessmen soon realized they could build one tall tower that would function as an antenna for an entire community. It picked up TV signals better than individual antennas and sent them through coaxial cables strung along telephone or utility poles directly into people's homes. Robert Magness, the founder of Telecommunications Inc., which would become the largest cable operator in the country, began by selling service door to door, then going out in the evening to string the wires himself. CATV (community antenna television), as cable television was called at first, was a cash cow. The costs were low: the cable operators paid nothing for the signal, the cost of wiring was a onetime charge, and the rental fee for the utility poles was minimal. Cable companies got involved in bidding wars to secure local franchises. Competitors offered to pay for local swimming pools, install television sets in schools, or pay towns a portion of their revenues. Giveaways were cheap at the price compared to the profits that lay ahead.

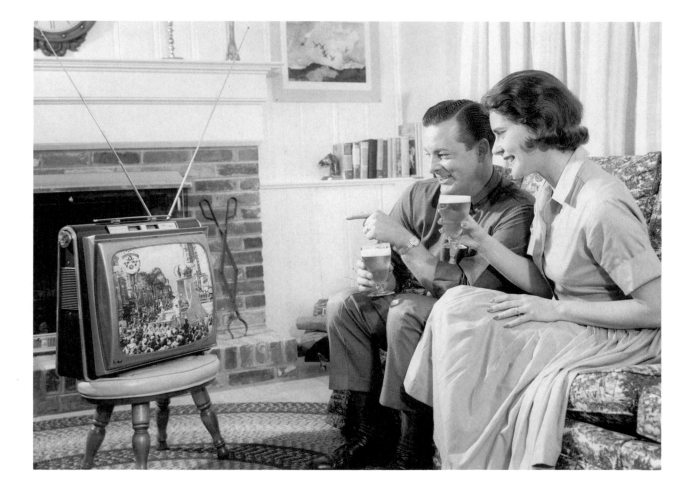

Cable reception was a revelation. Before Elmira, New York, was wired in 1965, viewers settled for two fuzzy channels, but subscribers to cable saw eleven clearly. By the mid-1960s, most rural areas and small towns were wired. The sales of television sets doubled when cable arrived. Because people no longer had to keep those ugly rabbit ears on top of their sets, they could tuck a TV inconspicuously into a bookshelf, or stash one on the kitchen counter beneath the wall cabinets.

By 1992, about sixty percent of American households had cable. The largest unwired areas remained in cities where cable companies and politicians still squabbled over enormously lucrative franchises. People without cable were enraged not to receive the thirty-five to forty channels that cable regularly delivered. Many installed their own backyard satellite dishes, which are motor-driven descendants of the old outdoor antennas that once cluttered the rooftops of American homes. □

INDOR TELEVISION ANTENNAS
Some Tips on Use

• For low channels, such as No. 2, it is generally advisable to pull out all rods fully and depress them to a flat position. If that doesn't work, experiment with other angles.
• Usually, it's best to orient the antenna at right angles to the transmitting station—touching only the bases; touching the rods affects the picture.
• It is all right to place the antenna on a metal TV cabinet, but keep it away from large vertical metal surfaces, such as window screens or refrigerators, which would materially affect the antenna's efficiency.
• Adjust the antenna each time you change channels.

—*Consumer Reports*, October 1958

Two-Newspaper Towns

On October 18, 1991, the *Arkansas Gazette,* a daily newspaper which had been published in Little Rock for 172 continuous years, printed its last edition. The *Gazette* was the oldest newspaper west of the Mississippi and one of the nation's finest. Under the editorship of Harry Ashmore in the 1950s, the paper had earned two Pulitzer prizes and national acclaim for its opposition to Arkansas Governor Orvil Faubus and its support for civil rights. Although a local magazine declared that the *Gazette* was "as implacable as a battleship, as inevitable as the sunrise," it was in fact a dead duck. The paper was done in by the loss of readers and advertising revenues, by a more aggressive local rival—the *Arkansas Democrat*—and by the tight pockets of its last owner, the Gannett Company.

The death of the *Gazette,* though particularly vexing, was hardly an isolated event. The number of American communities served by more than one local newspaper fell from over five hundred in the 1920s to under one hundred in 1992. Fewer than one of three Americans had access to more than one local daily paper. In 1991 alone, Dallas, San Diego, Knoxville, Charleston, and three cities in Virginia—Richmond, Roanoke, and Newport News—lost their second-ranked papers. Layoffs and closings made unemployment in the newspaper industry the worst it had been since the Depression. Sometimes, competing papers were consolidated, creating such mouthfuls as the *Nashville Banner-Tennessean.* In Little Rock, too, the publishers preserved the name of the older paper in their new morning daily, the *Arkansas Democrat-Gazette.* Following an industrywide trend, however, the new paper had jobs for fewer than one-third of the *Gazette's* employees.

In Dallas, the purchase of the *Times Herald* by the *Morning News* ended a rivalry between two particularly aggressive competitors. The *Times Herald* won Pulitzer prizes in 1964, 1980, and 1983, while the *Morning News* earned similar recognition in 1986, 1989, and 1991. During the 1970s and early 1980s, boom times in Texas provided enough advertising and readership to keep both papers running neck and neck. But with the protracted business slump of the late 1980s, the daily circulation of the *Times Herald* dropped to half that of the *News,* which began pulling away in the race for dwindling advertiser dollars.

For several decades, the long-term economics of the newspaper business had been discouraging. Costly investment in color presses and imaging equipment was not offset by payroll savings, as powerful unions successfully preserved many of the jobs their members would otherwise have lost. Advertiser dollars were diverted to an increasing number of television channels and throwaway suburban "shoppers." Retail advertising dropped during the early 1990s in the wake of department store closings and the general business downturn.

Readership had been declining steadily since the late 1960s. Barely half the nation's adults read a newspaper each day, and those who did were disproportionately among the older age groups. Younger people had grown up relying on television news. While the decline in readership may have leveled off in the early 1990s, there was no reason to think it would reverse itself significantly in the future.

The most vulnerable journals were those published in the afternoon. In 1991, morning papers had a total circulation of about forty-one million nationwide, while the afternoon dailies sold only half as many copies. In larger communities, many readers of afternoon papers were older blue-collar workers, whom upscale

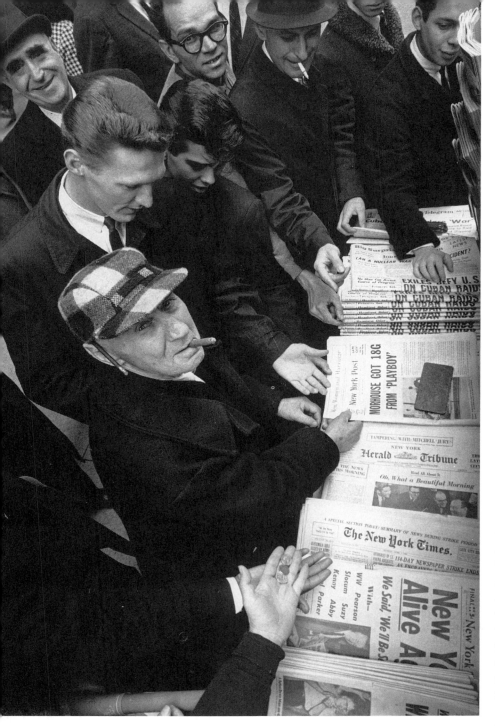

advertisers disdained. The only afternoon papers that were reasonably healthy were usually those published in small towns where there was no competition from local television.

What did communities lose when a paper died? Jobs, for sure, and often the crusading zeal that could be stimulated by circulation wars. *The Knoxville Journal*, a Republican paper, broke the scandal that sent Jake Butcher, a developer and Democratic candidate for governor, to jail. The afternoon San Diego *Tribune*, which was folded into the much more conservative morning *Union*, won Pulitzer prizes in 1979 and 1987 for editorial stands that challenged local opinion on air traffic safety and immigration reform.

Often the only potential buyer for a local paper was one of the nationwide groups like Gannett, Newhouse, Hearst, or Knight-Ridder. The giant groups and smaller chains collectively owned over seventy-five percent of the nation's dailies by 1991, reaching over eighty percent of total readership. In only twelve American cities were there at least two separate locally owned and fully competitive papers. Although some of the chain papers preserved a record of journalistic excellence, many cut costs by cutting local reporters.

To replicate the options of days gone by, many people began to read both a local and a national paper. Forward-thinking publishers, like those of the *Kansas City Star*, the *Hartford Courant*, or the *Chicago Tribune*, tried to develop regional readership. This may be the shape of things to come: small-town papers will prosper, one regional journal will survive in each metropolitan area, and a national press will serve the needs of people with more global interests.

It's quite possible that within the next decade general-interest newspapers as we know them will be replaced by more specialized information sources delivered via phone lines, cable channels, or home computers. When you want to know what happened at last night's school board elections, you'll order up a report from a local news-gathering organization. The latest scores? Dial a 900 number or tap into an on-line international sports-reporting service. The news behind the headlines from Singapore or Cheyenne will be available through a regular worldwide news service much like that operated by the United Press or the *New York Times* in their hey-days, but now custom-tailored and accessible on your video display rather than at the corner newsstand or delivered before dawn to your door. ☐

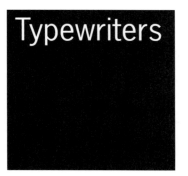

Typewriters

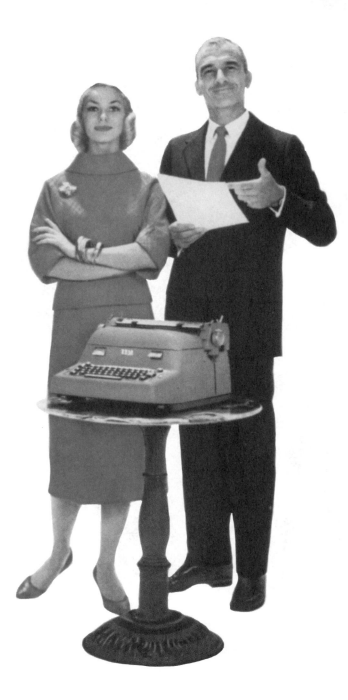

The typewriter as a labor saver . . . perfected the process which shorthand had begun—it completely emancipated the executive. It saved and conserved the very highest quality of brain labor. True, the busy man of affairs works as hard today as he ever did, but the typewriter has made his labor more productive. It has relieved him of the old pen drudgery, so that the greater part of his time may now be devoted to creative tasks. — *The Story of the Typewriter, 1923*

QWERTY—it's not a word, not a proper name, and not an acronym, but the order of these six letters is hauntingly familiar. They are the topmost lefthand letter keys on a typewriter, arranged in a seemingly random pattern that is anything but arbitrary. The assignment of letter to key was made by Christopher Latham Sholes, who studied spelling patterns as he worked to perfect his great invention, a mechanical writing machine. Sholes reasoned that keys frequently struck in sequence should be physically separated to prevent their locking together at the printing point.

Sholes, a Milwaukee printer and publisher, knew from his own trade how valuable a device to speed up the inscription of words could be. With two partners, he produced in 1867 a crude machine that, nonetheless, typed accurately and rapidly. A friend, James Densmore, soon joined the enterprise and gradually bought out the two minority partners. Densmore was as outspoken and driven as Sholes was shy and modest. He supported Sholes through twenty-five or thirty attempts to improve the machine until it was ready for production in 1873.

E. Remington & Sons, the noted gunmakers, contracted to manufacture these "type-writers," as Sholes called them, at its factory in upstate New York. Remington eventually purchased control of the company in exchange for a royalty on sales, and

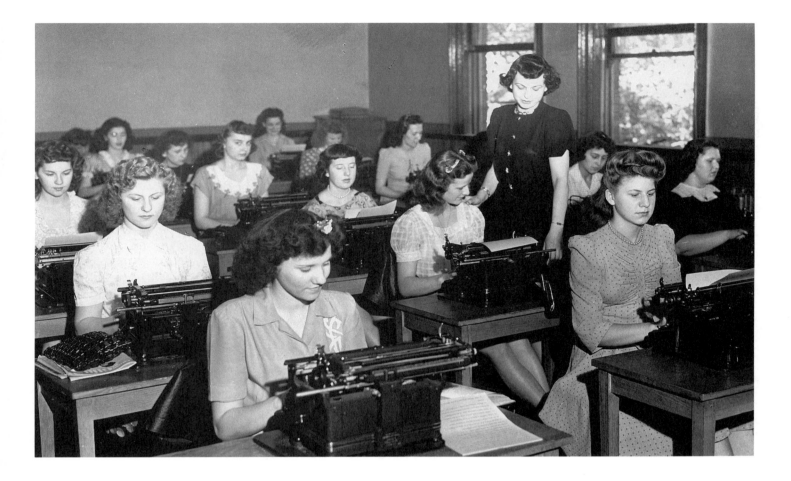

Sholes sold his royalty rights for $12,000—the only money he ever received for his invention and his years of work perfecting it.

Remington set its best men to the task of improving Sholes's machine for mass production. In 1874 the first commercial writing machine—the Model 1 Remington—was ready for sale. It looked strangely like a sewing machine; it even had a foot treadle to work the carriage return. Because it had no shift-key mechanism, it struck capital letters only. The Model 1 had what is commonly referred to as a universal keyboard—the so-called QWERTY arrangement that Sholes had devised.

An early catalogue describes the Model 1 Remington as "graceful and ornamental—a beautiful piece of furniture for office, study or parlor." "Persons traveling by sea," it suggests, "can write with it when pen writing is impossible." The catalogue lists prospective users in descending order of importance: reporters, lawyers, editors, authors, and clergymen. Almost as an afterthought, it states that "the merchant, the banker, ALL men of business can perform the labor of letter writing with much saving of valuable time."

One appreciative customer was Mark Twain (Samuel Clemens). Astonished that the contraption could type at the speed of fifty-seven words a minute, Twain plunked down $125 and had the machine shipped to his home in Hartford, Connecticut. On December 9, 1874, he typed a letter to his brother Orion:

DEAR BROTHER:
I AM TRYING TO GET THE HANG OF THIS NEW FANGLED WRITING MACHINE, BUT AM NOT MAKING A SHINING SUCCESS OF IT. HOWEVER THIS IS THE FIRST ATTEMPT I HAVE EVER MADE & YET I PERCEIVE I SHALL SOON & EASILY ACQUIRE A FINE FACILITY IN ITS USE. . . . THE MACHINE HAS SEVERAL VIRTUES. I BELIEVE IT WILL PRINT FASTER THAN I CAN WRITE. ONE MAY LEAN BACK IN HIS CHAIR & WORK IT. IT PILES AN AWFUL STACK OF WORDS ON ONE PAGE. IT DON'T MUSS THINGS OR SCATTER INK BLOTS AROUND. OF COURSE IT SAVES PAPER. . . .
YOUR BROTHER,
SAM

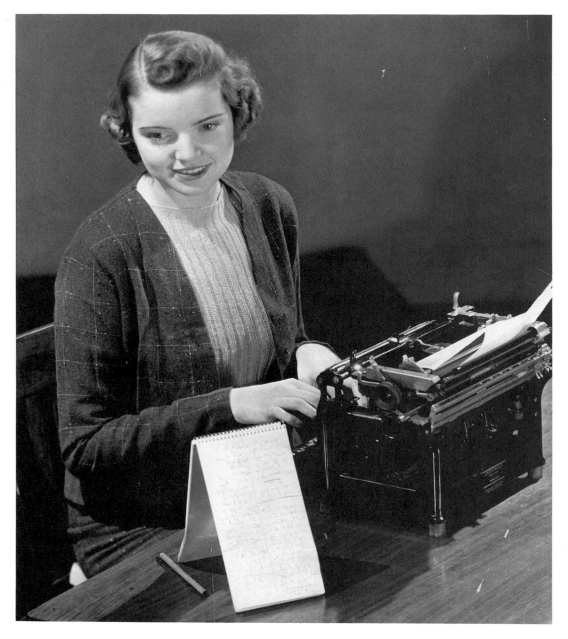

In an effort to attract other enthusiasts, Remington took a booth at the Centennial Exposition at Philadelphia in 1876. For twenty-five cents, a pretty girl would type out a brief message for the potential customer to mail back home. Long lines of people eagerly waited their turn to observe the workings of the wonderful new writing machine, but not a single one was sold. Fair-goers were much more impressed with the other new invention on display: the telephone.

For several years, typewriter sales lagged. It was clear to the company that it had to sell not just typewriters but a new *idea*. William Wyckoff, Remington's sales representative in Ithaca, New York, was particularly messianic in his zeal to get people to forsake pen and ink. When his own staff rebelled against the new machine, he told them, *"use it or quit."* By the mid-1880s, Wyckoff and two partners had bought the right to manufacture and distribute the Remington Type-Writer.

Although a typewritten personal letter was still unthinkable, progressive businessmen were coming to recognize that for their growing volume of office communications, mechanical writing was quicker, cleaner, and clearer. For the most part, however, men considered jobs as typists undesirable because of the relatively low pay. Then, in 1881, the Central Branch of the New York City YMCA decided to train eight young women in office skills. At the end of the six-month course, all eight were hired immediately, and the business world clamored for female typists, who were willing to work for low wages. To satisfy the need, private typing schools opened throughout the country. Their graduates swelled the growing ranks of office jobs, and at last the market for typewriters boomed.

Before the advent of the typewriter, few careers outside the home were available to respectable women. The small number who were educated might take up nursing or school teaching. The untrained and the uneducated could find employment in shops, factories, and domestic service. But these occupations did not provide economic freedom for the majority of women. To achieve real economic emancipation, they needed to enter the business community, which was dead set against letting them in.

Ironically, the typewriter—which later became a symbol of oppression for women who felt that they could not advance beyoud secretarial jobs—helped break the barriers against females in the workplace. By 1910, two million typewriters were in use in America, about one-third of them operated by young women in offices.

In the early years of the twentieth century, typing was still such a relative novelty that typewriting contests competed with sporting events for national attention. The Underwood company sponsored speed typists, giving them souped-up machines to train on and coddling them like Olympic athletes. Crowds flocked to the championships, sitting in rapt attention while the contestants pounded out as many as 140 words per minute.

> I like the tactile part of it. I like rolling the paper and pushing the lever at the end of the line. I like the bell that rings like an old train. It's a great piece of machinery. I even like crumpling up pages that don't work. One of our kids used to call them my "wrong pages." I don't like the idea that technology might fail me, and I don't like the idea that the words are not really on anything.
> — David McCullough, quoted in the *New York Times*, August 12, 1992

In the decades that followed, every office depended on typewriters, as well as a host of devices like adding machines, billing machines, cash registers, addressing machines, and calculating machines, all of which derived from the typewriter. The mechanical wonder moved into the home: friends typed letters to each other; students typed their term papers. Portable machines — light, compact, easy to carry—became a traditional going-off-to-college gift.

Since the turn of the century, inventors had been working on electric machines that would require less effort for a typist to operate, while producing a more uniform type stroke on the page. The first electric models cost two to three times as much as manual typewriters, without offering substantial benefits. Then in 1933, IBM, a manufacturer of tabulating equipment, bought a firm called Electromatic Typewriters Inc. IBM recognized a need to be filled: the expanding bureaucracy of the U.S. government produced reams of forms, invoices, purchase orders, etc., all with multiple carbon copies, which the keys of a manual typewriter could not penetrate. The first IBM electric typewriter, on the market in 1935, allowed a typist to produce twelve carbon copies, each of which looked as sharp and clean as the top page.

The new machines didn't please everyone. They hummed. They struck letters at the slightest touch, so that typists had to be careful not to rest their fingers on the keyboard. They required more servicing than the old mechanical models. Nonetheless, by 1954, over half of all typewriters in use were electric.

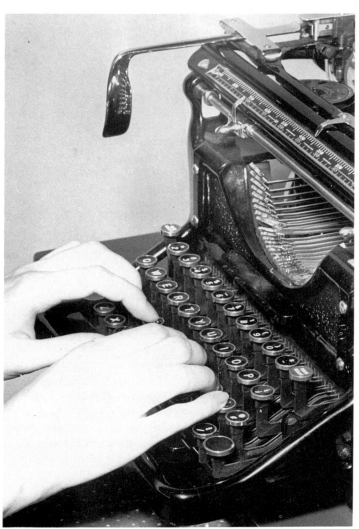

In 1961, IBM introduced the Selectric, the most popular electric typewriter ever marketed. It featured a "golf ball"-shaped element that eliminated the bars leading to the striking surface and did away with the moving carriage, which had been one of the parts of the old machines that was most likely to break down. The Selectric also used a ribbon enclosed in a disposable cartridge—no more messy carbon ribbon changes—and it offered the option of different styles and colors of type.

It was the development of the silicon chip that brought the reign of the electric typewriter to an end. The first blow was dealt in the late 1970s by "dedicated word processors," electronic typewriters with expanded memory capacity, which allowed a typist to read several lines of copy and make corrections before the text was printed. Frequently used paragraphs, like those found in standard contracts, could be stored and inserted without having to be retyped. A few years later personal computers offered a giant leap in the capacity to edit and store text. All typewriters—manual, electric, or electronic—were instantly obsolete.

Electronic typewriters remain convenient for addressing labels or envelopes, filling out preprinted forms, or typing short memos. Despite these uses, fewer than one million were sold in the U.S. in 1990, and industry analysts expect the market to shrink by an estimated three percent annually into the next century. In fact, many of those machines will be enhanced with disk storage and full-screen video monitors, making them computers in everything but name. □

The Unanswered Phone

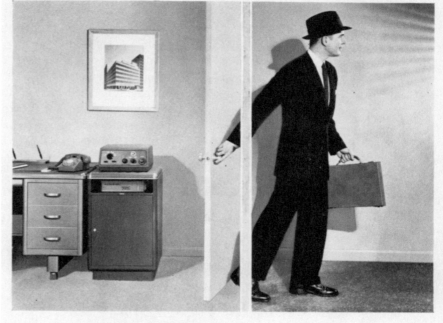

YOU'RE IN WHEN YOU'RE OUT

... with the new Telephone Answering set

Before there were answering machines, people indulged their imaginations. They convinced themselves that while they were out dozens of people had called to chat or invite them to dinner. There was the chance that He had been trying to get through. Or that someone out of the blue might have phoned to offer fame, free lessons, or, at the very least, a job.

Automatic answering replaced delicious uncertainty with sobering truth. The first answering machines were introduced in 1953 by the Bell System, which identified a huge potential market among small businesses and professionals who worked alone, such as doctors, psychoanalysts, free-lance writers, and photographers. The early machines were clunky and had to be wired into permanent phone lines. But by the 1970s, the installation of phone jacks, as well as lower prices and more practical designs, led to an enormous increase in the use and acceptance of the machines. They were a godsend for the very busy or the very shy. Unlike answering services, which charged a steep monthly fee, the machines were a onetime expense. They picked up after the first few rings, passed along every message, and were never rude.

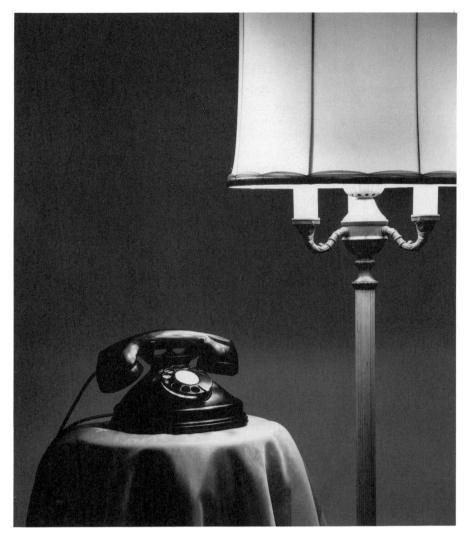

By 1973 an estimated six million Americans owned answering machines. According to one salesman, call girls were big customers. "They say they're actresses, but I don't know any actresses who could plunk down eight hundred dollars cash for the newest and the best."

An answering machine is essentially a tape recorder with two reels—one for the owner's announcement and one for incoming calls. At first, people were uncertain about how to leave a message. There were well-developed rules that governed telephone calls. The interjection of *uh-huh* and *okay*, for example, provided feedback that paced the conversation. When talking to a machine, however, callers often started out confidently, then trailed off because no one responded. They got flustered and finally blurted out a name and number just as the beep cut them off. Machine owners went to great lengths to avoid what was even worse—hang-ups. They had to fill thirty to fifty seconds of open tape before the caller could begin to speak. They told bad jokes or sang songs—anything to keep the caller on the line.

In the 1980s home answering machines took off. Single people and families with both adults working away from home discovered they couldn't live without them. In one year the sales of answering machines rose forty percent. No longer were callers reluctant to talk to the tape. Instead, they got annoyed when they *couldn't* leave a message.

By the early 1990s one in four American households was equipped with an answering machine. *Dog World* magazine suggested that animal owners get a machine so they could call their bored and lonely pets who were left alone all day. Dogs seem to respond to the "magical and mysterious sound of human voices speaking through the machine."

Voice mail, which has been called "an answering machine on steroids," has recently been adopted by American businesses. It is increasingly common to transact business with a bank, an insurance company, an airline, or a colleague down the hall, without speaking to a human being.

Unlike answering machines, which are attached to individual telephones, voice mail links a network of phones. With one call, an executive can send the same message to a dozen associates. When a person is away from the phone, voice mail can record incoming messages, then forward them at once. It can screen and hold calls. Voice-mail systems have replaced live switchboard operators with "automated attendants" that deliver instructions in a cheery but disembodied tone: "Thank you for calling the Acme Company. If you know the extension of the person you are calling, enter it now; for home delivery information, press 3; to place your orders, press 1; for sales information, press 5; otherwise, press 0 for the operator."

Voice mail got its start when an entrepreneur, Gordon Matthews, spotted a pile of "While You Were Out" pink message slips in the garbage. Matthews had the bright idea that a machine which allowed people to leave detailed messages in their own voices would cut down on reams of paper and eliminate garbled communication. Voice-mail systems became practical and affordable in the late 1980s because of inexpensive computers and devices that digitize human speech. Increased computer capacity meant more and more options, leading to "voice-mail jail," a endless loop of recorded messages giving instructions which never quite meet one's needs and from which the only escape is hanging up. □

Unfixed Domestic Male Animals

Tourists driving to Seville through southern Spain are startled to pass fields filled with young black bulls. Raised for the corrida, the Spanish bulls are among the few domesticated male animals allowed to keep their testicles past puberty. In the United States, it's hard to find a bull.

Early in the twentieth century, American dairy farmers began to breed their own stock rather than buy young cows from cattle drovers. They kept records of the best milkers and studs. Similarly, ranchers kept track of the best beef producers. By the 1930s, regional breeding associations maintained prized bulls and shipped refrigerated semen to the owners of top-ranked cows. In the late 1940s, it was accidentally discovered that semen mixed with glycerol could be frozen and preserved for years. The semen of one champion stud bull could be separated into thousands of units for use over generations. Artificial insemination allowed farmers greater control over their breed lines and saved wear and tear on the cows. It was also much less trouble. Unlike docile steers or oxen, bulls had to be housed and penned apart from the cows.

Until the 1960s, sexually intact mature male pigs, properly called hogs, had a place on the farm because the marketplace paid a premium for fat. Their testosterone enabled intact males to grow bigger and faster than gilts, or females. Although some buyers complained that they could taste an unpleasant boar taint, farmers continued to raise hogs for slaughter. More recently, however, diet-conscious Americans have demanded lean pork. Male piglets are now no more valuable to farmers than females and are usually castrated when they are a few weeks old.

For centuries, most male horses were gelded to make them more tractable work animals. Even today, when horses are kept mostly for pleasure, riders are usually more comfortable with a gelding than an unpredictable stallion. Stallions are rare except when the promise of a multimillion-dollar stud fee encourages a breeder to protect a male horse with the potential to be a big winner at the track or in the show ring.

Few people make a fuss about the castration of male animals. Animal rights advocates are less exercised about neutering than about other aspects of livestock raising, such as breeding pens, restricted movement, forced feeding, and overcrowding.

As hunting seasons have been shortened, wild deer have flourished. They come out of the forests to eat people's gardens and shrubs. They carry the deer tick that spreads Lyme disease to people and their pets. Since there are too many deer, many wildlife experts would like to allow hunters to thin the herds. But wild deer have been sentimentalized, especially by Disney, and popular opinion opposes slaughtering the excess animals. Meanwhile the deer make further inroads into suburbia. Recently it's been suggested that they should be prevented from breeding freely. Males could be stunned, sterilized or castrated, then sent back to the forest.

The oversupply of cats and dogs in America has already forced animal lovers to "fix" their pets. As many as ninety percent of male pet cats and fifty percent of male pet dogs are neutered either before they breed or after they father one litter. Public policy supports neutering. People feel sorry for the feral packs of abandoned cats and dogs that roam every city.

Animal shelters insist that people who adopt a waif must get their new pet neutered. Many communities force owners to pay a premium for animal licenses if their adult pet is intact. In Seattle, the license for an "unfixed" pet costs twice the price of a license for a neutered animal. Some parts of San Mateo County, California, require that owners of unneutered pet dogs buy a special permit and promise not to breed them.

Techniques are now available to make the few remaining adult male farm animals obsolete. For example, after the in vitro fertilization of a milk cow, male embryos are discarded. Female embryos are allowed to divide into eight cells and then the cells are separated. One is implanted in a surrogate mother cow; the others are frozen. After the calf is born and allowed to mature, her milk production is measured. If it is only average, the other cells are thrown out. If she is a champion, the remaining seven cells—her clone sisters—are implanted. Eight prize cows can result from one semination. Eventually 128 cells—and therefore 128 cloned cows—could be produced from one fertilized egg.

It will soon be possible to determine the sex of a single sperm. Breeders may want to eliminate any sperm that would produce a male offspring. At that point male farm animals could completely disappear. □

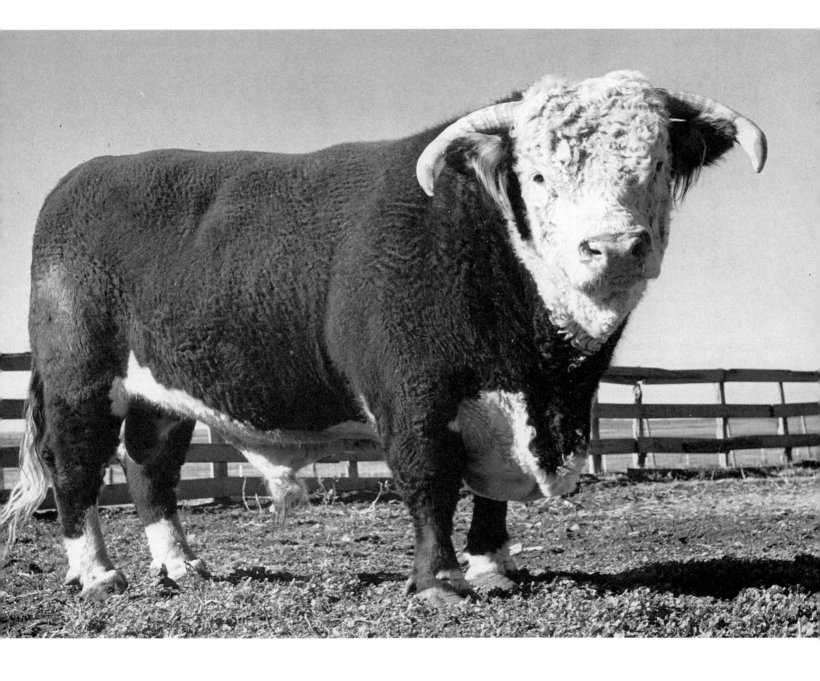

Vinyl Records

Some are stacked on the top shelf of the spare closet, next to shopping bags filled with finger paintings and clay figurines from nursery school. Others are piled in the stereo cabinet—in the back, untouched for over ten years. Probably they should be thrown out, but maybe someday they'll be valuable. Didn't people who got rid of their Tiffany lampshades live to regret it?

Vinyl records are disappearing from mass-market music stores. Fewer than twenty-five percent of new pop albums are released on vinyl, and the figure is even lower for jazz, classical, and country music. Almost all the music sold in America is on CDs and cassette tapes. Sales of CD players have grown faster than those of any consumer electronic product in history.

The concept of capturing sound on a disc, or record, was the brainchild of a young German immigrant named Emile Berliner. In 1894 Berliner's firm, the United States Gramophone Company of Washington, D.C., marketed the first records for fifty cents apiece. Early releases included vocals of "Old Folks at Home" and recitations of "Casey at the Bat." They were pressed on single-sided hard rubber discs, which were seven inches wide and had a playing time of two minutes. Because the rubber surface was often uneven, the phonograph needle skipped over the record. Berliner soon switched to records made of wax and shellac—a resin secreted by insects and imported from India.

John Philip Sousa's band recorded on disc, as did opera singer Enrico Caruso. In 1902 Caruso cut ten records for which he was paid a flat sum of a hundred pounds sterling. Later he demanded royalties. His twelve-inch solo records sold for three dollars. By the time Caruso died in 1921, he had earned over $2 million in recording fees.

The dance mania that swept the country between 1910 and 1920 transformed the record business. People danced the tango, the turkey trot, the hesitation waltz, the one-step. They danced in hotel lobbies, in restaurants, in nightclubs. They bought records so they could dance at home. They spent $27 million dollars on records in 1914; five years later they spent $160 million.

After the crash in 1929, the manufacture and sale of phonographs and records dropped precipitously and continued to languish for several years until a number of marketing decisions revitalized the industry. RCA Victor introduced an inexpensive record player that could be hooked up to a radio. Decca, Columbia, and RCA Victor devoted big budgets to promote popular and classical records. A huge audience listened to weekly radio broadcasts of the "Firestone Hour," the "Ford Sunday Evening Hour," the NBC Orchestra under Stokowski and Toscanini, and the Metropolitan Opera. Jukeboxes in bars and diners played the latest hits over and over. People who heard a pop song they liked hurried to buy their own record of it.

When America entered the war in 1941, the government curtailed the nonmilitary use of shellac, forcing a hiatus in record production. After the war, unrestricted shellac shipments resumed, and record factories were back in business. In 1947 consumers bought three and a half million combination radio-phonographs and four million records. The discs hadn't really changed in decades: the size, speed, and grooving were essentially the same; they scratched easily; and they played for only four minutes.

In 1948 Columbia Records announced "a revolutionary new product"—the long-playing record. The LP was a microgroove disc with a playing time of twenty-three minutes per side. Columbia officials showed reporters a stack of conventional records, nearly eight feet tall, and a pile of LPs, barely fifteen inches high. Each batch represented the same amount of playing time. Then they played an LP. There were no breaks in the middle of a symphonic movement, and the sound quality was as good, if not better. The new 33 1/3-rpm LPs didn't scratch as easily as the old 78s because they were made of Vinylite, a nonbreakable plastic. The following year RCA introduced seven-inch vinyl 45-rpm records, which became the standard format for pop singles. By 1950 the old 78-rpm shellac disc was history.

In 1955 RCA signed up Elvis Presley and sold ten million Presley singles within a year. Teenagers bought every rock-and-roll release they could get their hands on, especially those by Elvis, Jerry Lee Lewis, Carl Perkins, and Bill Haley and the Comets. On the weekly TV program "Your Hit Parade," Snooky Lanson and Dorothy Collins acted out the ten biggest hits of the week. Top 40 radio stations relentlessly hyped record sales.

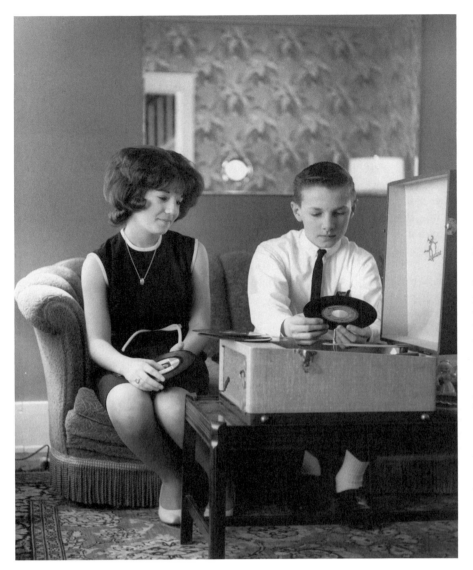

A decade later the Beatles gave pop music intellectual cachet. *Sgt. Pepper's Lonely Hearts Club Band* was the first concept album—a collection of songs bound together by a theme, rather than randomly chosen. When *Sgt. Pepper* was released in 1967, half the population of the U.S. was under twenty-five years old. The Woodstock generation defined itself by rock and roll. Each new release by the Who, the Rolling Stones, Janis Joplin, Jimi Hendrix, the Jefferson Airplane, or the Grateful Dead prompted a ritual: The devotee removed the LP from its paper sleeve, slipped it down the spindle of the record player onto the turntable, blew dust off the needle, watched the arm drop onto the record, consulted the cover to determine which musicians and vocalists performed each cut, then started to memorize the lyrics printed on the sleeve.

In the late 1970s audiotapes challenged the supremacy of the LP. Cassettes received an enormous boost with the growing popularity of Walkmans and other portable players. In 1983 the compact disc arrived, with its digitally recorded "perfect sound." CDs were small, durable, and easy to use. Although CDs typically sold for almost twice as much as LPs, they caught on fast. Record companies, responding to the higher profit margin for CDs, churned them out and stopped pressing LPs. Stores readily abandoned an item which was bulky and likely to warp and scratch.

Though CDs have been immensely popular, some purists hate them. Neil Young has complained that the CD reissue of his album *Everyone Knows This Is Nowhere* is inferior to the original vinyl LP. "Digitally recorded music is like ice cubes washing over you," says Young. "It's not the same." ☐

Shrevie: "Look. Pick a record, o.k.? Just any record, any record. What's the hit side?"
Beth: "'Good Golly, Miss Molly.'"
S: "O.K. Now ask me, what's on the flip side?"
B: "What is on the flipside?"
S: "'Hey Hey, Hey Hey.' 1958. Specialty Records. You see, you never ask me what's on the flip side. Every one of my records means something—the label, the producer, the year it was made, who was copying whose style, who was expanding on that. . . . Just don't touch my records, ever."
— *Diner*, written and directed by Barry Levinson, 1982

Wedding-Night Virgins

Virginity was the greatest gift a bride could bring to her groom. If word got out that a "nice" girl had "done it," she was damaged goods, and no decent young man would ever want to marry her. Wedding-gown white was taken seriously. Divorcées and even young widows were slightly tainted; they had to wear ecru or a subdued shade of gray if they walked down the aisle a second time.

In *Pillow Talk* (1959) and other comedies, Doris Day stayed out of Rock Hudson's bed until the gold band was firmly in place on her left hand. Art, or at least Hollywood, mirrored life. A happily married mother of three recalls her own priorities: "I was twenty-one years old. I got married because I couldn't have sex otherwise, and I really wanted to have sex. But before that ring was on my finger— nothing doing. I was a virgin out of fear. Fear of getting pregnant but, even worse, terror that someone would lose respect for me."

In the late 1950s, half of America's brides were twenty-one years old or younger. Between fifty and sixty percent of them were virgins, and most of those who didn't make it to the altar intact had slept only with their fiancés and only a few times before they married.

America's prevailing sexual mores at midcentury reflected a Victorian legacy. The arbiters of ethics in the nineteenth century were determined to protect home and family from the social and scientific revolutions that threatened them. A woman's nurturing role as a mother was separated from her sexuality, and the latter was ignored whenever possible. Although there were a few brave dissenting views, most gynecologists in the late nineteenth and early twentieth centuries believed that sexual desire in young brides was pathological and a sign of low moral character.

Well into the 1950s, *Ideal Marriage* by Theodore Van de Velde was a widely consulted marriage manual—the term for books that described sex acts in explicit, nonjudgmental terms. Dr. Van de Velde, a Dutch gynecologist who campaigned actively for sex education, believed that woman had the right to experience sexual fulfillment. Although he acknowledged that some women "do not enter married life as virgins," he believed that most new brides entertained a "profound and elemental dread" which "has deeper origins and significance than the fear of short physical pain." Popular opinion held that most young women were less passionate than their fiancés, and if they felt desire, they were often unsettled by it. Matching nightgowns and peignoirs were talked about; sex was not. A bride from the early 1950s recalls every word of her mother's premarital advice: "Remember, my dear, no matter how unpleasant it may be, you have to go through with it." Another young woman fainted during her wedding ceremony. "I was panicked about the night to come. It ruined the wedding for me."

Like so many other conventions, the standards of sexual behavior and morality were profoundly altered in the turbulent 1960s. Contempt for the power of authority and parental values were the primary reasons for change. Another was The Pill. After oral contraceptives became available at the beginning of the decade, couples no longer had to depend on condoms or the rhythm method. For the first time, women could take charge of protecting themselves against an unwanted pregnancy. Another factor was the declining risk of sexually transmitted disease: syphilis and gonorrhea could be cured; epidemics of chlamydia, genital herpes, and AIDS were still to come. Influenced by women's lib, as feminism was popularly known, young girls acknowledged their own desires and experimented sexually as much as their brothers did. Although a 1965 survey of college students revealed that one-third of the men and over two-thirds of the women believed that premarital sex was immoral, five years later nearly eighty percent of both men and women thought it was just fine. Topics that women barely discussed with their doctors in the 1950s were talk show staples twenty years later. The Latin names and Anglo-Saxon epithets for private parts and sexual practices, which had barely been whispered in polite society, were now shouted aloud.

Sex researchers have estimated that as many as ninety percent of unmarried women in the 1980s and 1990s had intercourse, often with more than one partner. Premarital sex—legally called fornication—is still illegal in thirteen states and the District of Columbia, but the laws are rarely enforced.

In preparing for marriage the bride should learn to cherish the brightness, the fire, the wholeness of her love and desire for her husband. This is creation, this is life, this is good. Sex experience before marriage dissipates the fire, shadows the light, and this is bad. . . . The tragedy of girls who have not understood this runs through the whole of their lives.
— Dr. Marion Hilliard, "Why Premarital Sex is Always Wrong," *The Ladies Home Journal*, September 1958

166

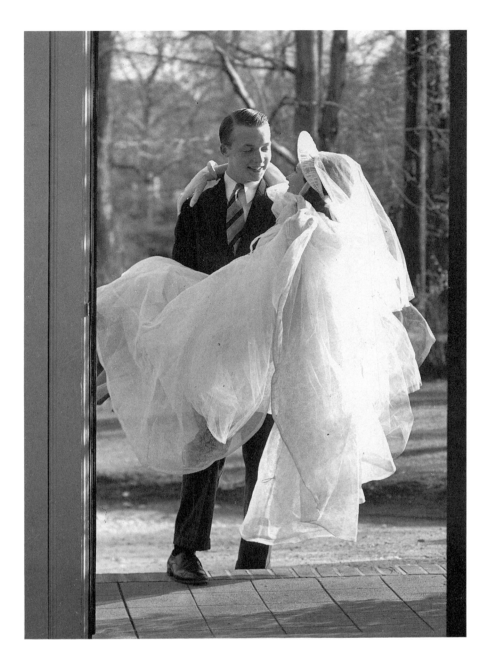

A modern bride is older than her counterpart of forty years ago, and she has probably slept with several men. She lost her virginity in her teens. For each young woman, that loss was a significant event, but one without consequences for her reputation. Today if a high school girl has a boyfriend, it is assumed that she is sleeping with him. Although people now often lead more judicious sex lives, at least partly because of the risk of sexually transmitted disease, there seems to be no revival of the moral order that made virginity a virtue. In fact, prolonged virginity often seems an anachronism, inviting pity or ridicule. One twenty-five-year-old woman, who is proud of her self-control, shudders when friends introduce her at parties by announcing, "This is Chris. She doesn't drink, and she's a virgin." □

He asked me to prove my love for him. But if I did, he wouldn't love me in the same way. . .And although I might be able to live with a man, I wouldn't ever again be able to live with myself. — "Virginity was My Problem," *Redbook,* **August 1961**

White Gloves

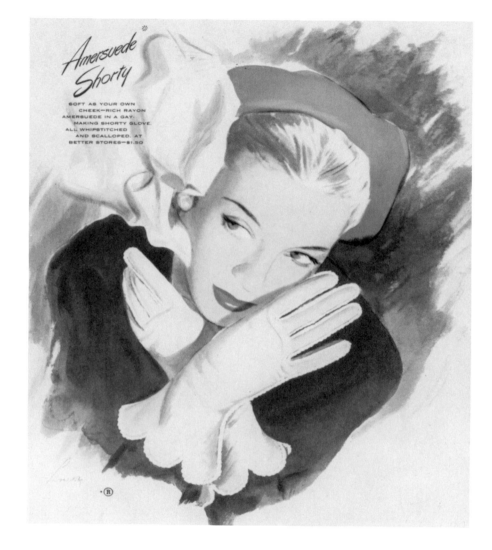

Young women armed with liberal arts degrees flocked to New York in the 1950s and early 1960s to work in publishing. They were called assistant editors, but they were secretaries. Every morning they traveled to the office on the subway. At noon they went out for lunch with friends. After work they ran errands and met dates for dinner. In mild weather—even on hot summer days—they never left a building without putting on short white gloves.

Each young woman owned a half-dozen pairs. Some were plain white cotton with a simple finish; others had perky buttons or colored ribbons or appliqued designs. A career girl never passed the glove counters in a department store without checking out the new styles. She wore each pair until the gray smudges that started at the fingertips were too noticeable, then washed the whole lot. She'd put on one pair, dunk her hands in soapy water, and rub one glove against the other, scrubbing the gray away. And so on until enough pairs were clean to get her through the next week.

Before the sixteenth century, gloves had been worn primarily by men. Catherine de Medici, the fashion-conscious Queen of France, is credited with popularizing gloves for herself and her ladies in waiting. She gave her favorites gloves of gossamer silk and leather, so fine they could be rolled into polished walnut shells.

Queen Elizabeth I loved gloves, and she had a special attendant to take care of her two thousand pairs. At a formal ceremony in Oxford in 1566, she wore remarkable white kid gauntlets, almost half a yard long and embroidered with gold, which, a courtier noted, "she pulled off more than a hundred times to display her hands, which indeed were very beautiful and very white." By the late sixteenth century, a glove given by a young woman to a gentleman meant that he was an accepted suitor, and the custom of wearing gloves had spread from the upper classes to the common people.

As elements of ecclesiastical dress, gloves were emblems of authority and chastity in religious ceremonies. Because white gloves were associated with purity, judges adopted them as a symbol of office, and brides wore them at their weddings. Nuptial guests and close family friends were given white gloves as mementoes of the occasion. Since gloves were expensive, the custom could be ruinous. At the wedding of Sir Philipp Harbet and Lady Susan in 1604, the guests included King James I and Queen Anne, as well as many lords and ladies of the court. The cost of wedding gloves was about one thousand pounds, which the fortunate couple recouped in presents of silver. Soon familes began to substitute white paper gloves for real ones as wedding souvenirs—a custom that survived for several centuries.

Nineteenth century English ladies considered gloves a symbol of gentility and wore them indoors and out, morning through evening. Queen Victoria preferred black kid for everyday wear and white kid for court functions. During her reign, women began for the first time to wear short white kid gloves. Mass-produced cotton gloves made it possible for women of lesser means to mimic the upper classes.

The early 1900s were truly "the age of the glove." A New York department store reported that it was not unusual for a customer to bring in thirty pairs at a time for cleaning. One social critic com-mented that "gloves have come to exercise a mild tyranny over us."

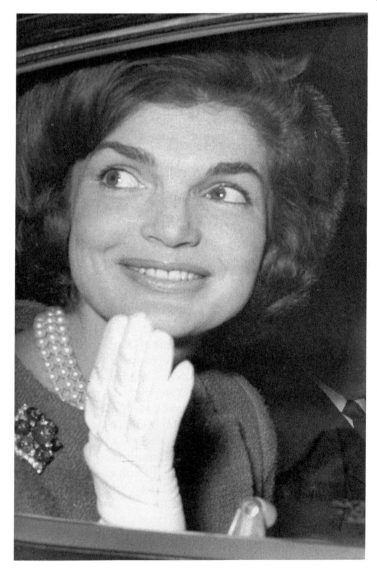

The tyranny persisted for decades. Through the 1950s the uniform of the day demanded white gloves. A serviceable, unadorned, double-woven cotton pair cost about two or three dollars. Crescendoe, a well-known brand, specialized in a better white cotton with embroidery, handwork, or applique, which cost between four and six dollars. Giant manufacturers like Kaiser and Van Raalte distributed thousands of dozens a month to department stores and specialty shops. Along with other companies like Shalimar, Dawnelle, and WearRite, they made white gloves of sheer fabric, crochet work, and cotton, ranging in price from one to twenty-five dollars.

After World War II, double-woven nylon was available for civilian use. Nylon came in two grades—seventy denier, which looked and felt like sueded leather but could be washed and dried fast, and fifty denier, which was less expensive. Top-of-the-line white gloves were still made of cotton, which was easier to trim.

In the Kennedy era, every woman in America longed to look like the First Lady in her pillbox hat and short white gloves. When she was photographed wearing long gloves at a formal White House reception, stores couldn't keep copies in stock. A pair of eight-button leather gloves, called the Jackie Kennedy, sold for sixteen dollars—a high price at the time. The style came in all colors, including white.

But even for gloves, Camelot came to an end. In the mid-1960s, sportswear took on fashion cachet. Women began to wear pantsuits, not only to the office but also to the theater or to church. With the advent of the miniskirt, the ensemble look of coordinated hat, purse, shoes, and gloves went out overnight. Manufacturers were left with huge cartons of white cotton gloves in the warehouse. "Today people buy gloves primarily to keep their hands warm," laments an industry executive. "Except as an accessory on formal occasions, they have become a utility, replacement item like underwear. We've lost a whole generation that grew up in the sixties, seventies, and eighties. Skirt lengths rise and fall. Shoulder pads come and go. But I don't see a renaissance for white gloves in my lifetime." □

Acknowledgments

The variety of subjects included in this book led us down many pathways of research. We uncovered much of the information we needed in the extraordinarily rich collections of the Research Division of the New York Public Library, the New York Society Library, and the Fashion Institute of Technology Research Library.

Additionally we drew on the resources of experts in diverse fields, among them Anna Blanco of Macfadden Publishing Inc.; Dr. William H. Bowen of the University of Rochester Department of Dental Research; Dr. John Cameron of the University of Wisconsin Department of Medical Physics; Dr. Richard Campana, plant pathologist at the University of Maine; Janet Carter of the Bank of America; Larry Chervenak; Betty J. Davis of the National Association of Soda Jerks; William Dermott of Exxon; Ray Ellis of the American Hotel and Motel Association; Edward Finfer of the U.S. Environmental Protection Agency; Joe Forsee of the International Circulation Managers Association; Roger Galliher; Thomas Greco of the American Bankers Association; Richard Heffner of the Motion Picture Classification and Rating Administration; Sheldon Hochheiser of the AT&T Archives; Wilson Hughes of the University of Arizona Garbage Project; Robert H. Hutchings; Samuel Kalow; Peter Kelly of the National Baseball Hall of Fame; Jerry Klotz of the Selective Service System; Nancy Knight of the Center for the American History of Radiology; Harold Koda of the Costume Institute at the Metropolitan Museum; Jim Kozak of the National Association of Theater Owners; John Laughlin; Beth Lerch; Phillip Majerus; Dr. Irwin Mandel of the Columbia University School of Dental and Oral Surgery; C. Eugene Mason of the National Marbles Tournament; Richard P. Mather and Keith Welkes of the Pennsylvania Deparment of Environmental Resources; Richard McComb and Irving Salero of FIT; Frank McGuire; Philip E. Meyer, professor of journalism at the University of North Carolina; Wayne Meyer AIA; Marjorie Miller of the FIT Research Library; Robert K. Otnes of the Oughtred Society; Amy Pagnozzi; George Pittman of Keuffel & Esser; Howard H. Prouty of the Margaret Herrick Library Academy of Motion Picture Arts and Sciences; Dr. Keith Reemtsma of the Columbia University College of Physicians and Surgeons; Gianpaulo Roma and Debby Lukasik of Texaco; Andrew Rowan of the Tufts University School of Veterinary Medicine; Ruth Sikes of the American Academy of Dermatology; Wilma R. Slaight of Wellesley College Archives; Yvonne Spalthoff of the Elm Research Institute; Harley Spiller; Dr. Stefan Stein, professor of clinical psychiatry at New York Hospital-Cornell Medical Center; John Thomas of NYNEX; Tom Tierney; Alan Truscott of the New York Times; Jane Varsalona of the Midwest Paper Doll and Toy Quarterly; and Charles Wilson of the American Contract Bridge League.

We are especially indebted to Daniel Cohen, Anne Tolstoi Wallach, and Dr. Wilbur Zelensky of the Department of Geography at Pennsylvania State University. We relied on their written work, and they were generous with their time and ideas as well.

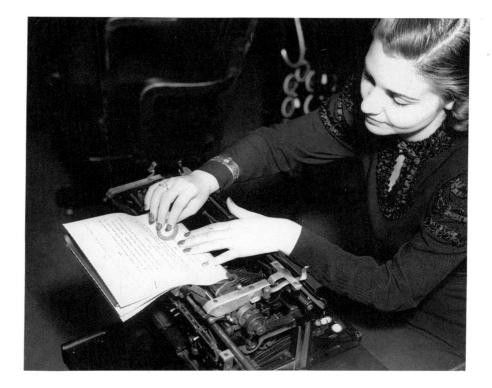

For their help in collecting the photographs reproduced in the book, we are grateful to Cristine Argyrakis and Paul Cunningham of FPG; Ronnie Brenne of the Bettmann Archive; Harriet Culver and Peter Tomlinson of Culver Pictures; Dale Connelly of the National Archives; Thomas Featherstone of the Wayne State University Archives of Labor and Urban Affairs; Roberta Groves of H. Armstrong Roberts; Cathleen Huck of the Conrad N. Hilton Archive & Library; Howard and Ron Mandelbaum of Photofest; and Eric Rachlis of Archive Photos.

We thank the following friends for their information and suggestions: Susan Balshor, Anne Crudge, Daphne Doelger, Alan Goldberg, Steven Goldberg, Eliot Hawkins, Rick Hostnik, Bettyann Kevles, Daniel Kevles, Carole Kismaric, Marilyn Minden, Victor Navasky, Norman Nelson, Judith Reemtsma, Natalie Robins, Anne Rogin, Janice Shapiro, Calvin Trillin, Lou Valentino, and Sheila Worthington. Above all we are grateful to Hugh Nissenson, who read every draft and made us weigh every word.

Finally, we express our appreciation to Caroline Herter, Jay Schaefer, and Judith Dunham of Chronicle Books, and Eric Baker of Eric Baker Graphic Design for their professional expertise and enthusiastic support. □

Credits

All pictures in the book are from FPG International Corporation except as indicated below.

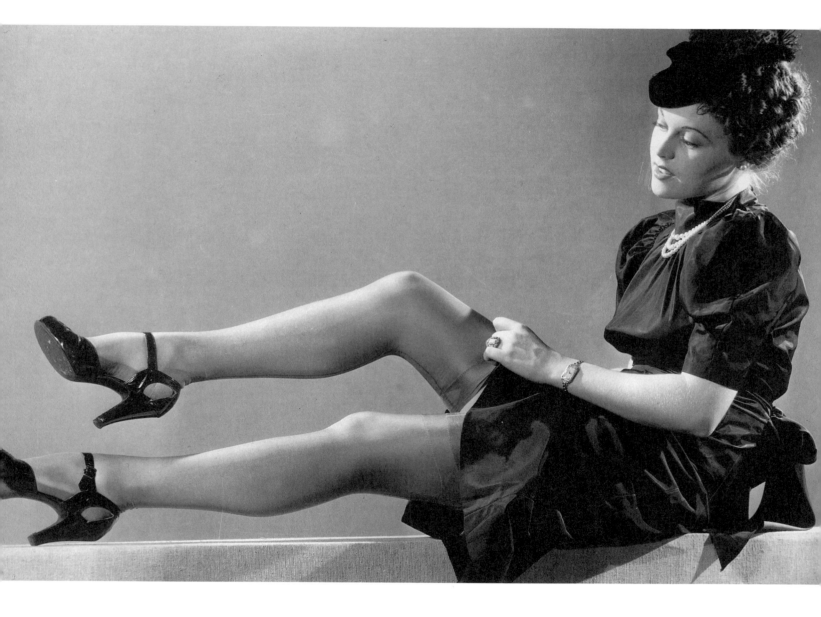

Bibliography

The articles and books listed below represent only a fraction of the published sources we read in the course of our research. We have chosen to cite those that were exceptionally informative about their particular subject and to identify the subject if the association is otherwise unclear.

Angell, Roger. *Five Seasons.* New York: Simon & Schuster, 1977. (Baseball Players Who Stay With One Team)

Arey, James A. *The Sky Pirates.* New York: Scribners, 1972. (Security-Free Airports)

Barson, Michael. *Better Red Than Dead.* New York: Hyperion, 1992. (Red Menace)

Blake, Virgil L.P., and Renee Tjoumas, eds. *Information Literacies for the Twenty-First Century.* Boston: G. K. Hall, 1990. (Card Catalogs)

Bliven, Bruce. *The Wonderful Writing Machine.* New York: Random House, 1945. (Typewriters)

Bogart, Leo. *Press and Public.* Hillsdale, N.J.: Lawrence Elbaum Associates, 1989. (Two-Newspaper Towns)

Bowen, Dr. William, "Dental Caries: Is It an Extinct Disease?" *JADA*, September 1991.

Braun-Ronsdorf, Dr. M. *The History of the Handkerchief.* Leigh-on-Sea, England: F. Lewis, 1967.

Brown, JoAnne. "A is for Atom, B is for Bomb: Civil Defense in American Public Education, 1948-1963." *Journal of American History*, June 1988.

Champlin, Charles. "What Will H. Hays Begat?" *American Film*, October 1980. (Motion Picture Production Code)

Cohen, Daniel. "For Food Both Cold and Hot, Put Your Nickels in the Slot." *Smithsonian*, January 1986. (Automat)

Cohn, Victor. *Four Billion Dimes.* Minneapolis: Minneapolis Morning Tribune, 1955. (Polio Scares)

Collins, C. Cody. *Love of a Glove.* New York: Fairchild, 1947.

Crain, Robert, Elihu Katz, and Donald Rosenthal. *The Politics of Community Conflict.* New York: Bobbs Merrill, 1969. (Cavities)

Cudlipp, Edythe. *Furs.* New York: Hawthorne Books, 1978.

DeLoca, Cornelius, and Samuel Kalow. *Romance Division.* Wyckoff, N.J.: D and K Book, 1991. (Typewriters)

Desowitz, Robert. *The Malaria Capers.* New York: Norton, 1992. (DDT)

DiMaggio, Paul. *The Hitchhiker's Field Manual.* New York: Macmillan, 1973.

Domhoff, G. William. *The Bohemian Grove and Other Retreats.* New York: Harper & Row, 1974. (Men's Clubs)

Donovan, Mary Ann. *Sisterhood is Power.* New York: Crossroads, 1989. (Nuns)

Ewing, Elizabeth. *Dress and Undress: A History of Women's Underwear.* New York: Drama Books Specialists, 1978.

———. *History of Twentieth Century Fashion.* Totowa, N.J.: Barnes and Noble, 1974.

———. *Fur in Dress.* London: B. T. Batsford, 1981.

Formanek, Ruth, ed. *The Meanings of Menopause.* Hillsdale, N.J.: Analytic, 1990.

Gelatt, Roland. *The Fabulous Phonograph.* New York: Macmillan, 1977. (Vinyl Records)

Gelman, Barbara, ed. *Photoplay Treasury.* New York: Crown, (c) Macfadden-Bartell, 1972. (Movie Magazines)

Geoghegan, Thomas. *Which Side Are You On?* New York: Farrar Straus & Giroux, 1991. (Organized Labor)

Golub, Sharon, ed. *Lifting the Curse of Menstruation: A Feminist Appraisal.* New York: Haworth, 1983. (Menopause Taboo)

Jones, Gerard. *Honey, I'm Home!* New York: Grove Weidenfeld, 1992. (Nuclear Family)

Laycock, George. "There Will Always Be Elms." *Audubon*, May 1990. (American Elms)

Lester, Katherine Morris, and Bess Viola Oerke. *Accessories of Dress.* Peoria, Ill.: Manual Arts, 1940.

Levin, Martin. *Hollywood and the Great Fan Magazines.* New York: Arbor House, 1970.

Mandel, Dr. Irwin. "Dental Caries: Another Extinct Disease?" *Cariology for the Nineties.* Edited by William H. Bowen and Lawrence A. Tabak. Rochester, N.Y.: University of Rochester Press, 1993.

Mann, Steve, and David Pietrusza. "The Business of Baseball." *Total Baseball.* Edited by John Thorn and Peter Palmer. New York: Warner Books, 1991.

Mariani, John. *America Eats Out.* New York: William Morrow, 1991. (Chop Suey)

———. *The Dictionary of American Food and Drink.* New York: Ticknor & Fields, 1983. (Chop Suey)

Martin, Richard. "Nightmare on Third Street." *Arkansas Times,* December 1991. (Two-Newspaper Towns)

McClure, Frank. *Water Fluoridation: The Search and the Victory.* Bethesda, M.D.: U.S. Department of HEW, National Institutes of Health, 1970. (Cavities)

McGill, Angus. *Live Wires.* New York: St. Martin's, 1982. (Telegrams)

Moley, Raymond. *The Hays Office.* New York: Bobbs-Merrill, 1945. (Motion Picture Production Code)

Morrison, Joseph. "The Soda Fountain." *American Heritage,* August 1962.

Morse, Hank. *Old-Time Milkmen: Their Labors and Loves.* Montebello, Calif.: Reyna Books, 1979.

Occhiogrosso, Peter. *Once A Catholic.* Boston: Houghton Mifflin, 1987. (Nuns)

Peltz, Leslie Klein. *Fashion Accesssories.* Encino, Calif.: Glencoe, 1986.

Probert, Christina. *Lingerie in Vogue Since 1910.* New York: Abbeville, 1981.

Schlebecker, John T. "An Informal History of Hitchhiking." *The Historian,* May 1958.

Schoeffler, O. E., and William Gale. *Esquire's Encyclopedia of Twentieth Century Men's Fashions.* New York: McGraw Hill, 1973.

Schwartz, David. "Life Was Sweeter and More Innocent in Our Soda Days." *Smithsonian,* July 1986. (Soda Fountains)

Segal, David R. *Recruiting for Uncle Sam.* Lawrence, Kans.: University of Kansas Press, 1989.

Severn, Bill. *Hand in Glove.* New York: David McKay, 1965.

Skolnick, Arlene. *Embattled Paradise: The American Family in an Age of Uncertainty.* New York: Basic Books, 1991. (Nuclear Family)

The Story of the Typewriter 1873–1923. Herkimer, N.Y.: Herkimer County Historical Society, 1923.

This Fabulous Century: 1950-1960. New York: Time-Life Books, 1970.

The Undercover Story. New York: Fashion Institute of Technology, 1982. (Girdles)

Vizzard, Jack. *See No Evil.* New York: Simon and Schuster, 1970. (Motion Picture Production Code)

Voda, Ann, Myra Dinnerstein, and Sheryl R. O'Donnell, eds. *Changing Perspectives on Menopause.* Austin: University of Texas Press, 1982.

Wallach, Anne Tolstoi. *Paper Dolls.* New York: Van Nostrand Reinhold, 1982.

Zelensky, Wilbur. "The Roving Palate: North America's Ethnic Restaurant Cuisine." *Geoforum,* vol. 16, no. 1, 1985. (Chop Suey)

Zorn, Eric. "Leisure Suits Him Now." *Daily News,* February 14, 1992. □